HARASSMENT AT WORK

HARASSMENT AT WORK

Vanessa Edmunds
Martin Hopkins
Audrey Williams

Solicitors, Eversheds

JORDANS
1998

Published by
Jordan Publishing Ltd
21 St Thomas Street
Bristol BS1 6JS

British Library Cataloguing-in-Publication Data
A catalogue record for this book is available from the British Library.

ISBN 0 85308 524 2

Typeset by Mendip Communications Ltd, Frome, Somerset
Printed in Great Britain by MPG Books Ltd, Bodmin, Cornwall

ACKNOWLEDGEMENTS

The authors and publishers of this book gratefully acknowledge the following:

- the permission of the Office for Official Publications of the European Community to reproduce the Commission's Recommendation and Code of Practice on the Protection of the Dignity of Women and Men at Work (92/131/EEC);
- the permission of the Equal Opportunities Commission to reproduce its Code of Practice on Equal Opportunity Policies, Procedures and Practices in Employment; and
- the permission of the Commission for Racial Equality to reproduce its Code of Practice for the Elimination of Racial Discrimination and the Promotion of Equality of Opportunity in Employment.

PREFACE

We have enormous sympathy for the huge number of businesss people and advisers who struggle to cope with the constantly shifting sands of discrimination law.

We know that harassment is becoming more and more of an issue for UK business. Not only does it offer a risk management challenge as claim frequency and compensation levels continue to increase but it also offers employers the chance to enhance the quality of the work environment by rendering it free of harassment. For these and a whole host of other reasons, it is more important now than ever that anyone responsible for people understands what harassment is and how best to deal with it.

We have therefore tried to help by writing this book. In doing so, we have tried hard to avoid the trap which catches out so many other lawyers whose books make things more complicated rather than simpler to understand. The book is a practical guide to the issues involved and offers down to earth advice on how to minimise, if not eliminate, harassment within the workplace. It is aimed at personnel managers and human resource professionals and explains what harassment is, how to recognise it, how to prevent it and what to do if and when it happens. It includes a draft harassment policy and draft sample letters as well as useful checklists.

In a way that only they understand, we are extremely grateful to our colleagues, Ian Cadogan and Elizabeth Gillow, who have done so much towards research and preparation. Without their contributions, this book would have stayed on the 'good ideas' shelf for years to come.

VANESSA EDMUNDS
MARTIN HOPKINS
AUDREY WILLIAMS

Eversheds

CONTENTS

TABLE OF CASES

References are to paragraph numbers

TABLE OF STATUTES

References are to paragraph numbers, except entries in *italics* which are to
page numbers

TABLE OF STATUTORY INSTRUMENTS, CODES OF PRACTICE AND GUIDANCE

References are to paragraph numbers

TABLE OF EUROPEAN MATERIALS

References are to paragraph numbers

TABLE OF ABBREVIATIONS

ACAS   Advisory Conciliation and Arbitration Service
CPS   Crown Prosecution Service
CRE   Commission for Racial Equality
DDA 1995   Disability Discrimination Act 1995
EAT   Employment Appeal Tribunal
EC Code   European Commission's Recommendation and Code of
               Practice of 27 November 1991 on the Protection of the
               Dignity of Women and Men at Work (92/131/EEC)
ECJ   European Court of Justice
EOC   Equal Opportunities Commission
EU   European Union
HSE   Health and Safety Executive
HSWA 1974   Health and Safety at Work etc Act 1974
MSF   Manufacturing Science Finance Union
RRA 1976   Race Relations Act 1976
SDA 1975   Sex Discrimination Act 1975

Chapter 1

INTRODUCTION

1.1 THE IMPORTANCE OF AVOIDING HARASSMENT

There are many studies and statistics supporting the business case for employers to take steps to avoid harassment at work. Many readers will recognise the reality which those studies reflect, that working in an organisation where there is harassment and bullying is not conducive to getting the best out of individuals and can result in a hostile work environment in which loss of creativity and motivation are the inevitable costs.

Beyond these internal costs, there are also wider implications of harassment at work. If employees do not feel valued or feel they are being abused, an organisation may face high levels of staff absenteeism and staff turnover. This can give the organisation a bad reputation in the recruitment market so, as it loses staff, it also has problems replacing them.

In addition to these practical, everyday problems, there are significant legal implications arising from the failure to tackle harassment and bullying which can result in claims against the organisation ranging from breach of contract, criminal liability, discrimination and personal injury. It is claims such as these which are considered in this book.

The most recent ACAS annual report (31 March 1998) identifies that for the year 1997, 107,000 industrial tribunal claims were issued, which is more than double the figure in 1990. In addition to this, ACAS has identified a growing trend of complaints which contain more than one claim; for example, an unfair dismissal claim may be brought in conjunction with a claim for breach of contract or discrimination.

Roughly 10% of these 107,000 complaints related to discrimination, of which a proportion will be claims of harassment. In addition, whilst two in five claims related to unfair dismissal, there has been a recognised increase in complaints about stressful work environments and bullying at work. The fact that bullying at work is being more fully recognised is illustrated by the efforts last year by one union, the Manufacturing Science Finance Union (MSF), to introduce specific legislation to tackle this problem within the workplace (the Bullying and Dignity at Work Bill). Although this was unsuccessful, employers should not be lulled into thinking that individuals cannot take action if they are concerned about bullying at work. Without the Bullying and Dignity at Work Bill or an equivalent specific piece of legislation, employees (and their advisers) are more and more seeking to fit bullying into the existing law across the entire spectrum of criminal law, employment rights and civil complaints. In support of its lobbying for the Bullying and Dignity at Work Bill, the MSF conducted a survey of 396 workplaces, which demonstrated that some 30% of employees described bullying as a 'significant problem'.

Add to this new trend the fact that, since 1996, we have had new legislation to protect disabled persons who, as well as complaining of bullying, could also complain under the new legislation of harassment at work, and the potential for employers to run into difficulties by failing to address, prevent and deal with harassment at work has increased significantly. Under the new Disability Discrimination Act 1995, according to a survey by the Equal Opportunities Review, there have been 2,000 applications in an 18-month period (from December 1996 to March 1998) and the current figures are running in the region of 200 claims per month.[1]

The aim of this book is to assist employers, as well as those subjected to harassment and bullying, to deal with the issues and problems which arise. First, the book considers exactly what amounts to harassment and bullying at work and what the law recognises. Then it looks at the extent of an employer's responsibility for harassment and bullying both inside and outside the work place. Finally, it considers the steps and preventative action which should be taken, and the financial implications which could arise.

The main message for readers, whether they are employers or employees, is that harassment at work is now an important issue which should be:

–   recognised;
–   prevented; and
–   taken seriously.

If any further persuasion was needed, a consideration of the court actions and remedies which an organisation might face will be convincing.

---

1   *Equal Opportunities Review* No 79, May/June 1998.

Chapter 2

SEXUAL HARASSMENT

Introduction – Legal definition – Why sexual harassment is unlawful – Sexual orientation and transsexuals – Third party harassment – Social gatherings and office parties – Office romances – Future changes – Future proposals

2.1 INTRODUCTION

'Sexual harassment pollutes the working environment and can have a devastating effect upon the health, confidence, morale and performance of those affected by it. The anxiety and stress produced by sexual harassment commonly leads to those subjected to it taking time off work due to sickness, being less efficient at work, or leaving their job to seek work elsewhere. Employees often suffer the adverse consequences of harassment itself and short and long term damage to their employment prospects if they are forced to change jobs. Sexual harassment may also have a damaging impact on employees not themselves the object of unwanted behaviour but who are witness to it or have knowledge of the unwanted behaviour.'[1]

The traditional view of sexual harassment is of a male employee leering at a female colleague who, more often than not, is a junior member of staff. Where the harassment extends beyond the visual, the male employee may begin to make unwanted verbal suggestions or unwanted physical actions.

Whilst a number of the early cases of sexual harassment fall into this category, the issue of sexual harassment at work has broadened over the years:

– it is no longer recognised as solely male conduct;
– complaints are being made of sexual harassment by females both from males and from other females, ie same sex harassment;
– there may not necessarily be a sexual motive behind such conduct, the motive may be related to the fact that the individual has a different sexual orientation, is changing sex, or is considered in some way to be 'different';
– most significantly has come the recognition that employees may be harassed because of sex, race or other personal characteristics by the customers, clients, suppliers, agents and consultants who deal with the organisation.

When one considers the range of individuals who operate within a work environment, the list can extend to a wide category of potential harassers.

The impact of harassment at work is quite often cited as leading to poor performance, increased levels of absence and poor motivation. Most employers recognise that these effects are not limited to the person who is being subjected to the harassment but their colleagues also may be affected.

With the development of the law on sexual harassment in the UK has come the recognition that whilst there are violent episodes and extreme cases of harassment, there are also less obvious cases.

---

1   European Commission Recommendation No 92/131/EEC.

Some of the most recent developments in the area of sexual harassment, particularly in terms of new law, has been with cases of harassment not by work colleagues, but by members of the public, and outside the work environment – often in circumstances where the harasser has come into contact with the individual via their work. Employees, of course, do and say things outside of the office which can impact upon working relationships at functions, conferences, courses, or simply on the way to or from work. The most sinister aspect of harassment which the law has sought to address is stalking with the introduction of the Protection from Harassment Act 1997. This piece of legislation (which will be examined in more detail in Chapter 7) now enables criminal and civil action to be taken against individuals who harass others by placing them in fear for their safety, and by stalking.

As if all of this was not enough for employers to have to tackle, there is also the problem where the dividing line between sexual harassment and the office romance shifts; particularly when an office romance goes wrong, and the previously welcome attention forms the basis of a complaint of sexual harassment. This can have difficult repercussions and employers need to be aware of personal animosity turning to harassment at work and take steps to prevent it.

2.2 LEGAL DEFINITION

2.2.1 Definition of sexual harassment

What does the law recognise as sexual harassment? As a concept, it has evolved over the years and is difficult to pin down precisely. One of the reasons for this is that the term 'sexual harassment' is not contained in any UK legislation and certainly not in the Sex Discrimination Act 1975 (SDA 1975) which deals with discrimination against employees at work because of their sex. Over the years, however, a number of cases (discussed below) have provided an outline of the nature of sexual harassment. Following these cases, the European Union has issued a Recommendation and Code (the 'EC Code') to identify harassment by reference to the motive of the harasser and how it affects the person who is subjected to the harassment.[1]

The EC Code contains terminology which describes sexual harassment as:

- offensive;
- demeaning;
- affecting a person's dignity.

Whilst the EC Code is not legally binding, it carries much influence and has been relied upon in the UK courts, as well as being recommended to tribunals to consider in sexual harassment cases.[2]

In addition to this, the importance of the EC Code has been emphasised indirectly by the European Court of Justice (the 'ECJ') which, in the case of *Grimaldi v Fonds Das Maladies Professionelles*,[3] stated that there was an obligation

---

1   European Commission Recommendation and Code of Practice 92/131/EEC OJ L49 (see
     Appendix 1).
2   *Wadman v Carpenter Ferrer Partnership* [1993] IRLR 374.
3   [1990] IRLR 400.

on the part of national courts – and in the employment context this includes employment tribunals, the Employment Appeal Tribunal (the 'EAT'), the Court of Appeal and the House of Lords – to consider any relevant recommendations. Thus, in dealing with a case of sexual harassment the Code is very relevant.

The definition of sexual harassment as contained in the Code is:

> 'conduct of a sexual nature or other conduct based on sex affecting women and men at work ...'

The Code goes on to make clear that such conduct is unacceptable in the workplace if:

- the harassment is unwanted, unreasonable and offensive to the recipient of the conduct;
- decisions regarding the recipient's training, employment, promotion or salary are dependent upon whether the conduct is rejected or accepted;
- the result of the conduct is to create 'an intimidating, hostile or humiliating' work environment for the recipient.

Bringing all of these concepts together, what seems clear is that the intentions of the harasser can derive from one of a number of motives: whether it is to embarrass the individual, and one way of achieving this is by sexually harassing the victim; or to exercise power or authority, particularly where this is linked to career decisions; or for the harasser's own sexual gratification or where they are seeking sexual favours.

2.2.2 Methods of harassment

As the EC Code recognises, sexual harassment can take many forms, ranging from verbal, non-verbal and physical. Non-verbal harassment, which is often by looks and gestures, can be the most difficult to establish and identify by a third person. The use of written materials, internal memoranda, and E-mail in this technical age, can also be a weapon for an harasser, as can photographs, cartoons and other visual material.

From the reported cases, sexual harassment has included:

- comments on a woman's anatomy;
- overtly sexual comments;
- touching a person's body;
- simulating sex;
- sexual assault;
- verbal threats.

The UK courts accepted, quite early on, that sexual harassment was not limited to physical conduct in the case of *Porcelli v Strathclyde Regional Council.*[1]

In that case, the first sexual harassment case before the Appeal Courts, the EAT wrestled with the concept of sexual harassment. The conduct which formed the basis of the applicant's complaint was wide ranging:

- she complained about comments made to her, where jars stored in a cupboard had to be reached with a ladder, such as 'If you can't climb a ladder, you shouldn't be in the f ... job';

---

1   [1984] IRLR 467.

–   one of the male employees would deliberately stare at her and follow her with his eyes when she moved around the room;
–   suggestive remarks would be made such as, picking up a glass rod holder shaped like a penis and being asked whether she had any use for it?;
–   openly and in front of her, comparing Mrs Porcelli's appearance to a nude female in the newspaper;
–   brushing against her.

The EAT was quite careful to lay down the fact that the nature of sexual harassment can take many forms and guarded against setting out a strict, all encompassing definition:

> 'We do not find it necessary to define the expression "sexual harassment" in precise terms. Unwelcome acts which involve physical contact of a sexual nature are obviously included. Such acts if proved would also amount to offences at common law such as assault or indecent assault. We consider that there can also be conduct falling short of such physical acts which can fairly be described as sexual harassment. As we have said the conduct of Coles and Reid [the two alleged harassers] in the incidents above quoted falls into this category. Although most of the incidents which the Tribunal found proved related to matters which did not have direct sexual overtones there can be little doubt that these two men subjected the appellant to sexual harassment as part of their campaign to have her removed from Bellahouston Academy.'

One of the reasons why the EAT did not seek to establish a precise definition of sexual harassment is because it can include a wide range of conduct. For this reason, in each case there needs to be an assessment of the particular conduct complained of to see whether it amounts to sexual harassment. This should be an assessment of the behaviour against the EC Code to decide whether it is offensive, demeaning or unwanted, and is either of a sexual nature or based on the complainant's sex.

Two questions commonly asked about the application of this definition to test whether the conduct is sexual harassment are:

(1) Does the conduct have to be offensive from an objective point of view, ie offensive to the reasonable person?
(2) Does it have to be repeated conduct or is one act of harassment sufficient? Otherwise, how does one know that the conduct is unwanted?

2.2.3 Objective or subjective?

In some ways these two issues are intertwined. The emphasis in the EC Code is on sexual harassment being unwanted behaviour which the individual finds offensive. This suggests a subjective test and certainly a number of cases emphasise this aspect.

> *Example* a female employee complained about salacious remarks and physical conduct. The tribunal took into account the evidence before it that she was an individual who wore 'scanty and provocative' clothes in the workplace. When Ms Wileman appealed against this approach, the EAT formed the view that the tribunal *could* take into account this aspect of the individual's character in deciding whether the harassment of which she complained was unlawful, in the sense that it did amount to a detriment (see later):

'If the girl on the shop floor goes around wearing provocative clothes and flaunting herself, it is not unlikely that other work people – particularly the men – will make remarks about it. It is an inevitable part of working life on the shop floor. If she then complains that she suffered a detriment, the Tribunal is entitled to look at the circumstances in which the remarks were made which are said to constitute that detriment.'

Although, on balance, in this case the tribunal concluded that Ms Wileman had been subjected to sexual harassment, it ordered only minimal damages for compensation.

Wileman v Minilec Engineering Ltd
[1988] IRLR 144

It appears that the test and assessment should be considered from the point of view of the harassed person. That means a subjective assessment is made of the conduct. Only if that person is offended or makes it clear that he or she is offended, will the conduct amount to sexual harassment.

However, the limitation to this approach is that it allows the argument that until an harasser discovers that the conduct is unwelcome to the other person, by 'testing out' the conduct or behaviour on that other individual, the harasser cannot tell that it is unwanted. This argument has been rejected, as the courts have recognised that there is an objective ingredient to defining sexual harassment. The objectivity is superimposed on the individual's reaction and involves recognising that some comments and conduct are of such a serious nature that they would be considered and categorised as harassment *even if done on one occasion only*.

This approach was explained in the case of *Scott v Combined Property Services Limited*[1] when the EAT declared that the test was both objective *and* subjective.

– it had to be objective to the extent that one had to identify the conduct as being capable of being offensive; and
– where the sexual nature of the conduct is readily recognisable, it would automatically be considered to be sexual harassment; and
– where the nature of the conduct might or might not be considered sexual in nature, the question is then whether, from a subjective point of view, the complainant found it to be offensive.

The suggestion that the use of the word 'unwanted' allows a harasser a 'testing ground' to gauge a response before the law expects the harasser not to repeat the conduct has been rejected. 'Unwanted' in this context has been more clearly defined as 'unwelcome or uninvited', in *Insitu Cleaning Co Ltd & Another v Heads*,[2] when, the EAT stated:

'whether a single act of verbal harassment is sufficient to found a complaint is also a question of fact and degree. It seems to be the argument that because the Code refers to "unwanted conduct" it cannot be said that a single act can ever amount to harassment because until done and rejected it cannot be said that the conduct is "unwanted". We regard this argument as specious. If it were correct it would mean that a man was always entitled to argue that every act of harassment was different to the first and that he was testing to see if it was unwanted: in other words it would amount to a licence for harassment. The evidence shows that what was said by

1   EAT No 757/96.
2   [1995] IRLR 5.

Brown was unwanted. If intention were relevant, and it is not, any sensible adult would know that the remark made would be unwanted unless there were very exceptional circumstances. The word "unwanted" is essentially the same as "unwelcome" or "uninvited". No one, other than a person used to indulging in loutish behaviour, could think that the remark made in this case was other than obviously unwanted'.

In the *Insitu* case quoted above, the remark was one comment, made to Mrs Heads by someone half her age, who on entering the room where a meeting was being held, said to her 'Hiya, big tits'. In the EAT's view a remark of this nature was objectively one which any reasonable person would find offensive.

2.3 WHY SEXUAL HARASSMENT IS UNLAWFUL

2.3.1 Sexual harassment

As we have already mentioned, the SDA 1975 does not identify sexual harassment separately as an act of unlawful sex discrimination. Harassment of this nature has been declared unlawful by the courts and tribunals by the application of the law of discrimination to this type of conduct.

Before examining exactly how this definition applies to sexual harassment, it is worth noting that generally there is a distinction drawn between sexual harassment and bullying. The key to this difference is the fact that sexual harassment is based on the sex (or arguably the sexual orientation) of the recipient, and that the sex of the recipient is always a factor in the treatment, either:

– because the comments are such that only a woman (or a man) would find them to be offensive;
– because only a woman (or man) is subjected to it;
– because the interest (in relation to sexual propositions and uninvited attention), is only directed at women (or men) or at a particular female (or male).

The law recognises that harassment amounts to 'less favourable treatment' and that it is directed because of the recipient's sex. This accords with the definition of sex discrimination under the SDA 1975 which states:

'A person discriminates against a woman in any circumstances relevant for the purposes of any provision of this Act if:

(a) on the grounds of her sex he treats her less favourably than he treats or would treat a man'

This is, in fact, the definition of what is known as 'direct sex discrimination'. It is worth mentioning that although the definition of discrimination in the SDA 1975 and the facts of many of the reported cases relate to discrimination and harassment against a female, the law does, of course, encompass the same protection for men. Thus it is also discriminatory to subject a man to sexual harassment because of his sex, and this could amount to less favourable treatment and unlawful discrimination. There are, however, two key requirements which must be established before an individual can complain in law of discrimination as a result of sexual harassment: first, it must be established that the treatment is less favourable; and, secondly, that as a consequence of the treatment, the individual has suffered a 'detriment'.

2.3.2 Less favourable treatment

The most common way of examining the less favourable treatment is to ask whether 'but for' the individual's sex he or she would have been treated in the particular, less favourable way. Thus in a claim of sexual harassment, can it be said that 'but for the fact that she was a woman she would not have been sexually harassed?' or is the reality that this unpleasant treatment was not truly less favourable, in the sense that it was directed at all, or a number of, individuals, regardless of their sex?

Care must be taken, however, in applying the 'but for' test, which was set out at an early stage in a House of Lords case known as *James v Eastleigh Borough Council*,[1] because this test is not entirely appropriate in the context of sexual harassment cases. This has recently been re-iterated by the EAT, emphasising that it is not a defence for an harasser (or the harasser's employer) simply to point out or argue that someone of the opposite sex would have been treated in the same, less favourable, way.[2] This is because the treatment of harassing an individual is characterised or determined by the sex of the recipient.

The care with which this particular test must be applied was recognised as early as the *Porcelli*[3] case which has already been referred to above. In that case the court emphasised that it was not just the fact of the less favourable treatment which rendered the sexual harassment discriminatory, but its sexual nature; in other words because the treatment had a sexual nature, this rendered the treatment less favourable on the grounds of sex.

In *Porcelli* the argument put forward by Coles and Reid (the two harassers about whom Mrs Porcelli complained) was that their conduct was due to their dislike of Mrs Porcelli and was part of a campaign to have her removed from the Academy. The tribunal reasoned that had Coles and Reid taken a similar dislike to a man, they also would have conducted a campaign to have him removed and thus, although the treatment of Mrs Porcelli was of a sexual nature, she could not establish that she had been treated less favourably than a man. This approach on the part of the tribunal, whilst superficially attractive, was recognised by the EAT as somewhat lacking in merit. The less favourable treatment of Mrs Porcelli arose because of the nature of the conduct against her, rather than the motive for that conduct, and she was susceptible to the particular actions because of her sex. For that reason she was treated less favourably. Indeed the EAT said quite clearly

> 'the aspects of the conduct of Coles and Reid towards the appellant [Mrs Porcelli] which had sexual overtones could have no relevance in their conduct towards a man.'

In *Insitu Cleaning Company*,[4] the employer sought to run a similar argument, that a remark about Mrs Head's breasts was not less favourable treatment due to her sex, when an equally offensive comment could have been made to a man about his bald head or beard. Again the EAT rejected this:

---

1   [1990] IRLR 288.
2   *British Telecommunications Plc v Williams* EAT No 1340/95.
3   *Porcelli v Strathclyde Regional Council* [1984] IRLR 467.
4   *Insitu Cleaning Co Ltd and Another v Heads* [1995] IRLR 5.

'A remark by a man about a woman's breasts cannot sensibly be equated with a remark by a woman about a bald head or a beard. One is sexual the other is not.'

Thus it is clear that in asking whether 'but for' the individual's sex he or she would have been subjected to the conduct in question, one is examining not the motive for the treatment, or even who the treatment was directed against, but more fundamentally, the nature of the treatment itself. This accords with the EOC's Code of Practice which defines harassment as occurring where there is unwanted conduct of a sexual nature or other conduct based on sex, ie conduct which an individual is susceptible to because of his or her sex, in a way which a person of the opposite sex would not be.

One case, somewhat surprisingly, has led to the view that there was no less favourable treatment.

> *Example*   A complaint was brought about calendars and visual displays of nude and partially nude women. Ms Stewart complained that she found these offensive, but the tribunal's view was that, as a man might also have been offended, there was no less favourable treatment on grounds of sex. The decision is disappointing because it fails to recognise that Ms Stewart found the items 'offensive' and, from both her subjective point of view, as well as (arguably) that of a reasonable person, she was offended because she was a woman. One might consider that such items are more likely to offend women and they are more susceptible to offence because they are female, ie because of their sex.
>
> Whilst, on appeal, the EAT did not consider it could interfere with the tribunal's view, there was a recognition of the sensitivities involved:
>
> 'It is crucial that complaints of the kind made by the Appellant are not treated as trivial. They should be taken up, investigated and dealt with in a sympathetic and sensible fashion.'
>
> *Stewart v Cleveland Guest (Engineering) Ltd*
> [1994] IRLR 440

2.3.3 Detrimental treatment

It is not enough for an individual to identify that the treatment to which she was subjected was less favourable, under the SDA 1975 she must also show that as a result of the less favourable treatment she suffered 'a detriment'. This again is because of the definition of discrimination under the SDA 1975 which states that employers are guilty of discrimination against a woman if by subjecting her to less favourable treatment she suffers a detriment.[1]

It is largely because of this provision that the courts have recognised sexual harassment to be unlawful discrimination. What is also evident, is that the courts have tried to avoid too technical a definition of 'detriment' when dealing with sexual harassment. In *Porcelli*[2] the EAT appeared to suggest that harassment itself did not amount to a detriment, because although an individual might be subjected to treatment which would be recognised as sexual harassment, that treatment would not be discriminatory unless it was unwanted in the sense that the individual found it offensive. It is here that the subjective element of the

---

1   SDA 1975, s 6.
2   *Porcelli v Strathclyde Regional Council* [1984] IRLR 467.

harassment again comes into play. Clearly, if the harassment is not offensive to the individual, she has not suffered a detriment. The matter was succinctly set out by the EAT in *Porcelli* who said:

> 'It was argued on behalf of the appellant that the words "subjecting her to any other detriment" was so universal that they covered acts of sexual harassment committed against her during her employment, without reference to any consequences thereof so far as her employment was concerned. The mere fact that they had been committed automatically placed her employers, perhaps vicariously, in breach of section 6(2)(b) and section 1(1) of the 1975 Act.
>
> We do not think that this interpretation is correct. The 1975 Act does not outlaw sexual harassment in the field of employment or elsewhere. That is left to the common law in an appropriate case. What it does outlaw in the field of employment is discrimination against a woman within the terms of her contract of employment on the grounds of sex. In certain cases, sexual harassment may be relevant in this connection. An employer who dismisses a female employee because she has resisted or ceased to be interested in his advances would, in our view, be in breach of section 6(2)(b) and section 1(1) of the 1975 Act for reasons arising from sexual harassment. Similarly if, for the same reason, he takes other disciplinary action against her short of dismissal, he will also be in breach. This action could be suspension, warning, enforced transfer, etc., all of which would be to the detriment of the female employee although open to an employer under her contract of service in a genuine case not associated with sexual harassment.'

This appeared to suggest that an employer could escape a complaint of discrimination where an employee was subjected to sexual harassment without more – that is to say, there had to be some other consequence, such as dismissal, suspension or transferral before a complainant could show a detriment. Later cases, however, have clarified this and the courts will now accept that the harassment itself, if unwanted and/or offensive, will amount to a detriment.

Reference has already been made to the case of *Wileman v Minilec Engineering Limited*[1] where the EAT's assessment was that a tribunal was entitled to take into account the complainant's own conduct, appearance and demeanour, when deciding whether the sexual harassment to which she had been subjected did in fact constitute a detriment. In that case, the EAT agreed that Ms Wileman had suffered a detriment and therefore had been discriminated against. She did not also have to show that there were other repercussions for her following the harassment.

Perhaps greater clarification of the matter has come in a case which examined whether an individual had suffered a detriment in the context of race discrimination. It is worth mentioning at this point that race discrimination (which will be examined in Chapter 3) has a similar test of discrimination, ie less favourable treatment which subjects an individual to a detriment. It is recognised and accepted that because the SDA 1975 and the Race Relations Act 1976 (RRA 1976) contain the same terminology, cases under the RRA 1976 can be used as guidance to assist in sex discrimination cases.

In *De Souza v The Automobile Association*[2] the harassment was alleged to be a racial insult about Mrs de Souza in a conversation between two managers which she was told about by a colleague. She complained that this amounted to discrimination. The Court of Appeal's assessment was that in order to complain

---

1   [1988] IRLR 144.
2   [1996] IRLR 103.

of a detriment, Mrs de Souza had to show that a reasonable worker would take the view that she had been disadvantaged, and thus objectively that there had been some detriment. It was not, however, necessary to show a tangible detriment

> 'in order for an employee to be said to be subjected to a detriment, however, it is not necessary that the result of the discrimination complained of was either dismissal or other disciplinary action by the employer, or some action by the employee such as leaving the employment on the basis of constructive dismissal or seeking a transfer. If such were the holding of the EAT in the sexual harassment case of *Porcelli v Strathclyde Regional Council* it was too limited an approach.'

If a reasonable employee could complain that the conduct amounted to a detriment, then the fact that the conduct has occurred is sufficient and it is not necessary to show any further consequences or action on the part of the employer.

One of the most serious cases of sexual harassment reported is *Bracebridge Engineering Ltd v Darby*[1] and the acts of harassment here illustrate the 'detriment' which the employee suffers when subjected to sexual harassment.

Mrs Darby was subjected to an extremely serious sexual assault by two colleagues who were in a supervisory position to her – a charge hand and a works manager. The two men physically carried Mrs Darby into an unlit room at the end of her shift, put her legs around one of them, threatened her with a warning if she resisted and then touched her private parts. Although this was a single act of harassment, the EAT (not surprisingly) concluded that it did amount to sexual harassment and a detriment. The *Darby* case also deals with the question of whether the acts of the two supervisors were committed in the course of employment and whether the employer should be responsible for those acts. This will be discussed further in Chapter 8.

Finally, it should also be borne in mind that the suffering of a 'detriment' can impact upon all aspects of the employment relationship and cover a variety of conduct and treatment. The case of *British Telecommunications Plc v Williams*[2] is interesting in this regard because Ms Williams complained about sexual harassment in an unusual context, namely the way in which an appraisal interview had been conducted by her manager; quite a different scenario from that which ordinarily would be recognised as an incident of sexual harassment. The particular complaint was that during the course of the appraisal interview, her manager stared at her legs, trapped her in the room, invaded her personal space and she claimed she found the interview 'sexually intimidating'. On the evidence, this was rejected by the EAT but the case does illustrate that all conduct should be carefully measured to avoid sexual harassment.

2.4 SEXUAL ORIENTATION AND TRANSSEXUALS

So far we have limited our examination of sexual harassment to the treatment of men and women at work, and in considering the discrimination principles, these have been applied to the sex of the individual. There have been cases where the substance of the complaint is not that the individual was subjected to harassment

---

1   [1990] IRLR 3.
2   [1997] IRLR 668.

because he or she was a man or a woman, but because that individual was homosexual or a transsexual. The question which arises is how far the law will protect these employees from harassment?

In this particular area, the law is likely to change considerably and the position as set out below may change in future, particularly with regard to homosexuals. Taking this into account, the current position and our prediction of the direction of future changes is outlined below.

2.4.1 The European influence

Before examining the specific protection which the law provides to each of these two categories of individuals, it is necessary to consider the law which exists and emanates from the European Union and which goes beyond the SDA 1975. There are a number of key EU provisions relating to anti-discrimination measures, which include:

– Article 119 of the Treaty of Rome which sets out an all-encompassing provision that men and women should receive equal pay for equal work;
– the Equal Pay Directive which reiterates and expands upon Article 119;
– the Equal Treatment Directive which states that there will 'be no discrimination whatsoever on the grounds of sex either directly or indirectly by reference in particular to marital or family status'.

There are, under the European law principles, complex rules about who is entitled to the benefit of European legislation. Every individual can rely upon the provisions of Art 119, however this Article is not relevant in the context of sexual harassment. Of the Directives, the Equal Treatment Directive may be of relevance when considering sexual harassment, because it deals with all matters of equal treatment at work (apart from pay, which is covered by the Equal Pay Directive and Art 119).

An individual who is working for a public sector employer, in many respects, has greater protection so far as the European legislation is concerned than one employed in the private sector. The reason for this is because the concept of 'direct effect'. The rationale behind 'direct effect' stems from the fact that the European Court of Justice (ECJ) has recognised that public sector employers are, in fact, State-owned or operated organisations who effectively are a part of the State or, to use the technical terminology, 'an emanation of the State'.

The purpose behind EU Directives is to require Member States of the European Union (each country) to introduce legislation to bring into effect the principles laid down in the Directive. Thus, if the UK enacts legislation to bring into effect all of the requirements and principles of a Directive, every employee will be able to rely upon that legislation. However, where there is a failure to introduce the Directive's provisions or perhaps where there are omissions so that not all of the requirements of the Directive are met by or introduced into the UK legislation, public sector employees may be entitled to additional rights. These rights are acquired because the ECJ considers that it would be wrong to allow one part of the State (ie the public sector employer) to benefit from the State's own failure to implement properly the Directive (ie Government and Parliament). To avoid a public sector employer defending a claim by arguing that a particular right was not covered in the UK – because the State had failed to introduce that right by properly complying with the Directive – the ECJ decided that Directives should have direct vertical effect. This means that a public sector employee should be able to rely directly upon the Directive, without having to wait until the domestic UK law is in compliance. In the context of sexual harassment, this may allow public-sector employees to rely directly on the Equal Treatment Directive. It should be noted, finally, that such direct reliance upon the Directive can only occur if the provisions in the Directive itself are clear and precise.

The position is very different with a private sector employee, who has lesser rights. A private sector employer is not held responsible for any failure on the part of the Government to introduce legislation and is only obliged to observe the UK law, in this context the SDA 1975. However, employment tribunals and other domestic courts are under an obligation to try and achieve the aims of both the ECJ and Europe as a whole. For this reason, when examining the SDA 1975, a tribunal must have regard to the Equal Treatment Directive and where possible, should read the SDA 1975 so that it is consistent with the terms and aims of the Equal Treatment Directive.

This rather complex situation needs to be understood because when considering homosexuals and transsexuals, the ECJ has had to interpret the Equal Treatment Directive. In turn, employment tribunals have to take that interpretation into account when considering individual cases and applying the SDA 1975, particularly when defining discrimination.

2.4.2 Transsexuals

It is clear that the law now protects transsexuals and that it is unlawful to discriminate against an individual because he or she is a transsexual. Care needs to be taken in this area and in particular it should be appreciated that there are important differences between transsexuals, transvestites and homosexuals.

Transsexualism (often described as a 'woman trapped in a man's body' or vice versa) is today recognised more readily as a medical condition and a much more sympathetic opinion is being formed. So far as discrimination law is concerned, this is one area where the UK has been influenced by Europe and the ECJ. The Equal Treatment Directive echoes in some ways the SDA 1975 but arguably whereas the Act talks about 'no less favourable treatment on the grounds of sex', the Equal Treatment Directive goes wider because it emphasises there shall be 'no discrimination whatsoever on grounds of sex either directly or indirectly'.

In 1996, the ECJ considered a case referred to it from the UK of a transsexual who complained of discrimination.

> *Example* 'P', a biological male, informed his employer (the County Council) that he was going to undergo gender re-assignment surgery (ie a sex change operation). Having completed the surgery he was dismissed on grounds of redundancy and complained that his dismissal was related to his gender re-assignment. The European Court agreed that the gender re-assignment was the reason for his dismissal and because it was a reason related to sex, this was unlawful as contrary to the Equal Treatment Directive:
>
> 'Accordingly, the scope of [the Directive] cannot be confined simply to discrimination based on the fact that a person is of one or other sex. In view of its purpose and the nature of the rights which it seeks to safeguard, the scope of the Directive is also such as to apply to discrimination arising as in this case, from the gender re-assignment of the person concerned.

Such discrimination is based, essentially if not exclusively, on the sex of the person concerned.'

P v S & Cornwall County Council
[1996] IRLR 347

In the UK, the *P v S* decision was followed by *Chessington World of Adventures v Reed*,[1] which was a case against a private employer, where it was not possible to place direct reliance upon the Equal Treatment Directive. In addition, this case directly concerned discrimination in the form of harassment.

Example   The campaign of harassment against Miss Reed in that case (a biological male) was repeated and sustained:

– her tools and coffee mugs were repeatedly stolen;
– she was verbally abused;
– her colleagues refused to help her with heavy lifting;
– her clothing and other property was defaced with lipstick;
– her car and motor bike were tampered with;
– a replica coffin with her name on it and the letters 'RIP' were left on her work bench.

She was then informed that her colleagues had collected together and agreed that £100 would be paid to whichever of them was successful in getting her to leave. Faced with this treatment she attempted suicide, resigned her employment and sued her employer for unfair dismissal as well as sex discrimination.

The EAT was quite clear that Miss Reed had suffered sex discrimination. The issue was not whether she had been treated 'less favourably' when compared to a man or a woman, but whether the reason for her treatment, ie the harassment in this case, was sex based. In the EAT's view, the harassment was sex based and for that reason it constituted sex discrimination. She had clearly suffered a detriment and the court concluded that this was a situation where no direct comparison could be made with a male employee.

Chessington World of Adventures Ltd v Reed
[1997] IRLR 556

It is interesting to note that the test of discrimination in this field moves away from the usual approach of comparing the treatment of an individual with the treatment or the hypothetical treatment of someone of the opposite sex.

Thus it appears that treatment which is offensive and unwanted, directed against an individual because of their transsexual status (which is sex based), amounts to unlawful sex discrimination.

Because of this development it is important that any harassment policy (see further Chapter 9) should include and have regard to the position of transsexuals within the workplace. Conduct which amounts to harassment of individuals because of the fact that they are transsexuals will be sexual harassment.

In January 1998, the Department for Education and Employment issued a consultation paper, in which it proposed introducing specific legislation to protect discrimination against individuals by their employer and in their employment, because of their transsexualism. The consultation period for the

---

1   [1997] IRLR 556.

paper ended on 13 March 1998. The Department recognises that the interpretation of the SDA 1975 to give protection to transsexuals is somewhat strained
and therefore considers it appropriate to introduce specific legislation which
contains detailed definitions, as well as particular exclusions.

The consultation paper recognises that transsexualism is defined in the
International Classification of Disorders as:

> 'a desire to live and be accepted as a member of the opposite sex, usually
> accompanied by a sense of discomfort with, or inappropriateness of one's anatomic
> sex and a wish to have hormonal treatment and surgery to make one's body as
> congruent as possible with the preferred sex.'

To gain protection under the proposed legislation, the consultation paper
suggests that an individual who has this desire, would only be protected if it could
be demonstrated that:

- the individual has formally recorded with a medical practitioner or a
  psychiatrist that he or she is a transsexual and identified an intention to
  achieve a new sexual identity;
- it can be shown that the individual is in the process of achieving a new sexual
  identity;
- the individual has, in fact, already achieved a new sexual identity.

If an individual is a transsexual as defined, then the regulations propose that
the individual would be entitled not to be subjected to discrimination, which
would expressly include harassment, and would be entitled not to be treated less
favourably. The proposal is to retain the less favourable test and to identify that
an individual could complain of harassment and less favourable treatment, if
subjected to conduct which is less favourable when compared with someone of
the sex to which the individual was 'deemed to belong before undergoing gender
re-assignment'.

It remains to be seen whether the legislation which is proposed will be
introduced and whether it will be introduced in the format being suggested.[1]

2.4.3 Homosexuals

The position with regard to homosexuals is less clear but may become clearer in
the future. The courts have drawn a distinction between treatment because of an
individual's sex on the one hand and treatment because of their sexual orientation
on the other. The argument has been that the harassment of a homosexual is not
based on the individual's sex but on that person's sexual orientation and
therefore it is not less favourable treatment on grounds of sex.

This has been the approach despite the wider definition of sex given by *P v S*[2]
and the transsexual cases, which suggest that one cannot limit the meaning of
'sex' solely to male/female.

The situation of homosexuals was considered in the case of *Smith v Gardner
Merchant*,[3] where the EAT clearly rejected an argument that harassment of a
barman because he was homosexual amounted to sex discrimination. This case
has recently been considered by the Court of Appeal which stated that Mr Smith

1   'Legislation Regarding Discrimination on Grounds of Transsexualism in Employment'
    Department of Education and Employment, January 1998.
2   *P v S & Cornwall County Council* [1996] IRLR 347.
3   [1996] IRLR 342.

would, in fact, succeed if he could show that he was treated less favourably than a homosexual woman, and that the treatment was based, not on his sexuality but his sex, as a male homosexual.[1]

Again, however, the ECJ has considered the matter, but on this occasion was firmly of the view that sex discrimination did not extend to prevent discrimination due to a person's sexual orientation.

> *Example*   This case concerned the exclusion of Ms Grant's lesbian partner from benefitting from travel concessions provided by South West Trains. Generally speaking, South West Train's policy is to provide travel concessions to employees, their husbands, wives and common-law opposite sex partners. Ms Grant argued that this amounted to sex discrimination because if she had a common-law or co-habiting partner who was of the opposite sex to her, that person would benefit under the terms of South West Trains' policy. Her partner was denied the benefit because she was female. The opinion of the Advocate General was that there was sex discrimination and that this was contrary to the Equal Treatment Directive.
>
> Somewhat surprisingly, however, the ECJ did not agree with the opinion of the Advocate General. In fact, the ECJ's view, quite clearly, was that the treatment of South West Trains did not amount to discrimination on the grounds of sex:
>
> 'since the condition imposed by the undertakings' regulation applies in the same way to female and male workers, it cannot be regarded as constituting discrimination directly based on sex.'
>
> Effectively, what the Court said was that for a lesbian employee to complain of discrimination she would have to show that a male homosexual employee would have been treated differently and not in that less favourable way. Provided that both male and female homosexual employees are treated in the same way, they are not subjected to different treatment based on sex. This decision has come as a grave disappointment to those lobbying for homosexual rights.
>
> *Grant v South West Trains Ltd*
> [1998] ICR 449

The current position, therefore, is that the answer to the question whether homosexuals can complain of sex discrimination based on their sexual orientation has been answered with a resounding 'no'.

The lobbying continues, however, with, in 1998, the introduction of a Private Members Bill (the Sexual Orientation Discrimination Bill) aimed at making discrimination against homosexuals unlawful. Until such time as legislation is introduced, or a new case establishes that a complaint of discrimination can be brought, the debate about whether an individual who is harassed because of sexual orientation can complain of discrimination, will continue.

It had been hoped that this question would be dealt with following the referral to the ECJ of one of a number of cases which have been brought against the armed forces and Ministry of Defence in recent years. These cases have sought to challenge those operations' expulsion of homosexuals. In the case of *R v Secretary of State for Defence ex parte Perkins*,[2] Mr Perkins complained that his employer,

---

1   [1998] IRLR 510, CA.
2   [1997] IRLR 297.

the Royal Navy, discharged him when it was discovered during an investigation that he was homosexual. The High Court Judge's view (as Mr Perkins was seeking a Court declaration) was that the European legislation (the Equal Treatment Directive) did protect an individual's sexual orientation because the statement that there shall be no discrimination whatsoever on the grounds of sex:

> 'extends the concept of discrimination'.

The judge in that case referred the matter to the ECJ for guidance but at the same time stated:

> 'homosexual orientation is a reality today which the law must recognise and adjust to, and it may well be thought appropriate that the fundamental principle of equality and the irrelevance of a person's sex and sexual identity demand that the Court be alert to afford protection to them and ensure that those of homosexual orientation are no longer disadvantaged in terms of employment, save and unless the discrimination is justified . . .'

Unfortunately, in the light of the outcome in the *Grant* case, the *Perkins* case has been withdrawn.

With continued lobbying it may only be a matter of time before discrimination protection is extended to homosexuals. This will mean that again, harassment policies, if they do not do so already, ought to expressly provide protection against harassment for homosexuals. Similarly employers must be aware that harassment in their workplace, meted out to individuals because of their homosexuality, may in future amount to sex discrimination, which certainly could not be justified.

The existing Code of Practice and Recommendation (the 'EC Code') specifically points out that 'gay men and young men are also vulnerable to harassment' as well as lesbians. Sexual harassment of homosexuals was contemplated by the European Commission as early as 1991, when the EC Code was issued.

Until such time as the law is changed, however, it may be that an individual's only remedy is to complain of infringement of their human rights, contrary to the European Convention on Human Rights. This will be introduced into the UK by the Government's Human Rights Bill. Article 8 of the European Convention states specifically that every individual has 'the right to respect for his private and family life, his home and his correspondence'. It is argued that this right to private life includes a right to respect sexual orientation.

Finally, there is the prospect of the European Union as a whole coming to the view that specific legislation should be introduced to protect homosexuals. The Amsterdam Treaty, currently in draft, contains a proposal allowing the European Commission and Parliament to take steps to outlaw discrimination based, amongst other things, on sexual orientation. Thus even without legislation in the UK or further case-law in this area, it may be that Europe steps in to introduce protection.

2.4.4 Homosexual harassment of non-homosexuals

By contrast to the situation concerning homosexuals themselves, there has been an interesting approach taken in one case concerning an employee who was not homosexual, where the nature of the sexual harassment involved homosexual acts.[1]

Although this is a tribunal decision and therefore of limited authority, it is nevertheless interesting in its approach. The employee in question was a 21-year-old male who had begun employment as a security officer. He complained that certain of his work colleagues subjected him to a campaign aimed at embarrassing him, making comments about his sexual organs (clearly conduct related to sex); on one occasion two male employees simulated sex, and on another occasion Gates was grabbed from behind by one of the harassers who attempted to simulate anal sex.

In the complaint of sex discrimination which was brought, the tribunal considered that the acts of harassment – some of which focused on homosexuality – was conduct of a nature to which the applicant, *as a man*, was susceptible and thus was conduct of a sexual nature and based on sex. On this basis the tribunal concluded that there had been less favourable treatment because Gates had been treated in a way that a woman would not have been treated and therefore he was discriminated against and subjected to a detriment. Although the focus of the case clearly remained gender discrimination, it is of interest because the nature of the acts of harassment themselves were such that a male employee was considered by the tribunal to be more susceptible to and offended by them than a woman. Equally, one might consider, a male employee who himself was a homosexual would be offended by such conduct.

The debate and distinction between these two approaches appears to be whether the conduct is solely because of the sex of the individual or solely because of his or her sexual orientation. It might be argued that harassment of an individual such as Mr Smith in the *Smith v Gardner*[2] case was a combination of both, that the comments and acts of harassment were in part due to the fact that he was homosexual but that the nature of the harassment was determined because he was a male homosexual.

A similar case, where the conduct was by a female supervisor against female members of staff, was considered by an industrial tribunal in *Johnson & Garbutt v Gateway Food Markets Ltd.*[3] The complaint concerned Ms Cooper (the applicants' supervisor) touching them; in each case they complained of being touched 'more like the touching of a boyfriend', on the leg and on the bottom.

Although complaints were made to their employer and Ms Cooper received a final written warning, both applicants complained of sex discrimination. The tribunal decided that what had occurred involved touching 'of a sexual nature', and as Ms Cooper had never and would not, in their view, touch a man in this way, both Garbutt and Johnson had been subjected to unwelcome conduct based on sex. In addition, the failure of Gateway to deal with the matter sufficiently seriously, as an incident of harassment, meant that both had been discriminated against unlawfully.

1   *Matthew Carl Gates v Security Express Guards, Security Service of Mayne Nickless (UK) Ltd* Case No 45/42/92.
2   [1996] IRLR 342.
3   Case Nos 4079/90 & 3041/90.

2.5 THIRD PARTY HARASSMENT

There are two further categories of individuals who need to be considered by employers when looking to prevent harassment in the workplace, particularly in the context of sexual harassment. This stems from the extent to which the law renders an employer responsible for discrimination at work. The strict legal test will be addressed in subsequent chapters (in particular Chapter 8) but, in general, employers must appreciate that they have wide obligations to protect employees, bearing in mind a number of different scenarios:

– employees at work may be harassed by colleagues who are not employees: for example, sub-contractors, agency workers, locums and temps, all of whom are in the workplace and to whom employees are exposed;

– employees may also be harassed by clients, customers, suppliers and other third parties with whom they deal;

– an employer's own employees may also harass colleagues who, although they are not employees of the employer, the employer might still be responsible for protecting against discrimination and, in this particular case, sexual harassment.

2.5.1 Non-employees/'workers'

The type of conduct which is discussed in this chapter can, of course, be committed by employees against others who are 'at work' but are not actually employees in the strict legal sense. It is for this reason that in this section the term 'workers' is used. 'Workers' carries a much wider meaning than 'employees' and under the SDA 1975 this extends the right to be protected from sexual harassment and discrimination in two key areas.

First, the scope of the SDA 1975 is such that an employer is responsible for anyone who is carrying out work in a 'personal capacity'.

This is because s 82 of the SDA 1975, which defines 'employee', protects a number of people, defining employee as someone who is:

– employed under a contract of service; or
– an apprentice; or
– working on a contract personally to execute any work or labour.

The last category may include individuals who are not employees in the way that common sense might assume, for example a person who comes to the office every day and who is paid a salary.

Secondly, the SDA 1975 protects contract workers who might be employed by a third party or agent but who are carrying out work for the organisation at the workplace. A typical example of this arrangement is a temporary secretary (a 'temp') who is provided to fill an absence. The temp is provided by a secretarial agency which actually employs the individual. Although the principal is not the employer of the temp, that contract worker is in the organisation or principal's workplace. If subjected to sexual harassment, the temp could complain and take proceedings against the principal who, after all, is responsible for the conduct of employees, where that conduct occurs in the principal's workplace. Section 9 of the SDA 1975 makes the principal, ie the person for whom or on whose premises the work is carried out, responsible for any discrimination, including harassment.

For all these reasons employers must take steps to ensure that these categories of workers are not sexually harassed or discriminated against and that they are also not allowed to sexually harass others.

There is a careful distinction in terms of the legal responsibility for such workers.

2.5.2 Responsibility for protecting against harassment

The SDA 1975 states that an employer must prevent its own workers and employees from discriminating against other employees, workers and contract workers and for this the 'employer' will be held responsible (subject to avoiding liability by proving the defences available; see further Chapters 9 and 12). The responsibility is to protect this wider category of worker and is illustrated by a case which, although not a harassment case or a sex discrimination case, applies the same principles.

> *Example* Mrs Remick and a number of her colleagues complained of racial discrimination by Harrods. In each case, Mrs Remick and her colleagues were not employed by Harrods but were employed by concessionaire companies who operated stands within the department store. Harrods had to give each individual 'store approval' and if approved, each employee could work for their employer on the employer's concession stand. Mrs Remick complained because Harrods refused to give her store approval and she argued that this refusal was because of her race and amounted to discrimination. As with the SDA 1975, the RRA 1976 provides that it is unlawful for a principal to discriminate against a contract worker by 'subjecting him to any other detriment'. The Court of Appeal was clear in its view that Mrs Remick could complain against Harrods on the basis that she was providing work 'for' Harrods even though the store was not her employer.
>
> *Harrods Ltd v Remick and Others*
> [1997] IRLR 583

Under the RRA 1976, a principal for whom contract workers work must not discriminate by subjecting the worker to a detriment – the SDA 1975 contains identical wording.

2.5.3 Responsibility for workers who harass others

By contrast, although obliged to protect this wider group of workers against sexual harassment, an employer is only responsible for the acts of its 'employees', ie those carrying out work in a 'personal capacity' under the vicarious liability principles. In certain circumstances an employer may be directly responsible for the acts of its agent (see Chapter 8). However, the law has extended further the employer's responsibility in the field of sexual harassment, by emphasising that in having to ensure that an employee is not subjected to a detriment, this includes a detriment in the nature of sexual harassment. Although the employer is not responsible for the acts of the third party (who is not a worker), this conduct is still something over which the employer has control. The concept is more easily examined in the context of two cases, one under the RRA 1976 complaining of sexual harassment and racial harassment, the second a sexual harassment complaint.

Example   *Burton and Rhule v De Vere Hotels* saw a complaint being brought against De Vere Hotels following a function at which the two waitresses (Burton and Rhule) served members of a local Round Table. During the dinner, the comedian Bernard Manning gave a performance in which he made racially offensive remarks while the waitresses were working in the room. The harassment was then continued by one or two of the guests, who made further offensive remarks.

The source of the complaints from both individuals was that their employer, in requiring them to work during Bernard Manning's performance, had 'subjected them to a detriment' which was both racial and sexual harassment. The EAT agreed because in its view the situation was under the control of the employer:

'The Tribunal should ask themselves whether the event in question was something which was sufficiently under the control of the employer that he could, by the application of good employment practice, have prevented the harassment or reduced the extent of it. If such is their finding, then the employer has subjected the employee to the harassment. We turn, as invited by the parties, to apply these principles to the Tribunal's findings of fact in this case. Mr Pemberton told the Tribunal that he would never allow young female staff to go into a function where he knew a performer might tell sexually explicit jokes. He was there clearly describing what he saw as good employment practice. The Tribunal said that he ought to have warned his Assistant Managers to keep a look out for Mr Manning and withdraw the young waitresses if things became unpleasant. He did not do so because he did not give the matter a thought. He should have done. Events within the banqueting hall were under the control of Mr Pemberton's assistants. If they had been properly instructed by him, the two young women would not have suffered any harassment. They might possibly have heard a few offensive words before they were withdrawn, but that would have been all.

We are unanimously of the view that on this occasion the employer "subjected" the applicants to racial harassment which they received from Mr Manning and the guests.'

Burton and Rhule v De Vere Hotels
[1996] IRLR 596

The point was reiterated in another EAT case, *Go Kidz Go Ltd v Bourdouane* (below).

Example   Go Kidz Go Ltd is an organisation which conducts children's parties at its premises. In that case, the third party was a parent of one of the children attending the birthday party. Ms Bourdouane, initially, was subjected to offensive comments and later to an assault, when the father who had made the lewd comments smacked and pinched her bottom and pressed against her. Between the time when the offensive comments were made and when the sexual assault occurred, Ms Bourdouane went to find her manager and complained. Because all staff were busy, her manager requested that she finish the party and told her that they would discuss the matter later. In sending her back to continue the party, the EAT was clearly of the view that this was a situation under the employer's control and accordingly she had been subjected to sexual harassment which was a detriment by her employer. The central theme in both these decisions is that the employer is responsible for the harassment in the widest sense possible.

The EAT recognised the difficulties with the complaint of harassment:

'The term "sexual harassment" may properly be applied to the treatment of Ms Bourdouane by the male parent on the facts of this case. However, sexual harassment per se does not give rise to a complaint under the 1975 Act. Further, the parent was not an employee of the Appellant [Go Kidz Go] for whose act the Appellant was vicariously liable, subject to the statutory defence, under section 41 of the 1975 Act. How does the Complainant establish unlawful direct sex discrimination against her employer arising out of acts of sexual harassment directed at her in the course of her employment by a third party not a fellow employee?'

The EAT then went on to list the following to explain the answer to this question:

- the employer must not treat an individual less favourably on the grounds of her sex;
- an employer must not subject an individual to a detriment – in the particular case there was sexual harassment and it was to the detriment of Ms Bourdouane;
- an employer has an obligation to take all reasonable steps to prevent discrimination occurring and to do that must anticipate when discrimination may occur and take steps to prevent the discrimination;
- in this case the employer could anticipate that there would be sexual harassment (indeed, following the complaint, the manager had been warned that harassment was taking place and at that point ought to have anticipated that the harassment would continue when Ms Bourdouane returned to the party) and in requiring her to return, had subjected her to harassment by failing to control the situation.

Go Kidz Co v Bourdouane
(1996) IDS 578, EAT

Thus it can be seen that employers now have placed upon them a high level of responsibility and that responsibility emphasises the employer's obligation to monitor and control conduct and behaviour within the workplace. An effective harassment policy should anticipate the possibility of third parties harassing individuals and ensure that those within the organisation managing the work or operation understand that they must deal with such complaints and prevent them.

2.6 SOCIAL GATHERINGS AND OFFICE PARTIES

It is worth mentioning at this point that employers may be responsible for acts of harassment at social events organised by the employer, such as office parties.

It is, of course, difficult to draw the line between the situations where an employer is in control of a particular environment and those where it is no longer responsible. Acts of harassment obviously can, and do, occur at social gatherings and much depends on how close a connection the event can be said to have had to the work environment. The responsibility, however, of an employer for acts of discrimination at such events is very different from the question of whether the employer is entitled to take disciplinary action against the employee concerned. Often, the decision to take disciplinary action will depend in large measure on the impact that the particular event or incident has on working relations.

There are obviously a range of different circumstances where the distinction between a work related activity and a social activity may become blurred. The following events are likely to be considered functions where the employer will be expected to carry some responsibility for the behaviour of employees, and therefore should be careful not to allow situations to become out of hand. These include:

- an office party;
- a Christmas party;
- training sessions events;
- celebratory events (for example, sessions to celebrate meeting sales targets);
- lunch celebrations.

Employers might also be held responsible for any injury caused at these types of functions where they could be considered to have been negligent. Although outside the scope of this book, negligence can of course apply not just to employees but also to guests who might be attending the party. There are a range of cases, not limited to complaints of harassment, where employers have been held responsible for untoward incidents at events of this nature, including fighting, abuse of alcohol and the use of drugs.

From an employment law point of view, there are two considerations: the potential for a discrimination complaint; and the possibility of a dismissal resulting from such conduct.

There have been cases where tribunals have concluded that an employer was justified in dismissing an employee, particularly bearing in mind the effect which the conduct had on subsequent working relationships. Whether responding by dismissing an employee is fair and reasonable (for the purposes of unfair dismissal) will, in part, also depend upon the employer's conduct; for example, a tribunal will take into account the extent to which control over the event was exercised by the employer, and whether the conduct was contributed to alcohol which the employer provided. There also obviously are important implications where clients of the employer are invited to the function.

On balance, and because of the extent of responsibility which can attach to these incidents, it is recommended that employers urge individuals on such occasions to enjoy themselves but to maintain some control of their behaviour. Assuming that the company harassment policy already makes clear what is acceptable within the workplace, it is advisable for employers to issue a gentle reminder to those attending that whilst the organisation wishes them to enjoy themselves, appropriate consideration must be given to other persons present at the event.

Bearing in mind the scope of responsibility outlined in cases such as *Bourdouane* and *Burton and Rhule*, the Court of Appeal has attempted to draw some distinction between social events where the employer does or does not bear responsibility for the conduct of employees in a subsequent case which was in fact a victimisation complaint (see Chapter 8) but which had its origin in a complaint of sexual harassment.

> *Example* A female police constable, PC Waters, was employed and had access to a room in the section house where she lived. On one occasion while she was off duty, a male colleague visited her and after they had returned from a walk, sexually assaulted her in her room. PC Walters complained about the assault and then complained that she had been

victimised because of various subsequent acts which she said were only carried out against her because of the complaint of harassment. The tribunal and later the Court of Appeal, first had to decide whether the sexual assault was an act for which the Commissioner of Police, as the employer, could be held responsible. In effect, this meant deciding if it could be considered to have been carried out in the course of employment. The Court of Appeal balanced the circumstances, timing and location of the incident in forming the view that it could not be considered to have been done in the course of employment and therefore the employer could not be held responsible for it:

'In my view, there can be no such doubt. T and the applicant were off duty at the time of the alleged offence. He lived elsewhere, and was a visitor to her room in the section house at a time and in the circumstances which placed him and her in no different positions from that that would have applied if they had been social acquaintances only, with no working connection at all. In these circumstances it is inconceivable, in my view, that any Tribunal ... could find that the alleged assault was committed in the course of T's employment'.

Waters v Commissioner of Police for the Metropolis
[1997] IRLR 589

More recently one industrial tribunal has emphasised that a social function with a work connection will place the employer at risk if harassment occurs.

Example A female police detective constable was seconded from Lincoln-shire to the regional crime squad, where one of her male colleagues began to flirt with her (standing close, touching her hair and clothes). When she rejected this attention his attitude changed and, she claimed, he became hostile. At a leaving do held at a public house he made a sexually offensive comment and later assessed her work performance as poor.

In concluding that Ms Stubbs had been discriminated against the industrial tribunal took the view that the incidents in the public house:

'were connected with the work and workplace. They would not have happened but for the applicant's work. Work related social functions are an extension of employment ...'

Stubbs v Chief Constable Lincolnshire Police & Others
Case No 38395/96

Thus, if the particular social gathering is more akin to a truly social occasion rather than a 'work's outing', it is less likely that the employer will be held responsible. A number of factors might point to a social event having a strong connection with the workplace; for example, a free bar provided by the employer, the presence of senior managers at an event, or the fact that the event is at the invitation of the employer as opposed to a gathering of peers organised amongst themselves.

2.7 OFFICE ROMANCES

Another area where there is a fine dividing line between social contact and harassment at work occurs where two people are involved in an 'office romance'. Particular problems can arise where the relationship begins to break down and what was previously consensual behaviour becomes unwelcome. Bearing in mind the definition of sexual harassment, when conduct becomes unwanted behaviour which causes embarrassment or offence, employers are at risk of a complaint of sex discrimination.

It is also worth bearing in mind that a complaint may not stop at sexual harassment. If, following the break down of a romantic relationship between two employees, decisions are taken regarding one or both employees which could amount to a detriment, such as dismissal or refusal of promotion, this may lead to a sex discrimination complaint on grounds of the individual's sex.

One example which illustrates that an employer can be over-zealous in policing harassment at work is *Brookes Explosives v Montgomery* (below).

> *Example*   An anonymous letter sent to the company alleged that their sales manager was having an affair with one of the company's female processor workers (in a more junior position). The rumour was apparently encouraged by suggestions that the two individuals had gone on holiday together.
>
> The employer decided that both individuals would be dismissed upon their return. The male sales manager was questioned before he was dismissed but the female employee was dismissed on the spot. Both individuals complained to the tribunal. The sales manager complained of unfair dismissal, because he had been employed for more than two years. The female employee, however, had not been employed for the requisite length of time and could not complain of unfair dismissal; therefore she complained of sex discrimination. The EAT and the industrial tribunal agreed that she had been dismissed on grounds of her sex because they were satisfied that if the male sales manager had been on holiday with a male employee, that man would not have been dismissed.
>
> *Brooks Explosives v Montgomery*
> EAT 141/91

If a relationship of this nature breaks down and conduct which previously was tolerated becomes unwanted, an employer is under an obligation to put a stop to it and to avoid continuing action which would amount to sexual harassment. If, on the other hand, the relationship leads onto other things, for example marriage, then, again, an employer must take care not to dismiss on that ground because, under the SDA 1975, it is unlawful to discriminate against married persons by treating them less favourably.

> *Example*   Ms McLean was dismissed when she announced that she was to marry the assistant manager within the company. She successfully complained of discrimination on the grounds of her sex, because the tribunal was satisfied that a man who had announced an imminent marriage to another employee would not have been dismissed.
>
> *JS McLean v Paris Travel Services Ltd*
> [1976] IRLR 202

Of course sex discrimination in these circumstances can arise if a decision to dismiss (or to transfer which could be considered to be a less favourable treatment) is taken not because the couple have announced an intention to marry, but because of the fact of the relationship itself.

One tribunal decision has, however, raised questions whether a legitimate complaint of sex discrimination does arise if one employee begins to treat another in an objectionable way because of a relationship breakdown.

Example   Anbryn Properties employed a female employee, Mrs Fullbrook, who had had a relationship with Mr Allen, the owner of the business. The relationship broke down and Mr Allen's affections then turned to another individual. On a number of occasions incidents of verbal and physical abuse were alleged by Mrs Fullbrook, following the breakdown of the relationship and as a consequence of it. When she complained of sex discrimination, however, the tribunal's view was that the treatment to which she had been subjected and of which she complained, was not on the grounds of her sex and the fact that she was a woman, but because she had been involved in 'an intimate sexual relationship'. On this basis the tribunal reasoned that a different employee, regardless of whether that person was a man or a woman, would not have been treated in this way. Thus Mrs Fullbrook could not complain of less favourable treatment on the grounds of her sex when the truth was that the less favourable treatment was on the grounds of the intimate relationship.

SA Fullbrook v (1) Anbryn Properties Ltd (2) M Allen
8125/96/A

The rationale in this decision could be open to question, given that the fact remained that an intimate relationship occurred as a consequence of the fact that she was a woman and the relationship was a heterosexual one!

It is clear that employers should guard against allowing personal factors to influence decisions relating to the employment of individuals and their positions within the workplace. However, this must be balanced against the overriding duty to prevent harassment in the workplace.

2.8 FUTURE CHANGES

Reference has already been made to the European Commission's *Recommendation and Code of Practice on the Protection of the Dignity of Women and Men at Work* (the 'EC Code').[1] Chapter 10 deals with the sort of steps which an employer should take in implementing policies and taking preventative measures to address harassment at work. However, it is useful at this point to make reference to the EC Code, particularly in the light of future proposals.

The 'recommendation for employers' section of this document is particularly useful as a starting point for any organisation which is considering addressing harassment in the workplace. It contains a number of key recommendations to prevent harassment, as well as providing some guidance as to how it can be recognised.

The preventative steps include:

–   issuing policy statements so that employees and workers are fully aware of what type of conduct is inappropriate;

–   ensuring managers, supervisors and those in line management positions, know what is expected of their colleagues, themselves and their juniors and can take appropriate corrective action where necessary;

---

1   See Appendix 1.

–   the policy must be communicated so that all employees are aware of its
     provisions so that they can ensure that their conduct does not infringe
     inappropriate behaviour and so they can be confident about making a
     complaint; this is particularly to encourage individuals to be aware that
     objecting to behaviour of this nature is not 'just them', that they are not being
     'over sensitive', but that they are entitled to expect a level of respect, dignity
     and consideration and to be treated accordingly;

–   in its policy and in dealing with harassment complaints, the organisation
     should make clear that it will take such matters seriously, it will support
     individuals and it will assist where necessary by providing advice and dealing
     with matters in a sensitive and confidential way;

–   procedures should be put in place to deal with complaints and those
     procedures should be tailored to sexual harassment which, because of its
     nature, often needs to be dealt with in a very different way to other
     grievances at work.

2.9 FUTURE PROPOSALS

One of the limitations of the EC Code is that it is at most, a 'best practice' guide
and it does not carry the force of law. Employment tribunals have been told that
they should take the Code into account but it carries no more weight than that.

The European Union has recently proposed strengthening this by introducing
legislation across the Member States of the EU on harassment, especially sexual
harassment. This proposal is under discussion and at the time of writing,
consultation papers have been issued in which opinions are being sought from
the Member States, businesses and trade union parties.

There are number of ways of introducing such legislation into the EU, and it is
outside the scope of this text to examine them in detail. However, two options
appear to be available for this particular harassment legislation:

(1) A collective agreement known as an 'agreement between the social partners'.
     This is effectively a way of collectively agreeing to introduce legislation
     between the employer's confederation (UNICE) and the European Trade
     Unions Confederation.

(2) Alternatively, a Directive could be introduced. We have referred already to
     the Equal Treatment and Equal Pay Directives. This would require
     Member States to introduce legislation to bring into effect the terms of the
     Directive.

Either way, the first change and point of impact proposed by this legislation
would be to create a binding, legal definition of sexual harassment. A second
proposal being put forward, which is a substantial move away from the current
legal position, is to place employers under a legal obligation to create and issue to
staff a policy on harassment and to have in place a system for counselling
individuals who are subjected to harassment at work.

Whilst there is little merit in examining in detail the consultation document, a
number of its key suggestions may well find their way into any subsequent
Directive if, as seems likely, the social agreement route fails.

First, 'harassment' is defined as:

> 'unwanted conduct of a sexual nature, or other conduct based on sex affecting the dignity of women and men at work. This can include unwelcome physical, verbal or non-verbal conduct'.

This is in identical terms to the existing definition contained in the EC Code.

Secondly, it is proposed to place an obligation on employers to provide confidential counsellors. This would be new in terms of a legal obligation, although many employers who take harassment at work seriously have already appointed counsellors and individuals within the organisation (such as welfare officers) whose role is to assist and act as a support for the recipients or complainants of harassment.

The proposal would also have the effect of rendering sexual harassment at work unlawful throughout all of the countries within the EU.

Chapter 3

RACIAL HARASSMENT

Introduction – Meaning of 'racial grounds' – Legal definition – Definition and methods of racial harassment – The comparator – Less favourable treatment – On grounds of race – Whose race? – A detriment? – Racist banter – In the course of employment – Dealing with complaints – Effects of racial abuse

3.1 INTRODUCTION

'For anyone who is a target of harassment, being at work means being in a permanent state of dread, being unable to concentrate, and failing to realise one's full potential. Worse the tension is contagious and invariably affects others, with ultimately damaging consequences for the organisation as a whole'.[1]

Compared to sexual harassment and sex discrimination, which has received much of its impetus from European law, there are fewer claims of racial harassment and, by comparison, this area of law is underdeveloped. The traditional view of racial harassment is of a white employee harassing a black employee or other individual from an ethnic minority. However, it is important to bear in mind that racial harassment can take the reverse form and can also occur between different ethnic minority groups.

There is no statutory definition of 'harassment' in the RRA 1976. The Act mirrors the provisions of the SDA 1975 and provides that it is unlawful to treat an employee less favourably or subject him or her to a detriment on what are termed 'racial grounds' in the legislation (see below).

Quite clearly, so far as harassment is concerned, harassment based on an individual's race (as defined in the RRA 1976) could amount to 'a detriment' and be unlawful race discrimination.

3.2 MEANING OF 'RACIAL GROUNDS'

Section 3 of the RRA 1976 defines 'racial grounds' as meaning colour, race, nationality, ethnic or national origins and a 'racial group' is also defined by these criteria. Although individuals may, for a variety of religious, social, or cultural reasons, consider that they belong to distinct groups and that they have been discriminated against because they belong to such groups, only individuals who have been discriminated against on one of the above grounds can claim protection under the RRA 1976. This is akin to the SDA 1975 where protection on the grounds of sex protects men, women and transsexuals, but not

---

1   Herman Ouseley, Chairman of the CRE: 'Racial Harassment at work: what employers can do about it'.

homosexuals. The RRA 1976 protects only individuals who are within a racial group.

3.3 LEGAL DEFINITION

Many of these sub-categories are self explanatory, particularly 'colour' and 'nationality'; however 'ethnic origins' and 'national origins' warrant more detailed examination. What does the law actually mean by these terms?

3.3.1 Ethnic group

The leading case, which defines what constitutes an ethnic group, is *Mandla & Another v Lee & Others* (below).

> *Example* The headmaster of a school refused a Sikh boy a place at the school because the boy insisted on wearing a turban rather than the school cap. The Court of Appeal refused to entertain the boy's complaint of racial discrimination, on the basis that Sikhs were a religious group rather than an ethnic group. The House of Lords disagreed and identified two crucial characteristics which must exist to establish a minority group as an ethnic group and thus protected by the RRA 1976:
>
> – a long-shared history, of which the group is conscious, distinguishing it from other groups and the memory of which it keeps alive;
> – its own cultural tradition, including family and social customs and manners.
>
> The presence of both of the above is necessary before a minority group can be identified as an 'ethnic group'.
>
> According to the House of Lords there are other factors which, although not essential, should also be considered when determining whether a group is to be regarded as an ethnic group, and which will weigh in favour of the existence of an ethnic group:
>
> – a common geographical origin or descent from a small number of common ancestors;
> – a common language (which does not need to be peculiar to the group);
> – a common literature;
> – a common religion distinct from that of the neighbouring community;
> – being a minority or an oppressed or dominant group within a large community.
>
> Not all of these 'non essential' criteria may be present and identifiable, but certainly one would expect some to be present. The House of Lords also added that members of an ethnic group could include converts to a religion or persons who marry into the group, whilst individuals who have left the group will be excluded. This is because it is necessary for the individual to demonstrate that he or she belongs to that group before (in the case of harassment) he or she can complain of being offended.
>
> *Mandla & Another v Lee & Others*
> [1983] ICR 385

The principles established in *Mandla* have been used in a number of cases to establish the ethnic origins of particular groups; these would be considered in order to establish whether there was race discrimination if an individual's ethnic origin or membership of an ethnic group led to harassment. The *Mandla* case also illustrates another key issue in the RRA 1976. It does not protect individuals against discrimination because of their religious beliefs or because they belong to a religious group or sect. It is only if their group, in addition to having a common religion, can also establish that it is an 'ethnic group' (ie the historical or cultural link) that protection under the RRA 1976 is achieved.

Religion alone is not included in the RRA 1976. Indeed, it is only in Northern Ireland, so far as UK law is concerned, that specific protection against religious discrimination exists.

3.3.2 Nationality

Section 78 of the RRA 1976 defines 'nationality' as including 'citizenship' It therefore covers not only an individual's nationality at birth but also an individual's current citizenship which may change from time to time

The original Race Relations Act 1965 did not refer to the word 'nationality' within the definition of racial grounds. The word was added in the amending legislation of 1976. The amendment was introduced following the decision in *Ealing London Borough Council v Race Relations Board* (below), which revealed a gap in the legislation as regards discrimination on the grounds of 'nationality'.

> *Example* Mr Zesko applied to be put on the council's housing list and was refused. The basis of the refusal was that Mr Zesko, who was of Polish origin, was not a British subject within the meaning of the British Nationality Act 1948 and this was a requirement by the council before an applicant would be placed on its waiting list.
>
> In rejecting Mr Zesko's claim of discrimination, the House of Lords stated that:

> ' "nationality" in the sense of citizenship of a certain State, must not be confused with "nationality" as meaning membership of a nation in the sense of race. Thus, according to international law, Englishmen and Scotsmen are, despite their different nationalities as regards race, all of British nationality as regards citizenship.'

> The House of Lords concluded that:

> 'the word "national" in "national origins" means national in the sense of race not citizenship.'

> Because at that time the definition was limited in that way, Mr Zesko had not been discriminated against on racial grounds; he was refused access to the waiting list not on account of his national origins (which were Polish) but on account of his nationality at the time when he applied, and this was not covered by the 1965 Act.
>
> *Ealing London Borough Council v Race Relations Board*
> [1972] 1 All ER 105

If he were to bring a similar complaint today, Mr Zesko would succeed because it is unlawful to discriminate against a person because of that person's nationality ie citizenship.

Until recently, the law in this area tended to examine discrimination against non-UK citizens generally, rather than against specific nationalities and formed the view that if all non UK citizens were treated the same, this did not amount to 'less favourable treatment'.

> *Example* Mr Tejani, who had been born in Uganda although he had since acquired a British citizenship, was required to produce a passport as means of identification before being granted a marriage licence. It was a custom of the Registrar to require sight of passports of applicants for a licence who were not born in the UK, although this was not a legal requirement. When Mr Tejani learnt that this was not a legal requirement he brought a claim for race discrimination. In rejecting his claim, the Court of Appeal concluded that the requirement for passports was applied to everyone from abroad in the same way:
>
> 'without any particular reference to a particular place or country of origin, he was not asked for it because of his racial origin, or his national origin, as defined in the Ealing Borough Council case.'

Thus the view of the Court was that all nationalities were treated the same way, save UK-born citizens. This analysis has limited appeal however, especially in cases of racially specific abuse and harassment and several recent tribunal decisions have considered the issue of discrimination as it applies against a specific nationality or national origin.

Tejani v Superintendent Registrar for the District of Peterborough
[1986] IRLR 502

> *Example* Mr Ruizo, an American of Spanish/Filipino origin, was referred to as a 'goddamn yank' by both colleagues and management. On occasions, by way of defending himself against such name calling, Mr Ruizo would reply 'bloody Brits'. In finding race discrimination, the tribunal concluded that Mr Ruizo had been subjected to this treatment because he was a US citizen, not because he was not British, thus his treatment was specific to his race.

Ruizo v (1) Tesco Stores & (2) Lea
[1995] Case No 53435/93, EOR Digest No 24

> *Example* Mr Milovanovic, who was of Serbian origin and had lived in the UK for 41 years, was subjected to racist comments referring to his Serbian origin, particularly after the start of the Bosnian war. The comments included,

- 'You're not in fucking Bosnia now. You're in England.'
- '. . . go back to Bosnia or wherever you belong and fight and die like a dog instead of our lads.'
- 'If all the foreigners or blacks go back to their own country we would have a better environment in this country.'

Mr Milovanovic eventually resigned and claimed race discrimination. An industrial tribunal found that the remarks:

'would only be made to an employee of foreign extraction and for that reason the applicant was treated less favourably on those occasions than other employees of British descent would have been, and that treatment was on racial grounds.'

Milovanvic v Hebden Dyeing & Finishing Co Ltd
[1995] Case No 29691/94, EOR Digest No 24

3.3.4 National origins

We referred earlier to the court's view that the English, Scots and Welsh are of the same nationality, ie UK citizens.[1] Thus a Scot who is subject to racial abuse because he is Scottish could not complain of racial discrimination based on his nationality. Instead, reliance would have to be placed on his national origins, that is to say, his Scottish ancestry.

> *Example* Mr Power applied for the position of Chief Constable of the Northern Constabulary in Scotland. When he was not short-listed for interview he claimed he had been discriminated against because he was English rather than Scottish. An industrial tribunal found that discrimination as between English and Scottish persons fell within the definition of racial grounds. Applying the authority of the *Ealing* case,[2] the tribunal accepted that the Scottish and the English are separate racial groups, defined by reference to 'national origins' in the sense that England and Scotland are 'nations'. The tribunal found in the alternative, that a claim *'could not be based'* on the Scots and English being different racial groups defined by reference to 'ethnic origins' on the Mandla test (see above).
>
> The EAT drew a distinction between 'national origins' and 'nationality'. Echoing the *Ealing* case, the EAT said that nationality was defined by reference to citizenship and accordingly the population of England, Scotland, Northern Ireland and Wales were all citizens of the United Kingdom. By contrast 'national origins' was wider:

'Nationality, we consider, has a juridical basis pointing to citizenship, which, in turn, points to the existence of a recognised state at the material time. Within the context of England, Scotland, Northern Ireland and Wales the proper approach to nationality is to categorise all of them as falling under the umbrella of British, and to regard the population as citizens of the United Kingdom. Against that background, what context, therefore, should be given to the phrase "national origins"? It seems to us, so far as there needs to be an exhaustive definition, what has to be ascertained are identifiable elements, both historically and geographically, which at least at some point in time reveals the existence of a nation. Whatever may be difficult fringe questions to this issue, what cannot be in doubt is that both England and Scotland were once separate nations. That, in our opinion, is effectively sufficient to dispose of the matter, since therefore we agree with the proposition that it is for each individual to show that his origins are embedded in such a nation, and how he chooses to do so requires scrutiny by the tribunal hearing the application'.

On the question of 'ethnic origins', the EAT concluded that the claim would not have succeeded on the alternative ground of 'ethnic origin' discrimination.

Northern Joint Police Board v Power
[1997] IRLR 610

---

1   *Ealing London Borough Council v Race Relations Board* [1972] 1 All ER 105.
2   *Ealing London Borough Council v Race Relations Board* (above).

This clear view from the EAT that the English, Scots and Welsh are not ethnic groups, echos an earlier EAT decision in *Boyce v British Airways Plc* (below).

> *Example* Four British Airways cabin crew of Scottish origin argued that they were discriminated against on racial grounds, on the basis that the English and the Scottish have different ethnic origins. The tribunal considered the test for ethnic origin set out in the case of *Mandla* (above) and concluded that the word 'ethnic' had a 'strong racial flavour' which was absent in the present case. It was therefore not open for the applicants to claim discrimination on grounds of ethnic origin.
>
> Agreeing with the tribunal's reasoning the EAT said that:
>
> 'given the wide variations in origin, background and, indeed race, within Scotland, all of whom can be categorised as "Scots", we cannot find that the common racial element within the group being addressed as Scots . . .'.
>
> *Boyce v British Airways plc*
> EAT 385/197

The judgment in the case of *Power*[1] is the first authorative decision which establishes that the English and the Scots are separate racial groups. Whilst some may find the decision surprising, it would be strange if this were not the case, given that the Irish and to a lesser extent, the Welsh, have been accepted as such.

An illustration of an Irishman complaining of racial harassment based on belonging to that national group and his national origins is *McAuley v Auto Alloys Foundry Ltd and Taylor* (below).

> *Example* Mr McAuley successfully claimed that he had been discriminated against on the grounds of his national origin when he was subjected to repeated anti-Irish comments from a supervisor. The comments included 'typical thick Irish' when he made a mistake and 'typical Paddy'. The tribunal found that:
>
> 'persons other than an Irish person would not have had such remarks made to them or about them and the remarks were undoubtedly derogatory towards and demeaning to the Irish and therefore to the applicant.'
>
> *McAuley v Auto Alloys Foundry Ltd and Taylor*
> [1994] Case No 62824/93, EOR Digest No 21

3.4 DEFINITION AND METHODS OF RACIAL HARASSMENT

3.4.1 Definition of racial harassment

Although the EC Code on the *Protection of the Dignity of Women and Men at Work* deals specifically with harassment based on sex, it can be used and adopted to define racial harassment as:

> 'conduct of a [racial] nature, or other conduct based on [race] affecting the dignity of women and men at work . . .'

---

1   *Northern Joint Police Board v Power* [1997] IRLR 610.

3.4.2 Methods of harassment

Racial harassment can take many forms and has included:

- the expression of racist views;
- racist jokes and banter;
- racist graffiti;
- racially derogatory remarks;
- display of racist publications;
- verbal threats; and
- assault.

But it is not just these more obvious methods by which harassment can occur. More sinister can be ostracising someone because of their race, or patronising them, belittling them and selecting them out for different treatment – which need not actually make positive reference to their colour or race, but where that fact is the underlying cause of the 'singling out'. Like sexual harassment, racial harassment can occur not just where the conduct is of a racially discriminatory nature, but where it is based on race, ie race is the cause of the behaviour, rather than the weapon itself. The strength of feeling which individuals have about such behaviour is illustrated by the following, extracted from evidence given in a race case in 1988:

> 'imagine the situation where a black man in a predominantly white office who for quite a while everyone saw as "good old Glen, he hasn't got a chip on his shoulder, he's one of the lads, I don't see him as a black man", that sort of attitude. "He's just Glen". It wasn't until the point where I started saying "I don't want to listen to these remarks anymore, they are offensive. I don't want to hear them", that the atmosphere changed. The reality is that anybody who refers to a black man as a "nigger", "coon", "spook", whether it be in jest or not, if that person went up to some ordinary black guy in the street and said that to his face, he would be looking at a fist in the mouth, never mind a grin or smile or an acceptance.'[1]

An example of a recent racial harassment case where the conduct was non-verbal is *Ruperting v Delphi Packard Electrical Systems Ltd* (below).

Example Mr Ruperting was of German origin and complained about swastika stickers being placed on a computer in his department and a number of colleagues (during the Euro '96 football competition) making Nazi salutes towards him. He complained successfully of racial harassment, although because the swastika incidents were out of time, he lost on this point.

Ruperting v Delphi Packard Electrical Systems Ltd
Case No 1301379/96

To complain in law of race discrimination, the victim of racial harassment must prove that:

- he or she has been treated less favourably;
- the treatment was on grounds of race; and
- he or she suffered a detriment (as a result of the less favourable treatment).

---

1   *Surinder Chima Singh v The Chief Constable of Nottinghamshire Constabulary* Case No 08807/88.

3.5 THE COMPARATOR

In order to establish discrimination, it will be necessary to compare the treatment of the individual with the treatment of another (real or hypothetical) person, to establish whether the treatment is less favourable. In order to be a valid comparison, the circumstances of the victim of discrimination and the hypothetical or actual comparator must be the same or not materially different. In cases of racial harassment, the relevant comparator is another employee of a different racial group. It is sufficient to show that a person of a different racial group would not have been treated in the same way.

3.6 LESS FAVOURABLE TREATMENT

Reference has already been made (in Chapter 2) to the case of *De Souza*,[1] where a black secretary was made aware of a racially insulting reference to herself in a conversation between two managers. The Court of Appeal found that, even though Mrs de Souza may have considered herself to have been treated less favourably as result of the insulting words:

> 'she could not have been treated less favourably within the meaning of s 1(1)(a) by whomsoever used the words unless he intended her to overhear the conversation, or knew or ought reasonably to have anticipated that the incident would be passed on or that [Mrs de Souza] would become aware of it in some other way.'

The Court's view was that Mrs de Souza, or the person in a like situation, would not be placed at a disadvantage in the circumstances and conditions in which they were working by the use of the word.

This decision can be criticised for its narrow definition of 'treatment'. It is also difficult to reconcile this analysis with the EC Code in that the racial insult could clearly have affected Mrs de Souza's dignity and created both an intimidating and humiliating working environment, particularly given that the comment came from a manager.

3.7 ON GROUNDS OF RACE

If the treatment to which the individual is subject to is racially specific or has racially specific connotations, then it will be 'on grounds of race', ie directed at that individual due to his colour, nationality, ethnic or national origins. As with sexual harassment, it is not relevant that the employer would also treat a person of a different racial group equally offensively.

The test of whether or not the harassment complained of was on racial grounds can be answered as in cases of sexual harassment: would a person who was not of that racial group have been vulnerable to the harassment? This is illustrated by the case of *Clark v B&Q plc* (below).

> *Example*   Mr Clark, a Portuguese national, was selected for redundancy on the basis of appraisals carried out by his store manager. One of the

---

1   [1986] IRLR 103.

comments was that Mr Clark did not participate in departmental managers' meetings unless pushed and that 'he is therefore a black sheep amongst other departmental managers'. Mr Clark sought to argue that the reference to 'black sheep' was a derogatory remark relating to his nationality.

An industrial tribunal disagreed. In the tribunal's view, the origin of the phrase as it was used by Mr Clark's manager, was:

'to indicate one in a flock of sheep that stood out in some way from the others, someone that was, as he described it a loner, the odd man out. Colloquially, of course it has come to mean somebody who is, in some way, disreputable. It has no reference to colour, ethnic origin, nationality or anything which is unlawful under the Race Relations Act. In our view, to try and interpret that remark as discrimination is false. No doubt the industry for political correctness might seek to argue that way. That simply discloses an ignorance of the linguistic use and derivation of the phrase.'

Clark v B&Q plc
[1996] Case No 56318/94, EOR Digest No 27

By contrast, derogatory comments which are not colloquial phrases risk being categorised as racial in nature.

Example Mr Sutton, who was of mixed race, was called a 'black bastard' by his general foreman at least 20 times over several months. The site manager, although aware of the abuse, did not speak to the general foreman and ask him to stop the abuse until Mr Sutton eventually complained. During a meeting between Mr Sutton and the employer's industrial relations manager, it was suggested to Mr Sutton that the words 'black bastard' were not unusual in the construction industry and could be regarded as words of camaraderie. An industrial tribunal rejected this suggestion. The tribunal found that:

'it is not correct to regard the use of such words as camaraderie and this tribunal does not accept that it is usual to call people who are black "black bastards". If that has been the situation in the past, it is no longer a tolerable situation and we strongly disapprove of any employers and particularly industrial relations managers who seek to sustain such language.'

Sutton v Balfour Beatty Construction
[1992] Case No 21650/90, EOR Digest No 12

Example An industrial tribunal upheld Mr Bellinfantine's claim of race discrimination on the basis that he had been called a 'black cunt' by a Mr Law, an employee of British Rail's subcontractor. The tribunal said:

'to call someone a black cunt is an abusive remark based on colour . . . it is unlikely that Mr Law would have called the applicant a white cunt if he had been white.'

Bellinfantine v British Rail
[1994] Case No 22829/92, EOR Digest No 21

3.8 WHOSE RACE?

Under the RRA, less favourable treatment 'on racial grounds' does not mean that it is necessary that the less favourable treatment is linked to the race of the individual bringing a discrimination complaint. In this respect the RRA 1976 is wider than the SDA 1975, in that a person may be discriminated against on the grounds of another person's race. Several EAT decisions illustrate this point.

In *Zarcznska v Levy*,[1] a white barmaid successfully complained of race discrimination when she was dismissed for serving a black customer against her employer's instructions. Similarly, in *Showboat Entertainment Centre Ltd v Owens*,[2] a white employee was dismissed for refusing to carry out instructions from his employer to exclude black people from an entertainment centre and successfully claimed for race discrimination. The EAT found it could not have been the intention of Parliament to leave an employee without a remedy in circumstances such as these.

The decisions have been criticised by commentators on the basis that it would have been open for the individuals to claim discrimination by way of victimisation, ie that they had been treated less favourably because they had done something under or by reference to the RRA 1976, such as refusing to obey a discriminatory instruction (see Chapter 7). The difficulty with a victimisation complaint in this context, however, is that it may be open to the employer to defeat such a claim by showing that the less favourable treatment was related to the employee's refusal to obey an order, rather than the fact that the order was a discriminatory one.

> *Example* A white employee was told, during her induction, that the company operated a special policy with regard to potential black and Asian customers. The instruction she was issued with was that if she received an enquiry from a potential black or Asian customer about hiring a vehicle, she should tell them that there were no cars available to hire. The following day she was asked by the director of the company whether the policy had been explained to her and a senior employee confirmed that it had. Ms Sargent resigned and brought a claim for race discrimination.
>
> Upholding the tribunal's finding of race discrimination, the EAT rejected the employer's argument that Ms Sargent had not been treated less favourably by the imposition of an unlawful instruction, but rather she had been treated the same as other employees and she had simply chosen to react differently. The EAT concluded that whilst the employer had imposed the policy on all employees equally, the instruction affected different employees in different ways. Miss Sargent, in the EAT's view, had been unfavourably treated as she did not regard herself as being able to continue to work with an employer who operated such a policy. Her conclusion on this and compulsion to resign amounted to less favourable treatment, when compared with an employee who did not take the same view of the instruction.
>
> *Weathersfield Ltd t/a Van & Truck Rentals v Sargent*
> [1998] IRLR 14, EAT

In the context of racial harassment, the principal applies equally and employers should be aware of this fact.

> *Example* An industrial tribunal upheld Miss Wilkinson's claim of race and sex discrimination based on sexist and racist remarks made to her because

---

1   [1979] ICR 184, EAT.
2   [1984] ICR 65.

she had an Afro-Caribbean boyfriend. The remarks included 'is it true about black men – are they all well hung?' The tribunal concluded that:

'the abusive remarks were not only directed at the applicant as a woman, but they were discriminatory in that they were directed against the applicant's boyfriend who was an Afro-Caribbean'.

Wilkinson v Oils & Soaps Ltd
Case No 26463/95

Thus organisations must take care if they receive any complaints about racial harassment from an employee. Just because the individual who complains is not, for example black, does not mean that the individual could not complain that he or she finds the behaviour offensive and/or embarrassing, and is therefore suffering a detriment.

3.9 A DETRIMENT?

An individual who has suffered less favourable treatment on the grounds of race must still establish that he or she has suffered a detriment in order to complain of race discrimination. As previously discussed, there are a wide range of circumstances where the less favourable treatment does not result in any tangible employment consequences, such as the loss of employment, salary or promotion. In the case of harassment, the fact that a hostile, upsetting or uncomfortable work environment prevails can, in itself, amount to a detriment.

In *De Souza*[1] the Court of Appeal found that a racial insult is not, by itself, enough to be a detriment, even if (as in Mrs de Souza's case) it caused her distress. She also had to prove that a reasonable worker would take the view that she had been disadvantaged in the circumstances in which she had to continue working. The court's finding that Mrs de Souza did not suffer a detriment appears to have been influenced by the fact that she was not intended to hear the derogatory remark and therefore could not be said to have been treated less favourably. The reasoning in *De Souza* was applied in *Elliot v Domnick Hunter Ltd* (below).

> *Example* Miss Elliot, who was of Afro-Caribbean origin, complained that she had been racially abused by her team leader who called her names such as 'fucking black bitch' and 'nigger'. On the evidence, the tribunal did not accept the allegations as true, although it did find that Miss Elliott was referred to as 'kizzy', a reference to a black baby born to a slave in the film Roots. The tribunal took the view that although the reference was offensive, Miss Elliott did not suffer a detriment within the meaning of the RRA 1976. The EAT refused to interfere with the tribunal's finding and rejected Miss Elliott's arguments that the abuse was racially insulting and that she had found it offensive. The tribunal stated that:

---

1   *De Souza v The Automobile Association* [1986] IRLR 103; see Chapter 2.

'in some circumstances it may be that a racial insult or insults would affect the working environment in some way and to such a degree that a detriment resulted.'

Elliot v Domnick Hunter Ltd
[1996] EAT No 1144/94, EOR Digest No 26

The idea or argument which both *De Souza* and *Elliot* put forward, that the offensive nature of a racial comment may not be sufficient to amount in law to a detriment, sits uneasily with the EC Code, which states:

'it is for each individual to determine what behaviour is acceptable to them and what they regard as offensive'

As we have seen, the Code defines harassment according to the perceptions and feelings of the recipient – embarrassing, offensive and unwelcome conduct.

In addition, this test has been adapted to assist in defining racial harassment. The Commission for Racial Equality (CRE) code defines harassment as:

'unwanted conduct of a racial nature, or other conduct based on race affecting the dignity of women and men at work'.[1]

The subjective/objective test has already been discussed in relation to sexual harassment in Chapter 2 and it has been seen that the assessment and test is both objective and subjective, although the emphasis in the EC Code is on the subjective approach. There will, however, be cases where the conduct complained of is so obviously offensive that a reasonable person could not but fail to find it so.

Example Mr Asante, a black manager, was racially abused by his store manager, Mr Rich. The abuse included an assertion that 'all black people are criminals'. Mr Asante's claim of racial discrimination succeeded before the industrial tribunal, who stated that such assertions 'would inevitably cause any reasonable black person to feel disadvantaged in the work place'. The tribunal firmly rejected the suggestion that the remarks could be regarded as banter; it found that Mr Asante's objections had been made clear, and Mr Rich could have been in no doubt that the remarks were offensive and could not be regarded as joking or banter.

Asante v (1) The Reject Shop and (2) Rich
[1996] Case No 36433/95, EOR Digest No 28

3.10 RACIST BANTER

Employers have sought to escape liability for racially offensive remarks by arguing that 'banter' of this nature is accepted by the workforce and commonplace in the particular work environment. Whilst it is true that the tribunals will assess abusive language in the light of commonly accepted standards in the relevant working environment, several tribunal decisions have illustrated that racial abuse cannot be justified in this way.

Example Mr Quaid was regularly subjected to racial abuse and called 'black bastard' and 'nigger'. Although the employer accepted that racist comments were regularly made, they sought to argue that such comments formed part of the everyday banter of their work environment as a fish processing

---

1   *Racial Harassment at Work: What Employers Can Do About It* (1995, CRE).

factory, that Mr Quaid gave as good as he got and had not objected to the comments. An industrial tribunal concluded that although other employees may also have been insulted, the nature of the language used was clearly on racial grounds. The tribunal said:

'the applicant's treatment was clearly less favourable than that other employees, if only because the language used to him was of a specifically different nature to that used to others. ... it is impossible to conceive that the applicant would have been called a "black bastard" or a "fucking nigger" if there had not been a racial element behind the terms used to him.'

Quaid v L Williamson (Shetland) Ltd t/a Sheltie
[1996] Case No 60642/95, EOR Digest No 29

Example An industrial tribunal found that the employer's management were aware of racist banter on the shopfloor, and

'considering there was no harm in it, ignored it, thereby effectively condoning it and for the purposes of the [Race Relations] Act, adopting it.'

Sattar v Aeroquip Automotive Operations Trinova Ltd
[1996] Case No 59628/95, EOR Digest No 20

Dismissing racial comments as part of everyday 'industrial language' therefore will not excuse an employer. However, one measure of whether such comments do amount to harassment and to a detriment will be the attitude of the person complaining: if he has participated in name calling of this nature it will be more difficult to demonstrate that it was found to be offensive.

This will still be carefully scrutinised by a tribunal because retorts of this nature may be simply a defence mechanism by the subject. We considered earlier the case of *Ruizo v Tesco Stores*.[1]

In accepting Mr Ruizo's complaint of race discrimination, an industrial tribunal found that the phrase 'goddamn yank' constituted racial abuse. The tribunal found that Mr Ruizo's retort of 'bloody Brits' did not mean he did not find the abuse offensive but was simply a defence mechanism. In the tribunal's view, the fact that he did not complain to management was irrelevant in determining whether Mr Ruizo found the phrase offensive. The tribunal said:

'it is hardly surprising that he did not complain to management when management used the phrase themselves, and were well aware of this and other racist remarks and seemed to condone it.'

Care must be taken to treat such complaints seriously and not just dismiss them as work 'banter'. The tribunal was particularly critical not only of Tesco's handling of the matter, but also of its handling of the proceedings; in particular that during the defence of the case, Tesco persisted in insisting:

'that the use of such phrases as "goddamn yank" and "black bastard" do not amount to racial abuse'.

Criticism was levelled at them because:

'They persist in referring to these phrases as innocent "banter". By failing to take any steps to eliminate the use of such language they have condoned racial abuse. It is no

1   *Ruizo v (1) Tesco Stores Ltd & (2) Lea* [1995] Case No 53435/93, EOR Digest No 24.

defence that the management do not find it offensive. It is no defence that no member of staff has complained about the use of this language. It is naive of any respondent company of the size of Tesco, to believe that unless it receives a complaint about the use of racial abuse there is no problem. To wait for a complaint is complacent at best, culpable at worst. The management are responsible for employees engaging in racial abuse. They were fully aware of it and condoned it.'

3.11 IN THE COURSE OF EMPLOYMENT

Liability for harassment is discussed in detail in Chapter 8. It is worth mentioning here, however, that employers have also sought to deny liability for racial harassment conducted by employees, on the basis that they are not vicariously liable for acts done by employees which are not in the course of employment.

Section 32 of the RRA 1976 provides that:

'Anything done by a person in the course of his employment shall be treated for the purposes of this Act . . . as done by his employer as well as by him, whether or not it was done with the employer's knowledge or approval.'

We have already seen that an employer will be liable for acts which it impliedly consented to by turning a blind eye to harassment of which it was aware or which involved members of its management. However, from the development of case-law in this area, it would appear that an employer will be liable even if it had no such knowledge. The highpoint in establishing the extent of the employer's responsibility came in *Jones v Tower Boot Company Ltd*.[1]

In *Tower Boot*, the Court of Appeal established that the distinction between acts which are unauthorised ways of doing authorised acts (for which the employer will be liable) and acts which are unauthorised (for which the employer will not be liable) is no longer relevant when assessing liability for discrimination.

Example Mr Jones, whose mother was white and whose father was black, was racially harassed by his work colleagues. The harassment took the following forms:

– physical assaults such as branding him with a hot screwdriver and whipping him with a piece of welt;
– racial abuse by being called names such as 'chimp', 'monkey' and 'baboon'.

The Court of Appeal stated:

'it would be particularly wrong to allow racial harassment on the scale that was suffered by the complainant in this case at the hands of his workmates – treatment that was wounding both emotionally and physically – to slip through the net of employer responsibility by applying to it a common law principle evolved in another area of the law to deal with vicarious responsibility for wrongdoing for a wholly different kind. To do so would seriously undermine the statutory scheme of the Discrimination Acts and flout the purposes for which they were passed to achieve.'

Jones v Tower Boot Company Ltd
[1997] ICR 254

---

1   [1997] ICR 254.

It will now be increasingly difficult for employers to argue that discriminatory acts done in the workplace or during working hours are not in the course of employment.

As with sexual harassment and discrimination, an employer may find himself liable for acts of racial harassment, abuse and racist comments and behaviour which occurs outside the factory, office or work area. If the place where such conduct occurs has a connection with the workplace, work relations or is under the employer's control, a court or tribunal will consider that the employer is responsible for ensuring that harassment and other unacceptable behaviour does not occur and is not tolerated. Examples of this are given in Chapter 2, but, briefly, this can include incidents which take place on a customer's premises, outside working hours, during a conference or in a social context during an offsite meeting or firm function. It is only where the incident happens in a purely social meeting or gathering, which has nothing whatsoever to do with work, that an employer can be excused from taking responsibility for it.

In Chapter 2, we considered the fact that employers will be responsible for any acts of sexual harassment to which employees are exposed in the workplace. Exactly the same rule applies where the harassment is racial in nature.

> *Example* A complaint was brought by a barmaid, who was black, after the owner of the pub where she worked played a video of a performance by Jim Davidson, the comedian, on the pub's television, at the request of the customers. The video contained a number of racist jokes which Ms Ampadu had to listen to whilst she continued working. The tribunal concluded that her employer had subjected her to racial harassment. Indeed the tribunal also found that her dismissal, which followed when she refused to continue working in the pub because of her embarrassment, was also unlawful and discriminatory (as victimisation – see Chapter 8).[1]
>
> *Ampadu v Mullane*
> Case No 33530/94

3.12 DEALING WITH COMPLAINTS

An employer who fails to deal adequately with complaints of racial harassment may be committing an act of discrimination under the RRA 1976. The CRE warns of 'subliminal discrimination' and ignoring grievances from members of racial groups. The CRE's 'Code of Practice for the Elimination of Racial Discrimination and the Promotion of Equality of Opportunity in Employment', makes a number of recommendations in relation to dealing with grievances, disputes and disciplinary procedures; including :

– warning employers against ignoring or treating lightly grievances from members of a particular racial group on the assumption that they are 'over sensitive' about discrimination;

– taking steps to avoid the intimidation of individuals, aimed at forcing them to leave the organisation. This can be on the basis that 'their face does not fit';

---

1   This should be considered in conjunction with *Burton and Rhule v De Vere Hotels* [1996] IRLR 596.

– implementing proper and effective disciplinary action against those responsible for harassment of this nature.

This warning was reiterated in a case which also demonstrates that an employer will be responsible for an employee being harassed by those who are not employees but with whom the employee comes into contact during the employment.

> *Example*   Over an eight-year period Mr Jenkins, a black college lecturer, complained to the college authorities of racial abuse by students of the college. The abuse consisted of calling him amongst other things 'nigger', 'kaffir', 'wog' and 'sambo'. Mr Jenkins' allegations were not believed, as his employer formed the view that due to his poor command of the English language the complaints were due to misunderstandings. The tribunal stated that:
>
> 'there was an innate tendency to disbelieve what Mr Jenkins said about the incidences concerned. That tendency was closely related to, if not based upon, racial considerations, relating to what was perceived to be his difficulties in understanding what was said or done in his presence. We consider that this was less favourable treatment of Mr Jenkins on account of his race'.
>
> *Jenkins v Burney & Others*
> [1994] Case No 4979/91, EOR Digest No 20

3.13 EFFECTS OF RACIAL ABUSE

We have already seen that courts are critical of employers who fail to recognise and treat seriously the problem of racial harassment.

However, it is not just the unpleasant nature of such conduct itself which can have a serious detrimental affect on the work environment and the individual. Other consequences may also flow from it, as illustrated in the case of *Bains v Amber Leisure Ltd* (below).

> *Example*   Mr Bains was a production worker, from an ethnic minority. Following a job-ranking scheme designed to reward employees according to their individual skills, merit and attitude, Mr Hickman (who performed the same job as Mr Bains) was paid £40.00 more than Mr Bains per week. Mr Bains complained but with no success. He was upset and demotivated and the company used his demotivation to justify its continued decision not to give him a pay rise each time he complained. Mr Bains demotivation was such that he discussed the possibility of taking voluntary redundancy and he was informed that he would be considered for any redundancies which arose in the future. When the company subsequently needed to effect redundancies, Mr Bains was chosen.
>
> In upholding Mr Bains' claim of racial discrimination, the tribunal was satisfied that Mr Bains' selection for redundancy was based on his request. However, it found that:
>
> 'the request was directly attributable to the treatment by the company of the applicant in a way which he perceived, and we agree, was discriminatory.'
>
> In the tribunal's view:

'it is a foreseeable consequence of discriminatory treatment of an employee that he will become upset and demotivated, and we have no doubt that the causative effect of the applicant's selection for redundancy was the company's detrimental treatment of the applicant.'

Bains v Amber Leisure Ltd
[1995] Case No 09972/94, EOR Digest No 23

It is common, understandably, for those subjected to racial harassment to become demotivated. For an employer this often leads to other problems at work. Branding the employee 'difficult' or uncooperative, commonly leads to other problems such as unhappiness with performance, poor appraisal reports and unresolved grievances. This in turn leads to lost promotion opportunities for the employee and the problems can escalate, leading to a catalogue of complaints, which are disruptive, wasteful of the employee's time and not in anyone's best interest.

Employers must guard against this situation by dealing with complaints promptly and effectively and ensuring that managers and work colleagues understand their errors and do not seek to blame the victim.

> *Example*   Mr Philogene, who was black, experienced racial abuse from his manager, Mr Locke.
>
> – on one occasion Mr Philogene was discussing England's performance in the test match against the West Indies with Mr Locke, when Mr Locke replied: 'Why don't you fuck off to the West Indies or Africa, wherever you come from, if it's that good out there?'. Mr Philogene jokingly replied that he was going back for four weeks to which Mr Locke said 'good, well stay there because we can do without fuckers like you here'.
> – on another occasion, whilst Mr Philogene was listening to a cricket match on a radio in his carrier bag, Mr Locke asked him whether the bag was his and threatened to throw it in the bin. Mr Locke was accompanied by the operations manager, Mr Forskitt, and Mr Philogene was asked by each in turn to allow them to look in the bag. Mr Philogene refused and walked away after being requested to stay where he was.

After the latter incident, Mr Philogene was disciplined and suspended for insubordination. At the disciplinary hearing, Mr Philogene alleged Mr Locke was conducting a witch-hunt against him on racial grounds. The allegation was not investigated and Mr Philogene was dismissed.

The tribunal formed the view that Mr Philogene's dismissal was not for insubordination but on racial grounds. The tribunal stated that the applicant's conduct was relatively minor and that Mr Locke's conduct was provocative. In the tribunal's view:

'the applicant's refusal to open his bag and his walking away from Mr Locke appears in a very different light when Mr Locke's previous racist comments and attitude to the applicant are taken into account. The charge of insubordination – later increased to gross insubordination – cannot be viewed in isolation from the relationship between the manager and employees. A black employee's reaction to the manager who racially abused him must be seen in a different light and if those factors had not been present.'

Philogene v (1) British Pepper & Spice Company Ltd
(2) Foskitt and (3) Locke
Case No 37647/96

Employers should be wary in case behavioural problems, poor performance or absenteeism are really a shield for the harassment problems which an employee is experiencing.

Chapter 4

DISABILITY HARASSMENT

Introduction – What is disability harassment? – Disabled person – Establishing harassment – Exclusion for small employers – Vicarious liability – Liability for the acts of third parties – Defence – Preventing disability harassment

4.1 INTRODUCTION

As with sexual and racial harassment, there is no legislation in the United Kingdom which deals specifically with disability harassment at work. However, as we have seen, it is well established that sexual or racial harassment may give rise to a claim under the SDA 1975 or the RRA 1976 on the grounds that the complainant has been treated less favourably due to sex or race and that the treatment amounts to a detriment.

A similar analysis applies to disability harassment, which would amount to unlawful discrimination because the DDA 1995 contains the same terms 'detriment' and 'less favourable treatment'. As yet there is no case-law on disability harassment although the principles established on sexual and racial harassment will apply equally to disability harassment under the DDA 1995.

There is little doubt, however, that it is only a matter of time before the case law on this new area begins to set out standards of acceptable and unacceptable conduct within the workplace. Since the coming into effect of the DDA 1995, it has been estimated that in total 2000 claims have been made to the tribunals.[1] A person's treatment in the workplace is bound to form part of the concerns of disabled employees, particularly their treatment by work colleagues. It will be interesting to see what develops. Because of the few reported cases as yet in this area, what follows in this chapter is necessarily an outline of the law and speculation as to what the legislation holds for the future.

According to a recent Government consultation paper which is looking to tackle the issue of rail transport for disabled persons, the category of individuals potentially protected is wide:[2]

– over 6 million people in the UK have some form of disability;
– this amounts to 12% of the population.

Admittedly a proportion of this group will not be in employment and some will be over retirement age (over two-thirds according to the Government paper are 'elderly').

---

1   *Equal Opportunities Review*, No 79, May/June 1998.
2   *The Rail Vehicles Accessibility Regulations 1998 Consultation Paper*, May 1998, Department of Environment, Transport and the Regions.

4.2 WHAT IS DISABILITY HARASSMENT?

We have already referred to the European Commission's Recommendation and Code on the *Protection of Dignity of Women and Men at Work* (the EC Code: see Chapter 2). As a reminder, this defines harassment as behaviour which is:

- unwanted, unreasonable and offensive to the recipient;
- where a person's rejection of, or submission to, such conduct on the part of employers or workers (including supervisors or colleagues) is used explicitly or implicity as the basis for employment decisions which affects that person's access to location, training, access to employment, continued employment, promotion, salary or any other employment decision; or
- is such as to create an intimidating, hostile or humiliating working environment for the recipient.

In order to bring a claim for harassment under the DDA 1995, an employee must establish:

- less favourable treatment on the grounds of disability (s 5(1)(a) of the DDA 1995); and
- that he or she has suffered a detriment (s 4(2)(d) of the DDA 1995).

Paragraph 6.22 of the Code of Practice on Disability Discrimination makes it clear that, although the DDA 1995 does not refer to harassment as a separate issue, harassing a disabled person on account of his or her disability will almost always amount to a 'detriment' under the Act.

4.3 DISABLED PERSON

In the previous Chapters examining sex and race discrimination, we have looked at exactly what the law means by the terms 'sex' and 'race'. We examined the fact that 'sex' is wider than just males and females and that 'race' covers more than just an individual's colour. When considering the meaning of 'disability' for the purposes of the DDA 1995, greater difficulties are faced. This is because the DDA 1995 has set out a complex definition which includes the medical considerations, as well as ensuring that minor disabilities do not enable people to complain under the Act. Indeed, the complexity of the new law in this regard has been subject to much criticism and is proving no easy task for the tribunals.

4.3.1 Existing registered disabled

The first category to gain protection under the DDA 1995 are those previously protected by the earlier disability laws, which the DDA 1995 replaces. That is the Disabled Persons (Employment) Act 1944 and the registered disabled system, commonly called the 'green card system'. The registration system has been repealed by the DDA 1995. However, those already registered at a certain date, who remained registered on the 2 December 1996 (when the Act finally came into effect) are automatically protected as disabled persons and do not have to satisfy the strict definition of disability, at least not for the first three years, ie until 3 December 1999. The two dates are key and registration must have existed on BOTH:

- 12 January 1995; and
- 2 December 1996.

4.3.2 Definition

Those who are not included automatically by their registration (and, in addition, all disabled persons who are registered as such after December 1999) have to demonstrate the following:

- first, that they have a physical or mental impairment;
- secondly, that the impairment is substantial; and
- thirdly, that the impairment is long term.

Each of these three prerequisites warrant further consideration.

4.3.3 Physical or mental impairment

The establishment of the existence of physical impairment is straight-forward. However, the extent of the impairment will have to be assessed to see if it satisfies the long-term and substantial tests, as the Act focusses on establishing the impact of a person's disability on their life, before they can seek protection.

It is more problematic to establish mental impairment, because under Sch 1 of the Act the requirement is that a mental impairment will only be protected if it is 'clinically well recognised ... by a respected body of medical opinion''. Many conditions will not be open to dispute, however, others may be more complex: for example, 'Gulf War Syndrome', which some medics assert is a mental condition. A huge debate is currently raging across both sides of the Atlantic as to whether the syndrome even exists, let alone whether it is a mental impairment.

For other conditions, one useful, reliable, guide, which a tribunal certainly will look at, is the World Health Organisation's International Classification of Diseases. Indeed, the DDA 1995 is supported by a series of Guides and Regulations, to help in implementation. A Code of Practice Guide issued by the Department of Employment[1] specifically states that a condition which has a listing in the World Health publication will, most likely, satisfy this element of the test.

4.3.4 Exclusions

During the course of the progress of the DDA 1995 through Parliament, a number of impairments were discussed and specifically excluded concerning who should and should not, be protected. Certain 'anti-social' conduct and behaviour, it was decided, should never allow an individual to claim protection under the Act. These include:

- voyeurism;
- pyromania and cleptomania: tendency to set fires and to steal;
- exhibitionism;
- paedophilia and tendencies to physically or sexually abuse others;

---

1   *Guidance on Matters to be Taken into Account in Determining Questions Relating to the Definition of Disability* (HMSO, 1996).

–   drug and alcohol addiction (unless this was due to the substance having been medically prescribed);
–   although severe disfigurements such as birthmarks are included, deliberately acquired disfigurements (such as tattoos, body piercing) are not.

4.3.5 The impact of the impairment

Detailed Codes and Guidance assist with the definition of a disabled person.[1]

This includes identifying whether the disability and the impact of the physical and mental impairment, has a substantial and a long-term adverse effect on 'normal day-to-day activities'. It is important to bear in mind, when considering this aspect of the DDA 1995, that the consideration is not whether the individual's disability substantially and adversely affects their work, but whether it affects their normal day-to-day activities. An all-inclusive list of normal day-to-day activities is set out in Sch 1 to the Act:

–   mobility;
–   manual dexterity;
–   physical co-ordination;
–   continence;
–   ability to lift, carry or otherwise move everyday objects;
–   speech, hearing or eyesight;
–   memory or ability to concentrate, learn or understand;
–   the perception of the risk of physical danger.

It is outside the scope of this book to go into detail as to how each of these items is to be assessed, for example looking at whether mobility is affected substantially and on a long-term basis. More detail is contained on this in the Guidance, which gives specific examples that can be used as a measure to identify the extent to which one or, taken together, all of these activities have to be affected before the effect can be considered substantial.[2]

The Act does give more detail on one of the definitions contained in this provision, which is the meaning of long term. An impairment will be treated as having a long-term effect if:

–   it has already lasted for 12 months or more;
–   it is expected to last for 12 months or more or is likely to do so, in the sense that it is more probable that it will last for 12 months or more than not;
–   if the condition is terminal and is likely to last for the rest of the individual's life;
–   if it is likely to recur.

4.3.6 Severe disfigurements

An individual with a severe disfigurement or perhaps a facial disfigurement could face distressing or offensive comments from work colleagues and others. The Act recognises that if an individual has a severe disfigurement – even though strictly

---

1   Disability Discrimination (Meaning of Disability) Regulations 1996, SI 1996/1455 and *Guidance on Matters to be Taken into Account in Determining Questions Relating to the Definition of Disability* (HMSO, 1996).
2   See also Brian Doyle *Disability Discrimination: Law and Practice* (Jordan Publishing, 1996).

such a disfigurement would not affect that list of normal day-to-day activities which is outlined above – the individual is to be treated, according to the DDA 1995, as a disabled person. The examples given include birth marks, skin diseases and deformities.

4.3.7 History of disability

Equally, a person who has had a disability in the past, but has subsequently recovered, may be subject to discrimination and less favourable treatment, because of his or her history. In this case, the Act again specifically provides that such individuals are to be protected, provided that the impairment affected them on a long-term basis as defined (taking into account both the 12-month measure and the likelihood of recurrence).

4.3.8 Progressive impairments

Finally, progressive conditions such as HIV infection are also specifically covered. Where conditions of this nature have some effect, albeit not initially substantial, they are to be treated as having a substantial effect as soon as the first symptoms start to impact. This is to avoid an individual who suffers some effect from such conditions not being treated as a disabled person because the symptoms are not yet substantial.

4.4 ESTABLISHING HARASSMENT

4.4.1 The principles for establishing harassment

The principles established in sexual and racial harassment cases are likely to apply equally to claims of harassment being discrimination and contrary to the DDA 1995.

The key to this type of harassment is probably illustrated by the case of *Porcelli*[1] mentioned earlier. This case (examined in detail in Chapter 2) concerned a woman who was subjected to a campaign of suggestive remarks and inappropriate touching by two male colleagues whose aim was to force her to leave her job.

The Court of Session decided that the woman had been subjected to the treatment on the ground of her sex even though the perpetrators did not have any sex related motive or objective. The treatment was found to be:

> 'a particular kind of weapon based upon the sex of the victim, which .... would not have been used against an equally disliked man.'

The motive of the perpetrators was not relevant in determining whether or not the individual had been the victim of sex discrimination. The key was whether the weapon used was one to which the individual was vulnerable because of her sex.

Applying this analogy to disability discrimination, any conduct which is offensive and based on a person's disability, regardless of the motive for the conduct, will amount to direct discrimination and less favourable treatment within the meaning of the DDA 1995.

---

1   *Porcelli v Strathclyde Regional Council* [1986] IRLR 134.

4.4.2 Comparator

In the case of *British Telecom Communications v Williams*,[1] the EAT stated that because conduct which constitutes sexual harassment is itself gender specific, there is no need to look for a male comparator. By analogy, where conduct is disability specific, there is no need to look for comparators to demonstrate that the treatment is less favourable.

4.4.3 A detriment

In determining whether or not a detriment has been suffered or, alternatively, the extent of the detriment suffered by the victim, the tribunal will look at the impact of the behaviour on the recipient. In the *Wileman*[2] case, it was found that the wearing of provocative clothes by the applicant was relevant in determining whether acts of sexual harassment constituted a detriment to the applicant. It is however difficult to imagine a situation where a victim of disability harassment could provoke the harassment.

4.4.4 Examples of detriment

Examples of harassment which amount to a detriment in sex and race discrimination cases have been given in previous chapters. The same examples, based on disability, would constitute disability harassment. Again, there is a range of methods and mediums which can be used to convey offensive or embarrassing comments or actions.

Derogatory comments, 'teasing' or singling someone out for embarrassing or humiliating comments or treatment, due to or based on their disability, would certainly be caught. Comments directed not to the disability itself, but some characteristics or aid used as a consequence of the disability could also be offensive. It should be borne in mind that a wheelchair and other aids forms part of a disabled person's body space. Leaning on a wheelchair, for example might well constitute disability harassment if the wheelchair user could show that it was intimidating or intrusive.

4.5 EXCLUSION FOR SMALL EMPLOYERS

One area that has been the subject of much debate in terms of an employer's responsibility and liability for disability discrimination, has been the size of the employer. The DDA 1995 as it currently stands, excludes all employers who are regarded as 'small' from the provisions of the Act. A 'small employer' for these purposes is defined as one which employs 20 or fewer employees at any relevant time. The relevant time is at the time of the act of discrimination.

In early 1998, the Government announced the creation of a review body to look into the various provisions of the DDA 1995, their impact and aspects as to enforcement. One of the areas which they are considering is whether the small employers exemption should remain or if the limit of 20 employees should be reduced.

---

1   [1997] IRLR 668.
2   *Wileman v Minilec Engineering Limited* [1988] IRLR 144.

Outside of this exemption, however, all employers are liable, as under the SDA 1975 and RRA 1976 for acts of harassment and discrimination against:

- applicants for employment;
- employees;
- workers, ie non-employees who are carrying out work in a personal capacity;
- agency and contract workers.

4.6 VICARIOUS LIABILITY

There are specific provisions contained in the DDA 1995 which make employers potentially liable for the acts of their employees during the course of their employment. These are examined in more detail in Chapters 2 and 8.

Under s 58(1) of the DDA 1995, anything done by a person:

> 'in the course of his employment shall be treated for the purposes of the Act as also done by his employer, whether or not it was done with the employer's knowledge or approval.'

The wording of this section is taken almost entirely from the SDA 1975, s 41 and the RRA 1976, s 32, which have proved troublesome in their interpretation.

Under common law, an employer is only liable for the wrongful or unauthorised mode of doing an authorised act of an employee(s). If the act itself is unauthorised, the employer is not liable. Given that acts of harassment rarely constitute an authorised act, the victim of such harassment was potentially denied a remedy against the employer or employee under the SDA 1975 and RRA 1976.

The issue was addressed most recently by the Court of Appeal in *Jones v Tower Boot Co Ltd*[1] which has been discussed earlier. The Court of Appeal recognised the injustice caused by the common law approach and found that s 32(1) of the RRA 1976 was not subject to the strict common law test of vicarious liability. Instead, it was held that the term 'course ... of employment' in the RRA 1976 and SDA 1975 should be given a broader construction. It is likely that tribunals will conclude that an employer is answerable for a wider range of disability discriminatory acts on the part of its employees than it would be under the test of vicarious liability under common law and even more likely that this term will be given the same, wider interpretation in the DDA 1995.

4.7 LIABILITY FOR THE ACTS OF THIRD PARTIES

Employers themselves may be held liable for committing an act of unlawful discrimination if they fail to protect staff from harassment by third parties, other than their employees, in circumstances in which the employer can control whether harassment occurs or by failing to adopt good employment practice. This principle has been established by two EAT decisions, *Burton and Rhule v De*

---

1 [1997] IRLR 168.

Vere Hotels[1] and *Go Kidz Go Ltd v Bourdouane*[2] discussed earlier (see Chapters 2 and 3).

Employers are therefore placed under a duty to implement preventive action, which will include making it absolutely clear that harassment of staff by other members of staff or by the public will not be tolerated.

4.8 DEFENCE

Under s 58 of the DDA 1995, the employer will have a defence in respect of an act of harassment by an employee if it can prove that it took such steps as were reasonably practicable to prevent the occurrence of harassment.

Employers are therefore recommended to introduce policies and training procedures in respect of disability discrimination and to put such policies into practice. Measures of this nature will both combat disability discrimination, and help to establish the employer's statutory defence in the event that a disability discrimination claim is brought against the employer.

4.9 PREVENTING DISABILITY HARASSMENT

Harassment may be verbal or non-verbal and, to a large extent, what constitutes harassment will be defined by common sense. Employers and employees should be sensitive to what disabled people might find offensive and remember that, although they might not intend offence by their comments or action, if such actions or comments are unwanted by the disabled person, they may amount to harassment. Motive is irrelevant.

Employers should also be sensitive to the types of images which may cause offence. For example, charity or other posters, particularly if they portray the disabled person in the role of a 'victim', may embarrass an individual.

Care should also be taken by employers and work colleagues alike, not to make assumptions about disabled workers which may result in excluding them from mainstream social, or work, activity. For example, even if a disabled person cannot participate in the activity itself he or she should be included in the occasion and made to feel a part of the team.

Employers should draft a full policy on disability harassment to make all employees aware of unacceptable behaviour and how complaints will be investigated. Taking steps to help other employees understand the issues, how to deal appropriately with disabilities and to appreciate what might cause offence, are recommended.

Below are some extracts from a booklet called 'Disability Etiquette' prepared by the Employer's Forum on Disability, which provides instructive guidance on dealing with disabled people, without the need to feel awkward:

– offer assistance to a disabled person if it appears appropriate, but wait until your offer is accepted before you help;

---

1   [1996] IRLR 596.
2   (1996) IDS 578, EAT.

- do not assume that you know the best way of helping, and listen to any instructions you are given from the disabled employee;
- do not be patronising and do not use gestures generally directed towards children;
- do not lean on a person's wheelchair – it is part of their body space;
- use the same physical contact as you would with anyone else, for instance offering a handshake or putting an arm around the shoulder;
- address your comments directly to the disabled person rather than to his or her companion;
- relax and try to make eye contact in the same way as you would with any other adult;
- do not be embarrassed about using common phrases such as 'see you later' or 'I'll be running along' even though this may relate to a person's disability;
- do not make assumptions about whether or not a person has a disability because some impairments may be concealed, for instance diabetes or mental health difficulties.

With regard to language, certain words or phrases may offend a person with a disability and this is key when considering harassment in the work environment. The Disability Etiquette Guide suggests the following should be borne in mind when talking to or writing about disabled people:

- the word 'handicapped' is regarded as offensive and 'person with a disability' or 'disabled person' should be used in its place;
- medical labels are undesirable, often misleading and tend to reinforce stereotypes;
- disabled people do not wish to be considered or portrayed as victims who are powerless and wholly dependent on the medical profession;
- it is de-humanising to refer to a person in terms of their condition;
- people should not be labelled as 'a spastic' or 'an epileptic'. Instead, people should be described as 'having cerebral palsy' or 'a person with epilepsy';
- do not use labels which pity, or imply frailty or dependence.

DO NOT SAY	DO SAY
'a victim of . . .'	'a person who has. . .'
'suffering from. . .'	'person with. . .'
'afflicted by . . .'	'person who experiences. . .'
'wheelchair bound'	'wheelchair user'
'confined to a wheelchair'	'person who uses a wheelchair'
'invalid' as this relates to illness and can be interpreted as 'not valid'	
'mental handicap'	'person with learning difficulties'

Just as employers are urged not to reject complaints of racial or sexual harassment by putting them down to the employee being 'over sensitive', the same applies to complaints of disability harassment.

Chapter 5

BULLYING AND OTHER FORMS OF HARASSMENT

Introduction – Sources of law – The employer's response – The Employment Rights Act 1996 – Prerequisites for a claim for constructive dismissal – Civil liability – Criminal liability – The future

5.1 INTRODUCTION

'Bullying: The use of strength or power to coerce others by fear.'[1]

Bullying is usually associated with school-boy behaviour in playgrounds. In recent years, workplace bullying has become recognised. Reference to bullying is becoming increasingly common in reported decisions and employers have started to acknowledge the extent of the problem, especially the costs to their organisations in lost time and production. According to research,[2] 53% of workers admit to having been bullied and a staggering 78% admit to having witnessed incidents of bullying in the course of employment. The research suggests that employees are more likely to be bullied while under the age of 25, by their line managers and following a change of job or appointment of a new manager. Unlike the playground bully who relies on physical strength, the tactics of his workplace counterpart include:

'offensive, intimidating, malicious, insulting or humiliating behaviour, abuse of power or authority which attempts to undermine an individual or group of employees to cause them to suffer stress.'[3]

An estimated 40 million working days[4] are lost through bullying in the work place each year at a cost of between £3–4 billion.[5] In addition, there are the hidden costs of treating victims who suffer from ill-health or psychological damage.

The law's response to this problem is open to criticism. Unlike victims of sexual, racial or disability harassment, the victim effectively has to exercise his or her rights through the framework of unfair dismissal legislation and without the support of commissions and other regulatory bodies. From the outset, the odds are stacked against the victim and those who do succeed will recognise the inadequacies of the method and calculation of compensation, especially the limits imposed by statute. From an employer's perspective, however, although less straightforward (in terms of a right to challenge in law) than sexual, racial or disability harassment, bullying which is permitted to occur in the workplace may

---

1   Oxford English Dictionary (Oxford University Press).
2   Charlotte Raynor, 'The Incidence of Workplace Bullying' (1997) *Journal of Community and Applied Social Psychology.*
3   Unison, *Bullying at Work.*
4   Professor Cary Cooper, University of Manchester Institute of Science and Technology.
5   NASUWT, *No Place to Hide – Confronting Workplace Bullies.*

result in complaints being lodged. In this Chapter, we examine the way in which the law deals with workplace bullying and the dilemmas and difficulties often encountered by victims.

5.2 SOURCES OF LAW

There is no legislation within the UK specifically concerned with workplace bullying. This leaves the victim with a range of Acts of Parliament and common law principles from which to obtain protection and a remedy from the effects of bullying. These include:

-   The Employment Rights Act 1996 (ERA 1996) – a victim may pursue a complaint of unfair dismissal should work place bullying cause the employee to resign from his or her employment.
-   The Sex Discrimination Act 1975 (SDA 1975) and Race Relations Act 1976 (RRA 1976) – a victim may pursue complaints of discrimination if the workplace bullying includes sexist or racist overtones – indeed there may be advantages for victims to pursue this if they can.
-   The Disability Discrimination Act 1995 (DDA 1995) – where the bullying relates to an individual's disability.
-   The Health and Safety at Work Act etc 1974 (HSWA 1974) – employers have a duty to ensure the health and safety of their employees at work. Breach of this legislation may result in criminal proceedings.
-   Civil law – an employee may also pursue his or her employer for negligence if he or she suffers personal injuries during the course of employment.
-   Criminal law – a bully may find himself or herself subject to the rigours of the criminal justice system if he or she is responsible for physical assaults and/or other forms of unacceptable behaviour.

5.3 THE EMPLOYER'S RESPONSE

With growing recognition of workplace bullying there has been a proliferation of policies and procedures within organisations in order to resolve complaints at an early stage and without recourse to litigation. However, while the majority of employers are *au fait* with their health and safety obligations, few feel comfortable with dealing with complaints of bullying. All too often the victims are looked upon as being inadequate and deserving of the treatment they have received.

UNISON in their guide 'Bullying at Work' say:

> 'working people faced with the problem of bullying in the workplace need to be confident that employers are aware of the possible problems and are willing to tackle them.'

Ideally, all employers should demonstrate their willingness to stamp out bullying by adopting harassment policies and procedures which extend to bullying.

Managers should be trained on all aspects of the policies and employees properly inducted so that they are aware of their rights. Employees should also be encouraged to report incidents of bullying that they witness, with the aim of reducing the staggeringly high percentage of witnessed incidents.

Above all, employers must recognise that bullying happens and the adverse effects it may have upon the organisation and its reputation. UNISON summarise the position succinctly as follows:

'it is bad management practice to allow bullying to continue.'

We now consider what may happen when bad management persists and action has to be taken.

5.4 THE EMPLOYMENT RIGHTS ACT 1996

5.4.1 Constructive dismissal

When the internal procedures fail, the first dilemma faced by a victim to decide is whether or not to resign and if so, whether to claim unfair dismissal.

Section 95(1)(c) of the ERA 1996 includes within the definition of dismissal, circumstances where:

'the employee terminates the contract under which he is employed (with or without notice) in circumstances in which he is entitled to terminate it without notice by reason of the employer's conduct.'

This is often referred to as a 'constructive dismissal'. To succeed with a complaint, an employee must prove that there was a fundamental breach of contract by his or her employer which caused the resignation and that the employee acted in response by resigning, without having affirmed the breach by remaining (the existence of these ingredients are often together termed 'repudiatory breach').

Even if an employee is able to prove a repudiatory breach of contract, a constructive dismissal will not necessarily be unfair. An employment tribunal is obliged to look at the conduct of the employer and consider whether or not the employer acted reasonably in the circumstances. It is usually easier to show that the employer's conduct was unreasonable when there is a clear breach of contract.

Western Excavating (ECC) Ltd v Sharpe[1] is recognised as the leading authority on constructive dismissal, in which Lord Denning said:

'An employee is entitled to treat himself as constructively dismissed if the employer is guilty of conduct which is a significant breach going to the root of the contract of employment; or which shows that the employer no longer intends to be bound by one or more of the essential terms of the contract. The employee in those circumstances is entitled to leave without notice or to give notice, but the conduct in either case must be sufficiently serious to entitle him to leave at once. Moreover, the employee must make up his mind soon after the conduct of which he complains. If he continues for any length of time without leaving, he will be regarded as having elected to affirm the contract and will lose his right to treat himself as discharged.'

This has become recognised as the established test for determining whether or not there has been a constructive dismissal although through recent decisions the

---

1   [1978] IRLR 27.

requirement to resign 'on the spot' has relaxed somewhat.[1] Interestingly, Lord Justice Lawton in *Western Excavating* took the view:

> 'Sensible persons have no difficulty in recognising conduct by an employer which in law brings a contract of employment to an end. Persistent and unwanted amorous advances by an employer to a female member of staff would, for example, clearly be such conduct. What is required ... is a large measure of common sense.'

5.4.2 What breach occurs with bullying?

Recognising a breach of contract in bullying situations is not always straightforward. Shouting, setting tight deadlines and criticising employees may often be interpreted as being the attributes required for an effective manager in some situations and industries. Also, bullies tend to operate over a period of time, often with minor actions which accumulate to create a hostile work atmosphere. Bullies are rarely caught out by the bullying equivalent of a 'one off unwanted amorous advance'.

In the vast majority of bullying cases, the victim has to demonstrate a breach of one of the implied terms of employment. The general rule is that a term will only be implied into a contract if it is necessary to give it business efficacy[2] or by law. Terms may also be implied if they are customary to the trade or calling or from the usual practice of the particular employer.

5.4.3 Breach of the implied term of trust and confidence

An employer has a duty not to destroy the relationship of trust and confidence between employer and employee. In *Courtaulds Northern Textiles Ltd v Andrew*[3] the duty was summarised by Mr Justice Arnold as follows:

> 'It was an implied term of the contract that the employer would not without reasonable and proper cause, conduct themselves in a manner calculated or likely to destroy or seriously damage the relationship of confidence and trust between the parties.'

While in *Woods v WM Car Services (Peterborough) Ltd*[4] Mr Justice Browne-Wilkinson described the relationship in the following terms:

> 'To constitute a breach of this implied term it is not necessary to show that the employer intended any repudiation of the contract; the Tribunal's function is to look at the employer's conduct as a whole and determine whether it is such that its effect, judged reasonably and sensibly, is such that the employee cannot be expected to put up with it.'

The sorts of behaviour which, from previous cases, constitutes conduct which employees are not required to 'put up with' include the following examples:

> *Example* Mr Bliss was employed as a consultant orthopaedic surgeon and refused to undergo a psychiatric medical examination. The Court of Appeal

---

1   Eg *Waltons and Morse v Dorington* [1997] IRLR 488.
2   *Liverpool City Council v Irwin* [1977] AC 239.
3   [1979] IRLR 84.
4   [1982] IRLR 413.

concluded that the Health Authority had acted in breach of their obligations under the contract of employment by requiring Mr Bliss to submit for a psychiatric examination without reasonable cause and by suspending him from duty on his refusal to submit to such an examination.

Bliss v South East Thames Regional Health Authority
[1985] IRLR 308

Example Miss Protopapa resigned as a telephone supervisor after being severely reprimanded by her immediate superior in front of other employees for making a dental appointment without first asking permission to be absent from work. The EAT's view was that Miss Protopapa had been unfairly dismissed on account of the humiliating, intimidating and degrading behaviour of her employer.

Hilton International Hotels (UK) Ltd v Protopapa
[1990] IRLR 316

5.4.4 The last straw

Bullying often takes place over a period of time. In isolation an individual incident may appear to be insignificant – however, when taken together with a number of other incidents it may constitute a fundamental breach. The leading authority is *Lewis v Motorworld Garages Ltd* (below).

Example Mr Lewis was employed as a 'Sales Manager' and was demoted to the position of Service Manager in 1981 which resulted in a change of salary, loss of an office and the withholding of salary increases. Mr Lewis chose not to resign. There followed a series of criticisms and a final written warning was issued in July 1982. Mr Lewis considered the criticisms and his demotion to be unjustified and resigned in August 1982. He complained of constructive dismissal arguing that his employers had breached the implied duty of trust and confidence.

The industrial tribunal and EAT both identified the demotion as a repudiatory breach, but held that the delay in resigning meant that Mr Lewis was unable to rely on the breach. The Court of Appeal overruled this and, in its view, even if an employee had not treated the demotion as a breach at the time, he was entitled to add it to other actions which, taken together, would amount to a breach of the implied term of trust and confidence.

Lewis v Motorworld Garages Ltd
[1985] IRLR 465

Lewis has been successfully applied by other applicants – for example in *Beaumont v East Gloucestershire NHS Trust* (below).

Example Mr Beaumont was a hospital cook who was subject to an 18-month campaign of bullying from colleagues. This included drawings and graffiti on lavatory walls, his locker being broken into and vandalised, his uniform being torn to shreds and placed under a running shower. Despite Mr Beaumont making formal complaints, his manager failed to intervene, investigate or even draw Mr Beaumont's attention to the trust's harassment policy. Mr Beaumont resigned when a colleague told him that the truth was written about him on the lavatory walls. While the final incident may be viewed as insignificant when compared to the others, the tribunal concluded that Mr Beaumont had been unfairly dismissed. The tribunal accepted that the series of events gave rise to the resignation. While the final incident itself was considered insufficient to justify a resignation, it had to be viewed against the background of previous incidents. The cumulative series of acts amounted to a breach of the implied term, to justify a finding of constructive dismissal.

Beaumont v East Gloucestershire NHS Trust
COIT 44973/96

Example   Ms Chivers worked as an administration manager and complained about a number of incidents involving the store manager including:

– tearing up a budget statement Ms Chivers had prepared;
– blaming Ms Chivers for not completing paperwork;
– accusing Ms Chivers of lying about a doctor's appointment; and
– shouting at Ms Chivers in front of members of staff.

The industrial tribunal was able to find that the cumulative effect of these incidents gave rise to a breach of the implied term of trust and confidence.

Chivers v Asda Stores Ltd
COIT 2917/222

However, a word of caution. Not all unreasonable conduct or behaviour will constitute a breach of trust and confidence.

Example   Fisher was employed as a dental hygienist. In support of her claim of constructive dismissal, she argued that she had been bullied by an associate dentist who had humiliated her in front of patients. Reliance was placed on one incident when the dentist had refused to make his nurse available to carry out an X-ray. The tribunal accepted the dentist's judgement that the patient did not require the X-ray and that no breach had occurred. The EAT chose not to interfere with that conclusion.

Fisher v L&S Leigh
EAT 717/91

Similarly, the use of bad language may not always amount to a breach of trust and confidence. In *Mayne v Armour Sealed Units (Bristol) Ltd*[1] a managing director's use of bad language did not provide grounds for constructive dismissal, while in *Gregory v Sheffield Garage and Engineering Co Ltd*[2] abusive language accompanied with violent behaviour was held to be in breach of trust and confidence.

A good example of where the use of foul language entitled an employee to terminate is *Palmanor Ltd t/a Chaplins Nightclub v Cedron* (below).

Example   Mr Cedron was employed as a barman. One evening he started work at 8.30pm by arrangement. The club manager approached Mr Cedron to enquire why he was late. In response to Mr Cedron's explanation, the manager started to insult him by calling him a bastard and using other expletives. The manager concluded by telling Mr Cedron to leave the club, telling him he would ensure he did not work in London again.

---

1   COIT 2836/192.
2   COIT 2935/168.

The EAT formed the view that the use of foul language gave rise to a constructive dismissal. In providing guidance for the future Mr Justice Flynn said:

'In a case of this kind the industrial tribunal is required to ask itself whether the employer's conduct was so unreasonable that it went beyond the limits of the contract. Although tribunals have to be careful not to attach too great importance to words used in the heat of the moment or anger, there comes a time when the language is such that even if the person using it is in a state of anger, an employee cannot be expected to tolerate it.'

Palmanor Ltd t/a Chaplins Night Club v Cedron
[1978] IRLR 303

Bad language may also be accompanied with criticism. In *Courtaulds Northern Textiles Ltd v Andrew*,[1] Mr Justice Arnold summarised the position as follows:

'Criticism, even as trenchantly expressed as was the criticism in the present case, of a workman's performance will not necessarily, and in every case, lead to the conclusion that the voicing of that criticism constituted conduct of a repudiatory nature so as to lead to constructive dismissal. Where criticism is made, however trenchantly, because criticism is thought to be appropriate, then the circumstances of each case would plainly have to be considered with a view to a decision of the merits on the particular matter whether or not the repudiatory conduct is made out.'

Much will depend on the circumstances of each case and also the working environment. Foul language may be more acceptable on the factory floor than within an office environment – although there are no hard and fast rules concerning this.

Humiliating behaviour may also result in a constructive dismissal.

Example   Mr Garner resigned after 26 years when his employer went back on a promise to increase his salary and following an incident in which Mr Garner felt as though he had been treated like an office boy.

The EAT upheld the tribunal's view that the employer's conduct amounted to a repudiation of the contract. Mr Justice Kilner-Brown's approach was as follows:

'What it means is that the employer is making it impossible for the employee to go on working for him – and that is as plain a repudiation of the contract of employment as there can be.'

A Garner v Grange Furnishing Ltd
[1977] IRLR 206

5.4.5 Ignoring complaints of bullying

A failure to deal with a complaint of bullying may also breach trust and confidence. In *Hatrick v City Fax*[2] an employee complained of a one-off incident of bullying. Management decided to take no action over what they perceived as a 'minor act of stupidity'. The industrial tribunal disagreed and held that the failure to respond amounted to a fundamental breach of contract.

---

1   [1979] IRLR 84.
2   COIT 3041/138.

Failure to provide and implement a grievance procedure has been held to be a breach of a contract of employment justifying an employer's resignation. In _WA Goold (Pearmak) Ltd v McConnell_,[1] Mr Justice Morrison described the failure as follows:

> 'The right to obtain redress against a grievance is fundamental ... failing to provide a procedure for dealing promptly with employee's grievances and instead allowing them to fester in an atmosphere of prevarication and indecision the employers were in breach of an implied contractual term which was sufficiently serious to justify the employees in terminating their employment.'

The failure of the employer to deal with the employee's complaints and draw the employees attention to the existence of a harassment policy was considered crucial in _Beaumont v East Gloucestershire NHS Trust._[2]

With growing awareness of bullying and the widespread use of harassment policies, similar conclusions will most likely be reached for failing to deal with complaints of bullying.

5.4.6 Breach of the implied duty to provide reasonable support

During the last two decades it has become accepted that there is an implied term in employment contracts requiring employers to take reasonable steps to support employees in their work, without harassment or disruption from colleagues.

An early decision recognising the implied duty is _Wigan Borough Council v Davies_ (below).

> **Example** Following disputes with work colleagues, Ms Davies was 'sent to Coventry' by colleagues who refused to cooperate with her at work. The Council took no steps to rectify the situation and Ms Davies resigned and claimed constructive dismissal.
>
> The EAT expressed the view that:
>
> 'The employer was in breach of contract by failing to correct a situation which was intolerable to the employee.'
>
> This amounted to a fundamental breach of contract entitling the employee to treat herself as being constructively dismissed.
>
> _Wigan Borough Council v Davies_
> [1979] IRLR 127

A similar conclusion was reached in _Adams v Southampton and South West Hampshire Health Authority_ (below).

> **Example** Following harassment and abuse for refusing to take part in industrial action, Adams invoked the grievance procedure and identified the individual who was responsible for the bullying. However, no action was taken and Adams resigned. The industrial tribunal found that the Authority had breached the implied duty of reasonable support.
>
> _Adams v Southampton and South West Hampshire Health Authority_
> COIT 1560/156

---

1   [1995] IRLR 516.
2   COIT 2836/192.

An employee's refusal to identify or name a bully, however may work against the employee should he or she resign and take proceedings.

Example Mr McCabe was a victim of bullying but refused to name those who bullied him. He complained to his foreman who in turn spoke to his workmates. The bullying persisted and McCabe resigned and made a complaint of constructive dismissal. The claim failed – the employers had taken reasonable steps and McCabe's refusal to provide names prevented them from taking further action.

McCabe v Chicpak Ltd
[1976] IRLR 38

Failure to support an employee in their work may also amount to a breach of the implied duty concerning reasonable support.

Example Ms Gulleys found herself confronted with a demanding position in having to work nearly double the hours required by her contract. Following the removal of two experienced members of staff, Ms Gulleys resigned and claimed unfair constructive dismissal. On appeal, the EAT confirmed that the employer's failure to provide support prevented Ms Gulleys from performing her contract.

Whitbread Plc t/a Threshers v Gulleys
EAT 478/92

Thus, for an employer to avoid legal complaints, not only must bullying be prevented at work, but when conduct of this nature is brought to the organisation's attention it must be dealt with and appropriate support given.

5.4.7 Breach of the duty to provide a safe workplace

This implied duty requires employers to provide a safe working environment.

Example Mrs Austin terminated her employment following her employers failure to provide special eye protectors fitted with prescription goggles. The EAT held that the employer's failure to investigate and take action on this issue entitled Mrs Austin to resign without notice.

British Aircraft Corporation Ltd v Austin
[1978] IRLR 332

Example Mr Evans was the victim of extremely unpleasant bullying. This necessitated attendances at hospital, and included injuries to his head and testicles, burns, interference with his car and tools. Mr Evans resigned and complained of constructive dismissal. Finding in Mr Evans' favour, the tribunal held that despite knowing about the bullying, the employer had taken no steps to prevent further incidents. This was in turn a breach of implied duties to provide a safe working environment and trust and confidence.

Evans v Sousley Packaging Company Ltd
COIT 2916/185

5.5 PREREQUISITES FOR A CLAIM FOR CONSTRUCTIVE DISMISSAL

A complaint of unfair constructive dismissal is administered within the framework of the ERA 1996. Certain conditions have to be met which are far more stringent than for either race, sex or disability harassment:

- the victim must be employed under a contract of employment (ie must be an employee), whereas those who complain of sex, race or disability harassment need not;
- the victim must be dismissed (in most cases this will involve a resignation), whereas those who suffer sex, race or disability harassment may pursue their complaints while remaining in employment;
- the victim must have been employed for the necessary qualifying period (currently two years) whereas those who are victims of sex, race or disability harassment are not subject to any qualifying period;
- the victim must lodge the complaint within three months of the effective date of termination of employment. The employment tribunal will only accept a complaint 'out of time' if it is satisfied that it was 'not reasonably practicable' for the applicant to lodge the complaint within the time-limit. Victims of sexual, disability or racial harassment must also lodge their complaints within three months of the time when the act complained of was committed. A complaint 'out of time' may be accepted if in all the circumstances the tribunal considers it just and equitable to do so – a far easier hurdle to overcome;
- a questionnaire procedure applies for sex, disability and racial harassment and support provided by the Equal Opportunities Commission and the Commission for Racial Equality. No such support or procedure is available for the victim of bullying – the victim is alone unless he or she qualifies for legal aid (in the form of limited green form assistance) or can afford legal representation;
- the remedies on a successful outcome are different. There is a huge disparity in the treatment of victims even though the facts relied upon are often similar. Name calling and physical assaults are a common feature of all forms of harassment. Bullied victims are left with the usual remedies for unfair dismissal – the basic and compensatory unfair dismissal awards (subject to the statutory maximum), reinstatement or re-engagement (see Chapter 12). No provision is made for 'hurt feelings'. In calculating compensation for sex, racial and disability discrimination, large sums may be awarded including for hurt feelings which can result in substantial awards. For example in *Armitage, Marsden and HM Prison Service v Johnson*[1] the EAT found no reasons for interfering with a tribunal's award of £21,000 as compensation for injury to feelings to an employee who had suffered racial discrimination over a long period of time. This included racist remarks, false accusations and ostracism by colleagues. Bearing in mind the obstacles faced by the victims of bullying in progressing their complaints to a hearing it seems grossly unfair that they should be prevented from

---

1   [1997] IRLR 162.

benefiting from compensation for hurt feelings, especially when the victim's treatment follows a similar form.

It remains an anomaly of the legislation that different treatment should be afforded to victims and the removal of these disparities must be addressed by future changes to employment legislation. The discrepancy concerning compensation limits may be explained by *Marshall v Southampton and South-West Hampshire Regional Health Authority (No 2)*.[1] Until 1993, awards of compensation in cases of discrimination were subject to the same statutory maximum as unfair dismissal cases. The ECJ in *Marshall* decided that limits on compensation meant that victims of discrimination did not have an 'effective remedy' and the upper ceilings were subsequently removed by legislation. Enactment of the Fairness at Work Act will, to some extent, address a number of the criticisms, although the absence of compensation for hurt feelings remains an anomaly. Removal of the upper ceiling on compensation for unfair constructive dismissal claims should mean a more 'effective remedy' in many cases.

5.6 CIVIL LIABILITY

Employers who fail to provide employees with adequate protection from workplace bullying expose themselves to personal injury claims. These claims are pursued in the civil courts and are subject to the civil rules of procedure, which are examined in more detail in Chapters 11 and 12.

Liability for physical injury has been established for some time.

> *Example* Hudson was tripped up by a colleague on a regular basis. The colleague was warned about his actions and despite this he persisted. Hudson was injured and the employer was held liable for the injury as it was reasonably foreseeable. The behaviour was potentially dangerous and yet no steps were taken to prevent it.
>
> *Hudson v Ridge Manufacturing Ltd*
> [1957] 2 All ER 229

The decision also demonstrates the legal concept of 'vicarious liability' in which an employer may be held responsible for the misbehaviour of its employees.

Establishing liability for psychological damage or injuries which are not physical has not been so readily accepted by the courts. However, in *Walker v Northumberland County Council*[2] the High Court held that the County Council was in breach of the duty of care owed to its employee who suffered a second nervous breakdown as a result of stress and anxiety caused by Mr Walker's job as a social services officer with a heavy workload, including child abuse cases. In his judgment, Mr Justice Coleman said:

> 'An employer owes a duty of care to his employees not to cause them psychiatric damage by the volume or character of the work which they are required to perform. Although the law on the extent of the duty on the employer to provide an employee

---

1   [1993] IRLR 445.
2   [1995] IRLR 35.

with a safe system of work and to take reasonable steps to protect him from harm has developed almost exclusively in cases involving physical injury to the employee, there is no logical reason why risk of injury to an employee's mental health should be excluded from the scope of the employer's duty. The standard of care required for performance of that duty must be measured against the yard stick of reasonable conduct on the part of the person in the employer's position. What is reasonable depends upon the nature of the relationship, the magnitude of the risk of injury which was reasonably foreseeable, the seriousness of the consequences for the person to whom the duty is owed of the risk and the cost and practicality of preventing the risk. The practicability of remedial measures must take into account the resources and facilities at the disposal of the personnel body who owes the duty of care, and the purpose of the activity which has given rise to the risk of injury.'

Before reaching the Court of Appeal a settlement was reached at £175,000.

A factor limiting the development of liability for psychological injury is that in *Walker*, the Court recognised that it was reasonably foreseeable that there was a risk of a recurrence of ill-health when the employee returned to the same work without any additional assistance. Similar considerations will apply in instances when an employee suffers from mental illness on account of bullying and the courts will apply the same test based on whether it was reasonably foreseeable that a recurrence would occur.

In *Petch v Customs and Excise Commissioners*,[1] Mr Petch unsuccessfully complained of mental ill-health caused by his treatment by his employers. Dilon LJ noted that an employer would have been liable for a first nervous breakdown if senior management had been aware or ought to have been aware that the employee was showing signs of impending breakdown, and had been aware, or ought to have been aware, that his workload carried the risk that he would have a breakdown. This would have resulted in a liability of negligence.

In *Johnstone v Bloomsbury Health Authority*[2] a junior hospital doctor complained of the effect on his health of having to work long hours. Within his pleadings, he complained of suffering from stress and depression, a loss of appetite and insomnia. The health authority applied to strike out the claim on the basis that he agreed at the outset, in his contract of employment, to work such hours. In rejecting their application, Browne-Wilkinson VC said:

'The Defendants could not lawfully require the Plaintiff to work so much overtime in any week as it was reasonably foreseeable it would damage his health.'

The case settled before trial for £5,600.

More recently, in proceedings brought against a county council by a schoolteacher, a bullying case for personal injury was settled for £100,000. The bullying complained of included:

–   being ostracised;
–   being embarrassed at the Christmas party by labelling his bottle of drink 'Randy Brandy';
–   being refused a set of keys to the school;
–   not being given responsibilities as deputy head teacher.[3]

---

1   [1993] ICR 789.
2   [1991] 2 All ER 293.
3   (1998) *The Times*, 17 July.

The above show that while the courts are recognising that liability exists, the pace of change of the common law has been slow. With the intervention of statute in the form of the DDA 1995 greater protection now exists for victims who suffer from this type of ill-health, and with unlimited compensation as a potential remedy, employers who ignore this legislation do so at their peril.

5.7 CRIMINAL LIABILITY

Bullies may find themselves subject to criminal prosecution, especially for serious physical assaults. These are examined in more detail in Chapter 12 but warrant brief consideration here. Actions are normally brought by the Crown Prosecution Service and offences include actual or grievous bodily harm, violent disorder and affray depending upon the circumstances.

Under s 241 of the Trade Union and Labour Relations (Consolidation) Act 1992, criminal offences have been created for 'intimidation or annoyance by violence or otherwise' which takes place during industrial action or picketing. The section states:

> 'A person commits an offence who, with a view to compelling another person to abstain from doing or to do any act which that person has a legal right to do or abstain from doing, wrongfully and without legal authority –
>
> (a) uses violence to or intimidates that person or his wife or children, or injures his property,
> (b) persistently follows that person about from place to place,
> (c) hides any tools, clothes or other property owed or used by that person, or deprives him of or hinders him in the use thereof,
> (d) watches or besets the house or other place where that person resides, works, carries on business or happens to be, or the approach to any such house or place, or
> (e) follows that person with two or more other persons in a disorderly manner in or through any street or road.'

A person guilty of an offence under this section is liable to imprisonment not exceeding six months or a fine of up to £5,000.

A limiting factor is inclusion of the word 'compelling'. The acts listed above must be done to compel the other person from doing an act. This does not prevent acts done to persuade the other person from working during industrial action.

The Protection from Harassment Act 1997 makes harassment a civil tort and a criminal offence. The aim of the Act is to provide a remedy for stalking and other acts of harassment. Sections 1 and 2 of the Act provide:

> '1(1) A person must not pursue a course of conduct –
>
> (a) which amounts to harassment of another, and
> (b) which he knows or ought to know amounts to harassment of the other.'
>
> '2(1) A person who pursues a course of conduct in breach of section 1 is guilty of an offence.'

Offences under the Act may be committed at work or away from the workplace. Under the civil jurisdiction, damages may also be awarded to victims. One benefit of the Act is that those workers excluded from the ambit of the anti-discrimination legislation (ie those not sexually or racially harassed) may now complain to the police concerning their treatment.

The Act also creates the criminal offence of putting people in fear of violence. The latter offence requires fear to have been caused on at least two occasions and the maximum penalty is a prison sentence of up to five years and/or an unlimited fine. The courts also have power to issue a restraining order similar to a civil injunction. Breach of an order is a criminal offence with a maximum penalty of five years imprisonment and/or unlimited fine.

5.8 THE FUTURE

Recognition of the problem of workplace bulling is growing and employers are recognising their responsibilities. The law's response is open to the criticism that it is inadequate. It provides limited support to victims of bullying when compared to the protection available to those who complain of sex, race or disability harassment. Some of these criticisms will be addressed by the Fairness at Work Act through the removal of the upper compensation limits and reduction of the qualifying period to one year. However, there are no proposals to change the basis for calculation of compensation so as to include injury for hurt feelings and victims will continue to be awarded their lost earnings and statutory redundancy entitlement only. Victims will also have to proceed under the framework of the ERA 1996 and this will continue until specific legislation is enacted recognising this form of harassment.

One country which has a enacted legislation is Sweden. The statutory provisions apply to all activities in which employees can be subject to victimisation. Victimisation is defined as:

> 'Recurrent, reprehensible or distinctly negative actions which are directed against individual employees in an offensive manner and can result in those employees being placed outside the workplace community.'[1]

Employers have an obligation to plan and organise work to prevent victimisation and to make clear that such behaviour is unacceptable in the workplace. In addition, employers are required to adopt routines and procedures to detect problems in the workplace as they arise.

No such legislation exists in the UK. Employers are not obliged to adopt harassment policies and have a degree of flexibility in how they respond to complaints.

While the UK law offers some protection to victims, it is obvious from the Swedish example that more could be done. While many employers are adopting policies to counter workplace bullying, there is no statutory compulsion requiring them to do so. It is clear from the research undertaken that bullies continue to operate. If it is bad management practice to allow bullying, then given the benefits for the employer, legislation dealing with this problem is long overdue.

---

1   *Statute Book of the Swedish National Board of Occupational Safety and Health: Victimization at Work.*

Chapter 6

THE RELATIONSHIP BETWEEN HARASSMENT AND STRESS

What is stress? – Employers' liability for stress – Harassment and stress – What can employers do?

6.1 WHAT IS STRESS?

Stress is, in short, an inevitable part of living which, in varying degrees, we all experience. In its most innocuous form stress is harmless and could be argued to be a necessary part of life. However, whether in a work or domestic environment, high levels of stress may be extremely damaging to an individual if, for one reason or another, that person cannot cope. It is estimated that, after back pain, stress is the second most common work-related health problem.[1]

The Health and Safety Executive (HSE) defines 'stress' in its handbook *Stress at Work*:

'Stress is the reaction people have to excessive pressures or other types of demand placed upon them. It arises when they worry that they can't cope.

Stress can involve:

- physical effects, such as raised heart rate, increased sweating, headache, dizziness, blurred vision, aching neck and shoulders, skin rashes and a lowering of resistance to infection;
- behavioural effects, such as increased anxiety and irritability, a tendency to drink more alcohol and smoke more, difficulty sleeping, poor concentration and an inability to deal calmly with everyday tasks and situations.

These effects are usually short-lived and cause no lasting harm. When the pressures recede, there is a quick return to normal.

Stress is not therefore the same as ill health. But in some cases, particularly where pressures are intense and continue for some time, the effects of stress can be more sustained and far more damaging, leading to longer-term psychological problems and physical ill health.'

There are many factors in the workplace which may cause stress and some of those factors may be stressful for one person but not for another; some people rise to a challenge and others prefer routines. Some people may already be involved in a difficult situation outside work, such as the breakdown of a personal relationship, family illness or problems with children. It may be that a person who

---

1   Report from the European Foundation for the Improvement of Living and Working Conditions (from an article in *The Irish Times*, 20 October 1997).

would normally rise to a challenge simply cannot take any more pressure on top of an already stressful situation.

The HSE handbook has suggested that harmful levels of stress are likely to occur in the following situations:

- pressures pile on top of each other or are prolonged;
- people feel trapped or unable to exert any control over the demands placed on them;
- people are confused by conflicting demands made on them;
- people feel a high degree of uncertainty about their work, their objectives or their job and career prospects;
- work schedules are inflexible and over-demanding;
- there is prolonged conflict between individuals, including possibly sexual or racial harassment or bullying, or where staff are treated with contempt or indifference;
- there is a lack of understanding and leadership from managers or supervisors;
- exposure to excessive noise, heat, humidity and vibration;
- the presence of toxic or dangerous materials or other obvious workplace hazards.

This chapter examines the relationship between harassment and stress. According to a report by the European Foundation for the Improvement of Living and Working Conditions, people, not machines, are responsible for most of the stress suffered in the modern European workplace. It reports that three million people are subjected to sexual harassment at work, six million to physical violence and 12 million to psychological violence through verbal abuse or bullying.[1]

Clearly the HSE also regards 'conflict between individuals' as a source of stress including, not surprisingly, 'sexual or racial harassment or bullying'. This would also include bullying an individual because of his or her sexual orientation. The HSE publication also regards as stressful the situation 'where staff are treated with contempt or indifference'. Treating someone with indifference may not, at first sight, be thought of as bullying but, as can be seen from the previous chapter, if it is done deliberately over a prolonged period, it could well be a subtle form of bullying. In fact, many of the other stressful aspects of work could be attributed to harassment or bullying carried out deliberately:

- piling pressures on someone;
- giving someone conflicting orders;
- leaving someone in the dark regarding work, objectives or career prospects;
- making work schedules inflexible and over-demanding.

People can often cope with stressful situations if they know they have support and that they are appreciated. If, however, they feel that the person who should be supporting them is actually the person who is making their life difficult, this is not easy to cope with and will very probably result in a stressful situation.

---

1   Report from the European Foundation for the Improvement of Living and Working Conditions (from an article in *The Irish Times*, 20 October 1997).

6.2 EMPLOYERS' LIABILITY FOR STRESS

Employers owe their employees a duty of care to keep them safe from harm. Employers have, for years, been aware that they may be sued by employees who are injured at work or who contract a work-related disease (such as asbestosis). However, the case of *Walker v Northumberland County Council* (see Chapter 5) has confirmed that employers have a duty of care for their employees' psychiatric well-being as well as their physical well-being. In other words, they may be liable for a stress-related illness due to conditions in the workplace, sometimes known as 'occupational stress'.

> *Example* Mr Walker was employed for 17 years as a social worker responsible for managing four teams of field workers in Northumberland, an area with a high concentration of child-care problems. In 1980, he came under increasing pressure as child-care problems multiplied with the increase in the population. He made repeated requests for more staff but his requests were ignored. At the end of 1986 he suffered a severe nervous breakdown and was off work until March 1987. When he returned to work he was promised an assistant but this additional help was provided for one month only. The heavy workload continued and, in addition, there was a backlog of paperwork which had built up in his absence. He made repeated requests for more assistance but to no avail. He soon suffered another nervous breakdown and in February 1988 his employment was terminated on the grounds of permanent ill health.
>
> Mr Walker brought a personal injury claim which he won in 1992. His claim for the amount of compensation was eventually settled out of court for £175,000. The judge said in the course of the judgment:
>
> > 'Although the law on the extent of the duty on an employer to provide an employee with a safe system of work and to take reasonable steps to protect him from risks which are reasonably foreseeable has developed almost exclusively in cases involving physical injury to the employee there is no logical reason why risk of injury to an employee's mental health should be excluded from the scope of the employer's duty.'
>
> > *Walker v Northumberland County Council*
> > [1995] IRLR 35

The issue of liability is dealt with in detail in Chapter 8. However, it is useful to point out here that Mr Walker's claim was based in negligence. As is the case in any negligence claim, Mr Walker had to establish five facts:

(1) that the employer owed him a duty of care;
(2) that the employer was in breach of that duty;
(3) that he suffered an injury;
(4) that the injury was caused by the breach;
(5) that it was 'reasonably foreseeable' that injury would result.

On the question of foreseeability of the risk of injury, the test advanced by the court was:

> 'whether it ought to have been foreseen that Walker was exposed to a risk of mental illness marginally higher than that which would ordinarily affect a social services middle manager in his position with a really heavy workload.'

The court, in response to that test, concluded that Mr Walker's first nervous breakdown was not necessarily 'reasonably forseeable' but the second certainly was. Mr Walker had returned to work after his first nervous breakdown 'more susceptible' and hence his employer should have foreseen the risk of a second nervous breakdown.

Ever since the *Walker* decision there has been growing concern throughout all sections of industry that claims for damages for occupational stress will become widespread. However, it should be remembered that the employer's common law duty is to take *reasonable* care for the welfare of its employees, not *all possible care*.

A question which has been asked is whether employers can override the common law duty of care with an express contractual term. This question was considered in the case of *Johnstone v Bloomsbury Health Authority* (below).

> *Example* Dr Johnstone was a senior house officer whose contract of employment required him to work a 40-hour week and to be available on call for up to a further 48 hours per week. As a result of the excessively long hours he worked he suffered symptoms of stress and depression. He sued his employers for compensation for the damage he had suffered and for a declaration that he could not be required to work 'for so many hours in excess of his standard working week as would forseeably injure his health', even if this was less than the 48 hours overtime stated in his contract.
>
> The three Court of Appeal judges all had differing views. One considered that the duty of care could not be overriden by the express terms of the contract; one considered that the 40 hours per week could not be cut down by the implied duty of care but that the additional 48 hours overtime should be exercised with discretion in a way which did not injure the employee's health; and the third considered that if Mr Johnstone had contracted to make himself available for 88 hours, then that express term could not be cut down by an implied term. However, they all agreed that if the express terms of the contract were to prevail they would arguably be rendered ineffective by s 2(1) of the Unfair Contract Terms Act 1977 which states that:
>
> 'a person cannot by reference to any contract term . . . exclude or restrict his liability for . . . personal injury resulting from negligence'.
>
> *Johnstone v Bloomsbury Health Authority*
> [1991] IRLR 118

Unfortunately the case never went to a full trial as it was settled for £5,600 plus payment of Dr Johnstone's legal costs. The law in this area therefore remains uncertain. However, although not given the status of a decided case, the Court of Appeal clearly expressed the view that the employers could not require the employee to work so much overtime during the course of any week as was reasonably forseeable would damage his health, irrespective of the express terms of his contract of employment.

6.3 HARASSMENT AND STRESS

The *Walker* and *Johnstone* cases illustrate how an employer can be liable for the stress-related illnesses of its employees. They are not, however, harassment cases. Can employers be liable for the stress suffered by their employees as a result of harassment? The short answer is yes. There is no reason why a nervous breakdown as a result of harassment should be treated any differently to a nervous breakdown as a result of overwork (see Chapter 8). But what about the situation where an employee does not suffer an actual nervous breakdown, but clearly suffers some sort of stress as a result of harassment?

6.3.1 Sexual and racial harassment and stress

There have been many cases of both sexual and racial harassment where the complainant has been awarded not only damages for the loss suffered but also damages for injury to feelings. Parliament has recognised that individuals who are subjected to unlawful discrimination generally find the experience hurtful, distressing and humiliating and often suffer stress and stress-related illness as a result. For this reason the SDA 1975, RRA 1976 and DDA 1995 specifically provide for compensation for injury to feelings in addition to any award for lost earnings.

The Court of Appeal stated in the case of *Alexander v The Home Office*[1] that damages for injury to feelings should reflect compensation for the consequences of the discrimination and that it 'should not be minimal because this would tend to trivialise or diminish respect for the public policy to which the Act gives effect'. Aggravated damages may also be awarded where the employer behaved in a high-handed, malicious, insulting or oppressive manner, for example where the employer failed to address the question of harassment or did not take it seriously, resulting in further stress for the employee.

Some examples of awards for injury to feelings in sex and race discrimination cases show how seriously the courts view the treatment meted out to victims of discrimination generally and/or harassment specifically.

> *Example* In *LSM v Royal Navy* the industrial tribunal awarded Ms LSM damages of £65,377 which included £25,000:
>
> 'for injury to feelings, for the humiliation and stress suffered, an element relating to the personal injury arising directly from the harassment in the form of depression, and an element for the loss of congenial employment.'
>
> Ms LSM joined the navy as a 17-year-old recruit. She suffered almost four years of constant harassment during which time she had been sexually assaulted, forced to mimic oral sex, bullied and made to jump into water so that her clothes became transparent. By July 1994 she had been diagnosed with clinical depression and was suffering from severe headaches, sleep-lessness and lack of energy. She took a paracetamol overdose in 1995 and was shortly afterwards discharged as being 'temperamentally unsuitable' for service.
>
> *LSM v Royal Navy*
> Case No 55542/95

The size of the award no doubt came as a shock to the Royal Navy. Since 1993, however, when the ceiling on sex discrimination awards was lifted (the race discrimination cap was lifted in 1994), some awards have been very substantial.

---

1   [1988] IRLR 190.

An illustration of compensation for injury to feelings for racial harassment is given in *Chan v London Borough of Hackney* (below).

Example   Mr Chan, who is of Chinese origin, was employed as a team leader in the borough valuer's department. He started work there in 1984 and in 1991 Mrs Collins was appointed borough valuer. Before Mrs Collins was appointed, Mr Chan had been promoted twice and had been temporarily promoted to act as group valuer. His work was praised on several occasions. Within a short time Mrs Collins formed the view that he was 'lazy, incompetent and a liar'. She piled him with work and was totally unsympathetic to his concerns.

A few months after her arrival, a new group valuer, Mr Davies, was appointed and Mr Chan reverted to his old post as team leader under him. Mr Chan arranged a meeting with Mr Davies to discuss the treatment he was receiving from Mrs Collins. However, Mr Davies cancelled the meeting and, instead, served a notice of disciplinary hearing on Mr Chan. The notice alleged inadequate and negligent work performance and refusal to obey legitimate instructions. The notice was approved by Mrs Collins.

Mr Chan went on sick leave and took out a formal race grievance against Mrs Collins and Mr Davies. He took medical retirement and brought a claim for race discrimination in the industrial tribunal. The tribunal awarded him £113,964 compensation (together with interest of £16,298) which included £25,000 for injury to feelings (including £5,000 aggravated damages) plus £8,500 interest. They found that 'as far as Mrs Collins was concerned, the applicant's face did not fit'. The applicant had been put under considerable pressure by both Mrs Collins and Mr Davies with a view to building up a disciplinary case against him.

Chan v London Borough of Hackney
1996, Case No 40002/92

A further example of an award including an amount for injury to feelings is found in *Armitage, Marsden and HM Prison Service v Johnson* (below).

Example   Mr Johnson, who is English born of Afro-Caribbean origin, was employed as an auxiliary prison officer at Brixton Prison. From mid-1991 he was ostracised and subjected to racist remarks by fellow prison officers after he objected to the manhandling of a black prisoner by other prison officers. He brought a discrimination claim and was awarded £28,500 damages, £21,000 of which was awarded by way of compensation for injury to feelings and £7,500 aggravated damages because of the way in which the employers investigated the complaint.

Armitage, Marsden and HM Prison Service v Johnson
[1997] IRLR 162

An illustration of how important the issue of stress has become is given by a claim brought by trainee solicitor, whose employers settled the matter out of court for a very large sum.

Example   Ms Harrison took her law firm to an industrial tribunal in 1997 after being bullied and sexually harassed since joining the firm in 1995. She was placed in a department working with two senior male colleagues. She says:

'It started off just about work. One would shout at me to come and get him a file, when it was on the floor next to him, tell me to exchange contracts then deny that he'd said that, deliberately get me into trouble and tell me my work was all wrong. Then it became more personal, about my appearance and my relationship with my boyfriend. The other one sat through it all and said nothing.'

She became unwell with the stress and sought medical help. She was signed off, suffering from nervous disability and soon resigned. After hearing Ms Harrison's evidence, the law firm agreed to pay her £50,000 plus her legal costs and also agreed to pay for counselling for her.

Harrison v Laurence Murphy & Co
(unreported, 1997)

There are many more examples of large sums awarded for injury to feelings as a result of sexual or racial harassment. Stress induced by harassment is clearly an aspect of discrimination which courts take extremely seriously.

6.3.2 Disability harassment and stress

There have not, to date, been any examples of disability harassment claims being brought, but there have been awards for injury to feelings. Section 8(4) of the DDA 1995 specifically allows for compensation for injury to feelings and it is suggested that such an element of damages will be appropriate in most cases.

Example Ms Tarling had a club foot which had resulted in a progressive disturbance of her bone structure. Her job required her to stand for long periods of time which she found increasingly difficult. The employers were advised that a special chair was available which would help Ms Tarling to do her job. Taking into account the available grants, the chair would cost the employers £200. The employers did not buy the chair and dismissed Ms Tarling for poor performance. The tribunal found that the employers had failed to make a 'reasonable adjustment' within the terms of the DDA 1995 and awarded Ms Tarling £1,200 for injury to feelings.

Tarling v Wisdom Toothbrushes
COIT 3400/150

It must be borne in mind that certain manifestations of stress may fall within the definition of a disability for the purposes of the DDA 1995. If someone suffers a heart attack and consequent heart problems as a result of stress at work, then clearly this could qualify as a physical impairment under the Act (see Chapter 4). However mental impairments are not so easy to define. The Act states that an impairment resulting from or consisting of a mental illness will only constitute a mental impairment if the illness is a clinically well recognised illness. Thus a nervous breakdown or clinical depression may constitute mental impairments, but lesser manifestations of stress may not.

If an employee is suffering from stress, an employer should consider making reasonable adjustments to the employee's working conditions, such as allowing the employee to work part time or allocating less stressful duties. Such an employee should be monitored and regularly consulted so that the best approach can be agreed. If an employer dismisses an employee who is absent because of a stress-related illness without making reasonable adjustments to relieve the stressful situation, he may find himself subject to a claim under the DDA 1995. In any event an employer should, before dismissing an employee who is absent from work for a stress-related reason, investigate the medical condition so that the prognosis can be established, together with an estimate of how long the employee is likely to be away from work and whether the condition is likely to recur if the employee returns to work.

6.3.3 Bullying and stress

Unlike sex, race and disability discrimination, there is no specific legislation outlawing bullying. Unless the bullying is on the grounds of sex, race or disability, therefore, a bullied employee cannot bring a claim in an employment tribunal unless he resigns and brings an (unfair) constructive dismissal claim (see Chapter 5). Note that, although it is proposed that the qualifying period be amended to one year only, as the law stands at the moment, employees generally need two years' qualifying service in order to bring a claim of constructive dismissal. As discussed earlier, all employers have a duty under the contract of employment to have regard to the health and safety of employees and not to destroy or damage the relationship of mutual trust and confidence.

> *Example* Ms Fry was a florist's assistant. She claimed that she had been forced out of her job by her employer's behaviour and that she had suffered from Bell's Palsy as a result of the stress of working with him. In particular she complained that her employer had made her work in such cold conditions that she suffered arthritis in her hands and feet; disciplined her in a threatening and abusive manner; required her to work longer hours than those contractually specified and cancelled her occupational pension without her agreement.
>
> The tribunal found that the employer had been guilty of a number of breaches of contract entitling Ms Fry to resign and claim constructive dismissal.
>
> *Fry v Ashton Decor and Garden Centre*
> Case No 23299/91

Alternatively bullied employees who suffer stress as a result of bullying could bring their claim as a personal injury claim (ie a negligence claim) in the County Court or High Court. An example of such a case is that which Mrs Ballantyne brought against Strathclyde Council in 1996 (below).

> *Example* In June 1996 Mrs Ballantyne accepted an out-of-court settlement of £66,000 for the stress which she suffered at work. She claimed that she was humiliated and countermanded by her supervisor in front of residents at the home for the elderly where she worked, and that her employers did nothing to address the problem. Frequent criticisms led to Mrs Ballantyne taking days off work on grounds of ill-health because she experienced panic attacks, for which she received medication. Eventually she suffered a major panic attack at work and was forced to take early retirement. She brought a claim against her employers for personal injury.
>
> *Ballantyne v Strathclyde Council*
> (unreported, 1996)

It was clear that Mrs Ballantyne's employers had been put on notice of her problems but that her pleas had been ignored. As in the *Walker*[1] case, the employer failed to take reasonably practicable measures to keep its employee safe from mental harm. Had the case proceeded to a full trial it is likely that the court would have found in favour of Mrs Ballantyne following the judgment in the *Walker* case.

So, again, the employer is liable for the stress caused to an employee as a result of some form of harassment – in this case, bullying.

What of the stress caused by victimisation, when an employee has taken action in relation to an act of harassment, and is bullied or picked on in retaliation?

6.3.4 Victimisation and stress

Imagine having eventually plucked up the courage to do something about your boss's 'wandering hand'. What a relief to have told someone about it. But, you soon realise that, rather than being all over you, your boss is now studiously ignoring you and giving you all the worst jobs to do. You also notice that your boss's 'allies' all stop talking when you enter the room and you imagine (probably correctly) that he has told them what he has been accused of and by whom. You are being victimised for bringing a complaint of harassment and you feel more and more ostracised and become depressed. The situation at work becomes intolerable and you are eventually signed off from work by your doctor.

Victimisation is a form of discrimination (see Chapter 7) and is outlawed by the SDA 1975, RRA 1976 and DDA 1995. It is not uncommon for a person to react adversely when a claim is made against them. However, every attempt should be made by employers not to discriminate against someone who has brought a complaint or given evidence in connection with a complaint or done anything else in connection with one of the Acts and to ensure that none of their employees do so.

> *Example*   One of Ms Pereira's colleagues alleged that a company director had attempted to rape her. Ms Pereira had herself been sexually harassed by the same director. When the colleague told Ms Pereira about the incident, Ms Pereira started to gather evidence from witnesses relating to the attempted rape, and was dismissed for so doing. As a result of her dismissal, Ms Pereira became severely depressed. She brought a claim of victimisation to the tribunal who awarded her £4,000 for injury to feelings and stated that this was a 'very serious case of victimisation'.
>
> *Pereira and Another v (1) Marissa Ltd (2) Lopez*
> 1995, COIT 3137/233

It is difficult to envisage a situation where victimisation would not cause stress and, provided the claim is made out, awards will almost always be made for injury to feelings as well as damages.

6.3.5 Failure to take complaint seriously

A failure on the part of the employer to take an allegation of harassment seriously or to deal with it properly could give rise to a further complaint of discrimination. In addition, the failure on the part of the employer to deal properly with a

---

1   *Walker v Northumberland County Council* [1995] IRLR 35 (see para 6.2 above).

complaint of harassment might lead to the employee suffering stress and possibly resigning.

> *Example*   Ms Powell, who was black, was employed as a head chef at a Nottingham Pizzaland. An assistant manager from another Pizzaland visited Ms Powell at her place of work and asked her who she was working with that day. Ms Powell told him and the assistant manager commented 'There's three niggers working together'. Ms Powell complained on a number of occasions to her manager who took no steps to investigate the complaint. She began to suffer from depression and eventually went off sick. While off sick she made an official complaint to her area manager under the Company's grievance procedure. An investigation took place but no formal disciplinary action was taken. The employers refused to give Ms Powell details of the investigation and told her that if she wanted an apology she would have to ask the assistant manager for one herself. Ms Powell resigned and claimed race discrimination and constructive dismissal. She was successful on both counts. The tribunal found that the Company's failure to investigate Ms Powell's complaint properly and to tell her what measures had been taken amounted to a fundamental breach of mutual trust and confidence entitling her to resign and claim constructive dismissal.
>
> *Powell v Pizzaland International Ltd*
> COIT 2913/29P

6.3.6 Stress of accused harasser

It should never be forgotten that the accused harasser also has employment rights. Being accused of sexual, racial or disability harassment, bullying or victimisation can be a very stressful experience, particularly if the allegation is unfounded. Consideration should always be given to the effect that an accusation will have on the accused person's morale. A situation should never be pre-judged and all sides of the story should be heard and carefully considered; an accusation of harassment does not mean that the person is guilty. Wrongly assuming that a person accused of harassment is guilty might result in a stress-related personal injury claim or a constructive dismissal claim (see Chapter 7). If confidential counsellors are available, the accused harasser should be given the opportunity to speak to a counsellor.

In *White v Commissioner of Police for the Metropolis* (below) an employee took his employer to the tribunal following an accusation made against him.

> *Example*   Mr White was a sergeant with the Metropolitan Police. A female police constable, PC McGinley, was posted to Mr White's station and came under his supervision. PC McGinley brought a grievance alleging that Mr White had made derogatory remarks about her to her peers. During the course of the grievance, Mr White himself raised a grievance in respect of the allegations and the way in which they were being handled. Mr White was asked to apologise to PC McGinley but refused to do so and, as a result, was transferred to another police station. For most of the period during which PC McGinley's grievance was being pursued, the applicant was on sick leave suffering from stress and depression. He brought a sex discrimination claim in the industrial tribunal.

The tribunal upheld his claim finding that Mr White was given no opportunity to put his side of the story. They found that there was no proper investigation of the original grievance nor was his grievance dealt with adequately at all. They also found that the transfer was perceived by him and by others to be a punishment. The tribunal inferred from these facts that Mr White was treated in the way he was because he was a man and that every effort was made to placate PC McGinley because she was a woman.

Mr White was awarded £15,000 compensation for injury to feelings. The tribunal said:

'There is no doubt that he has suffered considerably at the hands of the respondent. His confidence has been eroded, particularly in dealing with women police officers, and he has also lost trust and confidence in his senior officers.'

The tribunal also awarded him legal costs amounting to £24,000 against the police, who, said the tribunal:

'had behaved unreasonably in defending the proceedings.'

White v Commissioner of Police for the Metropolis
1996, Case No 54225/95

6.4 WHAT CAN EMPLOYERS DO?

Employers want to get the best from their employees. To do this they must create a working environment in which employees can achieve their full potential. This means that the factors which cause unnecessary stress must be removed, and where this is not possible, stress should be managed in such a way that its adverse effects are minimised.

In order to avoid any *Walker*[1] type claims for personal injury, employers must demonstrate that they took reasonable steps to prevent the stress-related injury occurring. So how can employers protect their employees and themselves from injuries and claims arising from stress-related illnesses induced by harassment or bullying? The Chairman of the HSE says:

'Managing work-related stress is like managing anything else. Once the legitimacy of the issue is recognised you must find out the scale of the problem, decide what to do, do it and then check that what you've done is effective.'

6.4.1 Risk assessment

Given the potential liability for stress, employers should ensure that they are aware of the conditions under which their employees operate. Employers should make every effort to be in touch with what is happening in their workplace and must, at the least, fulfil their statutory duties. Managers are advised to keep in mind the following list of points:

– Communicate effectively and regularly with your team.
– Keep your eyes and ears open – a problem could be very apparent.
– Be prepared to re-distribute work loads if necessary.

---

1   *Walker v Northumberland County Council* [1995] IRLR 35 (see para 6.2 above).

-   Are you under-staffed? Could a temporary employee help to clear a backlog?
-   Consider providing stress counselling.

Employers of more than four employees are under a statutory duty pursuant to s 2(3) of the Health and Safety at Work etc Act 1974 to prepare and keep up to date a written statement of health and safety policy. At the very least, therefore, employers should have a policy covering general health and safety issues. Furthermore, under the Management of Health and Safety at Work Regulations 1992 (MHSW 1992), SI 1992/2051 (regs 3 and 4) an employer of more than four employees is required to assess the risks to health and safety of employees whilst at work and prepare a written report. This should cover the main findings of the assessment, give details of the steps taken to reduce the risks which have been found and should identify any individuals found to be especially at risk.

The health and safety assessment will, of course, cover items such as dangerous chemicals or machinery used in the workplace. However, ill-health resulting from stress caused by an aspect of the working environment should be treated in the same manner as ill-health resulting from physical causes. This means that employers have a legal duty to take reasonable care to ensure that the health of their employees is not placed at risk through excessive and sustained levels of stress arising from the way in which work is organised, the way in which their employees deal with each other at work or from the day to day demands placed on the workforce. In other words, stress should be treated like any other health hazard.

The risk assessment, which will probably take the form of a questionnaire, could be carried out as part of a health and safety assessment (as required by reg 3(1) of the MHSW 1992). Alternatively, it could be included in a harassment questionnaire such as that suggested in Chapter 10, or it could be the subject of a completely separate questionnaire. Work-based stress factors may include some or all of the following (taken from the ACAS booklet on Health and Employment):

-   poor working relationships;
-   restricted social contact;
-   lack of training;
-   poor communications and consultation;
-   poor or inconsistent management;
-   change of job;
-   too many bosses;
-   no control over pace or content of work;
-   organisational or technological change;
-   acting as a supervisor;
-   under or over-promotion;
-   too much or too little responsibility;
-   unreasonable time pressures or deadlines;
-   poor working conditions;
-   excessive noise;
-   uncertainty about role;
-   mismatch between tasks and resources;
-   too much or too little work;
-   irregular or long hours;

- lack of feedback or acknowledgement; and
- lack of job security.

Once the questionnaire has been completed and the results compiled, employers should study the results to find out the extent of stress and stress-related illness in their workforce. They should identify the factors which are causing stress and the probability of stressful incidents occurring in the future. Employers should also try to identify whether there are certain employees or categories of employees who are particularly vulnerable to stress. Note that if certain categories of employees are identified as being at risk then, inevitably, this will be evidence of the fact that harm to those employees was reasonably foreseeable. If a claim is then brought against them, employers will have to rely on the fact that all reasonable steps were taken to prevent the employees suffering any harm.

Having assessed the risk of the workforce and identified the sources of stress, the employer must then implement protective and preventative measures in order to minimise or eliminate the hazards which have been identified. The risk assessment should be reviewed and revised on a regular basis.

6.4.2 Protective measures

The best way to protect employees from stress and stress-related illnesses is good management. As the HSE handbook says:

> 'Ordinary plain good management and regard for people may well be as effective a way of dealing with stress and reducing its effects as a high profile approach to stress such as a company stress programme.'

It goes on to say:

> 'Employers do, however, need to set in motion procedures to ensure that the problem is understood and taken seriously; that excessive stress is not seen as a personal problem but an issue which managers, staff and the organisation as a whole are committed to addressing. It is important that individuals are not made to feel guilty about their stress problems and are encouraged to seek the relief and support they may desperately need.'

In order for any such procedure to be set in motion the support of senior management is crucial. Any stress programme must have, and be seen to have, the support of the managing director (or equivalent). In addition, if senior management adopt a bullying style of management, this will inevitably be passed down to lower levels of management, resulting in stress being suffered by a large number of employees. Organisations should therefore make it clear from the top, and by way of example, that autocratic management styles are not acceptable and that bullying is a disciplinary offence.

The HSE handbook suggests in Table 4 that there are a number of things that can help in a positive approach to stress reduction, including:

General management and culture
- Clear company objectives.
- Good communications.
- Close employee involvement, particularly during periods of organisational change.

–   Good management support and appropriate training and development of
    staff.

Relationships at work
–   Training in interpersonal skills.
–   Effective systems for dealing with interpersonal conflict, bullying and racial
    or sexual harassment, including:
    –   agreed grievance procedure;
    –   proper investigation of complaints.

The elements under the heading 'General management and culture' relate to
the reduction of stress generally. However, deliberately omitting any of these
elements could amount to bullying. So deliberately failing to give clear company
objectives, deliberately failing to involve an employee in company matters or
deliberately failing to support, train and develop staff could all possibly amount
to bullying. The elements under the heading 'Relationships at work' clearly relate
to any form of harassment or bullying and advocate an 'effective system for
dealing with interpersonal conflict'.

6.4.3 Stress policy

Chapter 10 sets out in some detail the requirements for an effective system for
dealing with interpersonal conflict including advice on how to draft and
implement a harassment policy and the training and communication required to
make the policy effective. Many of these issues will relate equally to a stress
policy.

The main benefits of such a policy will be to help management to recognise
stress and to provide guidance on what they should do if they find that it is
occurring; and to reassure employees that their concerns about occupational
stress will be taken seriously. A stress policy could be a separate policy or an
expansion of an existing health and safety policy, or it could possibly be included
as part of a harassment policy. The most obvious advantage in forming and
implementing a stress policy, apart from reducing the stress of the employees, is
that it provides a tangible example of an organisation's attempt to protect its
employees from risks which are reasonably foreseeable (such as those in the
Walker[1] case).

The following points should be made clear in the stress policy:

–   The employer takes its duty to provide a safe and secure workplace
    seriously.
–   There is a commitment on the organisation's behalf to take all reasonable
    steps to protect employees from harm to their health caused by stress.
–   Employees have a duty to bring such stressful circumstances to the
    employer's attention.
–   Individuals should not feel guilty about suffering problems related to stress
    and should be encouraged to seek any relief and support that they may need.
–   Any issues relating to stress raised by an employee will be taken seriously and
    as far as possible these will be dealt with confidentially.

---

1   *Walker v Northumberland County Council* [1995] IRLR 35 (see para 6.2 above).

–   The policy should identify who (for example a line manager or confidential counsellor) should be approached if an employee feels that he or she is suffering from stress.
–   A commitment that a full investigation will be carried out into any complaints made (for example of unfair allocation of work, bullying, victimisation or lack of support from superiors).
–   Details of the type of support services that the organisation is able to provide (such as stress management courses, confidential telephone helplines, counselling services etc).

It would be perfectly feasible to include stress-related issues within a harassment policy, and to assess the risk of stress at the same time as assessing the incidence of harassment and bullying. It should also be borne in mind that, as with harassment and bullying, records should be kept of all meetings and actions taken when dealing with stress-related problems since this will help to show due diligence of the employer.

6.4.4 Training

The HSE Guide suggests that staff should be encouraged to attend stress awareness and stress management courses so they are better able to handle the pressures they may encounter. It also suggests that, where problems have developed, line managers should be able to provide support and, if necessary, refer the person on for further help. If line managers are to be expected to provide support, they must be trained how to do so. They must be taught to recognise the symptoms of stress such as an increase in sickness absence, loss of motivation and commitment, erratic or poor time-keeping, tension and conflict between individuals, poor decision-making etc. They must be told that the organisation views the matter as a serious issue and that any complaints of stress must be taken seriously. They must be told that the matter should be treated sympathetically and confidentially and must know who to pass the matter on to if further help is required.

Some employers are now introducing Employee Assistance Programmes ('EAPs'). These are confidential personal counselling services where individuals can discuss work or non-work related problems. EAPs can be run in-house, contracted out to counselling organisations or managed from within the organisation using external counsellors. If existing members of the workforce are used as counsellors they should receive appropriate training.

Chapter 7

THE LEGAL BASIS OF A CLAIM

Who can bring a claim? – Sexual harassment – Sexual orientation and transsexuality – Racial harassment – Disability harassment – Victimisation – Bullying – Public Order Act 1986 – Protection from Harassment Act 1997

7.1 WHO CAN BRING A CLAIM?

It is important to define what category of person can bring a claim of harassment against their employer. In order to be protected against unfair dismissal, a person must be an employee under a contract of employment[1] and must normally have been continuously employed for a period of two years. However, it should be noted that a Government White Paper *Fairness at Work* has proposed that the qualifying period for unfair dismissal claims be reduced from two years to one. At the moment there is a statutory limit on the maximum compensatory award for unfair dismissal (see Chapter 13), but the White Paper also proposes a removal of this cap so that compensation for unfair dismissal claims would be unlimited.

The SDA 1975, RRA 1976 and DDA 1995 extend their protection beyond the scope of the ERA 1996 to cover not only employees employed under a contract of employment but also workers under a contract for services (self-employed workers) provided they execute the work personally, and contract workers (for example staff provided by an agency). There is no qualifying period of employment for cases brought under the SDA 1975, RRA 1976 or DDA 1995. Complaints of unfair dismissal, sex, race or disability discrimination must be presented to an employment tribunal within three months of the incident. However an employment tribunal can extend this time-limit for discrimination claims if it considers that it is 'just and equitable' to do so (in discrimination cases) or, in an unfair dismissal, if satisfied that it was 'not reasonably practicable' to meet the three-month deadline. In *Mills and Crown Prosecution Service v Marshall*[2] the time-limit for a transsexual's claim of sex discrimination was extended to three years after the alleged act of discrimination because the court recognised the uncertainty of the law in this area until quite recently.

Workers under a contract for services are covered by s 82(1), s 78(1) and s 68(1) of the SDA 1975, RRA 1976 and DDA 1995 respectively, which state that protection is afforded to those in:

> 'employment under a contract of service or of apprenticeship or a contract personally to do any work'.

Self-employed people must be employed under a contract *personally* to execute any work. They will not be protected by the employment provisions in

---

1   ERA 1996, s 230(1).
2   [1998] IRLR 494, EAT.

the SDA 1975, RRA 1976 and DDA 1995 if they allow someone else to do the work for them – even if they remain responsible for seeing that the work is carried out. To be within the scope of the legislation, self-employed people must be obliged to do all, or the majority, of the work themselves.

Contract workers (often known as agency workers) are also covered by the discrimination legislation. Section 9(1) of the SDA 1975, s 7(1) of the RRA 1976 and s 12 of the DDA 1995 each have a section headed 'Discrimination against contract workers'. The SDA 1975 and RRA 1976 define contract work as follows:

> '... any work for a person ("the principal") which is available for doing by individuals ("contract workers") who are employed not by the principal himself but by another person, who supplies them under a contract made with the principal.'

The DDA 1995 defines principal, contract work and contract workers as follows:

> '"principal" means a person ("A") who makes work available for doing by individuals who are employed by another person who supplies them under a contract made with A;
> "contract work" means work so made available; and
> "contract worker" means any individual who is supplied to the principal under such a contract.'

A common example of this situation is a temporary secretary (a 'temp') who is employed by and paid by an agency (the employer) but who might carry out work for a different organisation (the principal). The temp, an employee of the agency, is protected against discrimination by the agency because he or she is an employee of the agency. Because of the contract between the agency and the principal, the temp is also protected against discrimination by the principal. If the temp is harassed by any of the employees of the agency or the principal, he or she will be able to bring a claim in the employment tribunal against the agency or the principal.

The race discrimination case of *Harrods Ltd v Remick*[1] established a broad construction of 'contract worker' and held that staff employed by con-cessionaires at Harrods store could sue Harrods in respect of alleged race discrimination since they were contract workers who worked 'for' Harrods within the meaning of s 7 of the RRA 1976, even though they also worked for their employer.

7.2 SEXUAL HARASSMENT

7.2.1 Definition of sexual harassment

As can be seen from the previous chapters, there is no legislation which deals specifically with sexual harassment at work. There is, however, a plethora of case-law which clarifies what an employee needs to show in order to bring a claim of sexual harassment against his or her employers based on discrimination legislation. The European Commission has also issued a Recommendation and

---

1   [1997] IRLR 583.

Code on the *Protection of the Dignity of Women and Men at Work*.[1] This Code, which is referred to as 'the EC Code', is not legally binding but does carry much persuasive influence and has been relied upon in UK courts, as well as having been recommended to tribunals to bear in mind when considering sexual harassment cases.

The EC Code defines sexual harassment as 'unwanted conduct of a sexual nature, or other conduct based on sex affecting the dignity of women and men at work'. This is not a legally binding definition but is a useful one. In fact sexual harassment is merely a convenient term for a particular form of direct sex discrimination and any question on whether or not an employee has suffered sexual harassment should always refer back to the wording of the SDA 1975. (The SDA 1975 also legislates against indirect sex discrimination, ie the application of a condition or requirement which appears to apply to all groups equally, but which has the effect of discriminating against one group of persons.) The relevant sections relating to direct discrimination are ss 1(1) and 6(2)(b) of the SDA 1975. Section 1 defines discrimination and s 6 shows what sort of discrimination is unlawful in the employment field. In order to fit sexual harassment within the legislation, the relevant parts of the two sections must be read together.

'1(1) A person discriminates against a woman in any circumstances relevant for the purposes of any provision of this Act if –

(a)   on the ground of her sex he treats her less favourably than he treats or would treat a man ...'

'6(2) It is unlawful for a person, in the case of a woman employed by him at an establishment in Great Britain, to discriminate against her –

...

(b)   by dismissing her, or subjecting her to any other detriment'

There are thus three elements which need to be satisfied in order for an employee to bring a successful sexual harassment claim:

(1)   she must have been treated less favourably than an actual or hypothetical man in similar circumstances;
(2)   that treatment must be on the grounds of her sex; and
(3)   the treatment must have resulted in a detriment.

These provisions apply equally to a man discriminated against because of his sex.

7.2.2 Less favourable treatment

In sex discrimination cases a woman must compare the treatment she has received to the treatment a man would have received in a comparable situation. The requirement of a comparator has caused difficulties in cases of sexual harassment as there are certain forms of treatment to which women are particularly vulnerable.

---

1   See Appendix 1.

An example of a successful harassment claim where the treatment of an employee amounted to less favourable treatment than a man in a comparable situation is *H v P t/a R* (below).

> *Example*   H was a female cleaner whose duties included cleaning the men's lavatories. She would knock loudly on the door before entering and call out "Is there anybody there?". On one occasion, having called out and received no reply, she entered the lavatories and found a man urinating at an open urinal. Another time, after first calling out, she entered and found a man apparently masturbating. H made a number of complaints to her employers but nothing was done. She was eventually dismissed for an unrelated matter and subsequently brought a claim for sexual harassment. The tribunal found that a man in a comparable situation cleaning men's or women's lavatories would not have been subjected to the same treatment. She therefore made out her case of less favourable treatment based on the fact that she was a woman and her claim was upheld.
>
>

H v P t/a R
COIT 2989/186

An example of the difficulties caused by the requirement to compare like with like is the case of *Strathclyde Regional Council v Porcelli* (below).

> *Example*   Ms Porcelli was subjected to a campaign of various types of abuse by two male colleagues. They did not like her and wanted to force her to resign. Their campaign included actions of a sexual nature such as suggestive remarks and deliberate brushing against her. In the industrial tribunal the argument put forward on behalf of the two male colleagues was that they would have treated a man whom they disliked in a similar way and that she was not therefore treated less favourably than a man would have been. The tribunal held that she was not treated less favourably on the grounds of her sex as a man in her position would have been treated in a similar way.
>
> The EAT overturned the decision, however, and the Court of Session in Scotland upheld the EAT's ruling. It was held that, although the campaign persued against Ms Porcelli did not have a sex-related motive or object, the method of ill treatment was chosen precisely because she was a woman: 'It was a particular kind of weapon, based on the sex of the victim, which … would not have been used against an equally disliked man.'
>
>

Strathclyde Regional Council v Porcelli
[1986] IRLR 134

7.2.3 On the grounds of sex

This element of a sexual harassment claim is closely linked to the element of less favourable treatment. Many claims of sexual harassment will undoubtedly satisfy the requirements of less favourable treatment based on the sex of the complainant. Often sexual harassment will betray a sexual motivation on the part of the harasser. There are many examples of 'sleep with me and I'll promote you' types of harassment or offensive sexual remarks such as 'Hiya big tits' (as in the *Insitu* case referred to later in this chapter). But harassment can take a much more subtle form which makes it far more difficult to determine whether or not a particular type of behaviour constitutes sexual harassment. It might have been used out of animosity towards the recipient or it might be motivated by bullying. It might not have been intended as harassment at all.

For example, in *Stewart v Cleveland Guest (Engineering) Ltd*[1] a female worker objected to pictures of nude females displayed on the walls. In this case, the EAT held that the display was neutral since a hypothetical man could have been equally offended, and thus it was not discriminatory. Note that a similar case was brought in America where the outcome was that lewd pin-ups did constitute sexual harassment.

Less favourable treatment on the grounds of sex is sometimes known as the 'but for' test. Would she have been treated that way but for the fact that she is a woman or is it the case that all employees were treated in the same way, regardless of their sex?

The 'but for' test was set out in *James v Eastleigh Borough Council* (below).

> *Example* Eastleigh Borough Council offered free swimming to people of pensionable age (ie at that time, 60 years of age for a woman and 65 for a man). Thus, Mr James, who was 61, had to pay to swim at the pool while any woman aged 60 or over could use the pool without having to pay. He brought a sex discrimination claim arguing that it was unlawful discrimination that he had to pay to use the pool while a woman of the same age did not. The case went to the House of Lords which held that, but for his sex, Mr James would have been entitled to free swimming. The majority view was that motive and intention were irrelevant and that the key issue was simple causation.
>
> *James v Eastleigh Borough Council*
> [1990] 2 All ER 607

Would Mr James have been treated that way but for the fact that he is a man? Answer – no. The detriment he suffered was based purely on his sex. It does not matter that there was no intention to discriminate against him.

7.2.4 Suffering a detriment

In order for a harassment claim to be actionable, it must not only fall within the definition of discrimination (s 1(1)) but must also be accompanied by an action or event which makes the discrimination unlawful. In the case of harassment, this event is being subjected to a detriment (s 6(2)(b)). There is no definition in the SDA 1975 of 'detriment' but the judge in the case of *Ministry of Defence v Jeremiah*[2] said that it meant nothing more than 'putting under a disadvantage'. Detriment will include demotion, warnings, transfer, loss of status, racial insults and sexual harassment. In the context of sexual (and also racial) harassment it is not necessary to show that the harassment led to any other detriment such as transfer or dismissal; harassment can itself amount to a detriment.

It is now clear that a single remark or incident can, if sufficiently serious, amount to sexual harassment and therefore be a detriment within the meaning of the Act. In the case of *Insitu Cleaning Company v Heads*,[3] Ms Heads was greeted

---

1   [1994] IRLR 440.
2   [1980] ICR 13.
3   [1995] IRLR 5.

with the remark 'Hiya big tits'. This was deemed to constitute sexual harassment even though there was only one incident of harassment.

The most recent case to discuss the issue of detriment is the case of *Scott v Combined Property Services Ltd.*[1] In that case the industrial tribunal held that certain remarks about a female employee did not constitute sexual harassment. The EAT upheld the finding. In so doing, the EAT stated:

> 'The conduct complained of must at least be capable, as an objective test, of being categorised as offensive. In many cases, if that test is satisfied, nothing more need be considered; but, in cases where the conduct might be regarded as neutral or such as to be regarded by some people as offensive if not by others, the subject element comes into the equation in order to assess the reaction of the victim.'

So the effect of the conduct should be considered first from a purely objective point of view. If, objectively, the behaviour constitutes harassment, then the test of detriment has been satisfied. If, objectively, it is thought that no detriment was suffered or it is unsure whether any detriment was suffered, the matter should be looked at subjectively from the viewpoint of the alleged victim of harassment. This has the advantage for the complainant that his or her sensitivity can be taken into account when assessing whether or not there has been any detriment, but the potential disadvantage (for the complainant) that the tribunal will be able to hear evidence as to the individual's character which may be unfavourable.

In *Snowball v Gardner Merchant Ltd,*[2] the tribunal was entitled to take into account evidence concerning the complainant's general attitude to sexual behaviour (in particular the fact that she referred to her bed as a 'play pen' and mentioned her black satin sheets in conversations with fellow workers). The reasoning was that such evidence was relevant for the purposes of deciding whether she had, in fact, suffered any *detriment* as a consequence of the alleged acts of sexual harassment. This is important both with regard to the question of liability and compensation.

The issue was also discussed in the case of *Wileman v Minilec Engineering Ltd*[3] where it was held that women have a choice about what behaviour they accept and from whom. A female employee of Wileman Engineering complained she had been sexually harassed by one of the company's directors. The harassment was found to consist of salacious remarks and physical harassment. In the words of the tribunal:

> 'An employee may well consider herself to have been harassed by Mr A by conduct which she would not have objected to if done by Mr B or Mr C.'

The viewpoint of the alleged victim should therefore be taken into account.

7.3 SEXUAL ORIENTATION AND TRANSSEXUALITY

7.3.1 Sexual orientation

According to a survey conducted by Stonewall, the gay rights group, many gay men and lesbians said they had been harassed at work because they were known

---

1   1996, EAT 757.
2   [1987] IRLR 397, EAT.
3   [1988] IRLR 144.

or suspected to be gay. However, there is no legislation specifically outlawing discrimination (and therefore harassment) on the grounds of sexual orientation. The SDA 1975 says that a woman is discriminated against if a person:

'on the grounds of her sex ... treats her less favourably than he treats or would treat a man'

and a man is discriminated against if a person:

'on the grounds of his sex ... treats him less favourably than he treats or would treat a woman'.

Thus if a gay man were taunted by his colleagues by being called offensive names, he would not, as the law currently stands, be able to bring a sex discrimination claim as the harassment was not based on his sex but on his sexuality. He would not be able to show that the detriment he suffered was on the ground of his sex and would not therefore get past the 'but for' test.

Claimants have, in the past, tried to argue that the comparator for a gay man should be a heterosexual woman – ie that a woman with a sexual preference for men would not have been treated in the same way as a man with a sexual preference for men. However, tribunals have held in these circumstances that the relevant comparator is not a heterosexual woman but a lesbian. If a lesbian woman would have been treated in the same way, there has been no unlawful discrimination.

> *Example*   Mr Smith, who is gay, was a barman in a pub. He claimed he had suffered sexual harassment in employment by reason of his homosexuality and that he had also suffered less favourable treatment when he was dismissed for being gay. The EAT drew a clear distinction between discrimination on grounds of sex and discrimination on grounds of sexual orientation. The EAT held that discrimination on the grounds of sexual orientation was not covered by the SDA. It therefore followed that the taunting of a gay man did not amount to unlawful discrimination because the action against him was based on his sexuality and not because he was a man.
>
> *Smith v Gardner Merchant Ltd*
> [1996] IRLR 342, EAT

There has been a much publicised ECJ decision about the right to equal benefits for a lesbian worker's partner – *Grant v South West Trains* (below).

> *Example*   South West Trains offered travel concessions to the legal spouse or common law opposite sex unmarried partner of employees. However, it refused to extend these concessions to the same sex partner of Ms Grant. The ECJ held: that there was no direct discrimination on the grounds of sex because a male homosexual couple would have been treated in the same way; that same sex relationships are not the same as opposite sex relationships; that South West Trains' policy was not discriminatory on the grounds of sex and that EC law does not cover discrimination on the grounds of sexual orientation.
>
> *Grant v South West Trains Ltd*
> [1998] ICR 449

> *Example*   A non-homosexual man was harassed by two homosexual

colleagues, who carried out acts of harassment of a homosexual nature. An industrial tribunal decided that the applicant, as a man, was more susceptible to these acts than a woman would have been and thus the applicant had been treated less favourably because of his sex, and his claim of sexual harassment was therefore upheld.

Gates v Security Express Guards
1993, Case No 45142/92

7.3.2 Transsexuality

A transsexual is someone who has undergone, or is in the process of undergoing, or has declared an intention to undergo, surgery to change his or her sex (also known as 'gender reassignment'). A transsexual should not be confused with a transvestite, who is someone who dresses in clothes normally associated with the opposite sex, without wishing to change his or her sex. Unlike homosexuals or transvestites, transsexuals are now protected by law against discrimination on the grounds of their transsexuality. This is because of the ruling in the case of *Chessington World of Adventures v Reed* (below) which has been discussed in Chapter 2.

> *Example*   Mr Reed began working for Chessington World of Adventures in January 1987. In July 1991 she announced her intention to change her gender identity from male to female. Following her declaration some of her male colleagues subjected her to a campaign of harassment.
>
> It became clear to her managers that she was experiencing serious difficulties at work because of her transsexuality. However no real investigation was carried out and no steps were taken to protect her or to prevent the harassment. No disciplinary action was taken against those responsible for the harassment. In October 1991, Miss Reed submitted a claim to the industrial tribunal complaining of sex discrimination (as well as unfair dismissal and unlawful deduction of wages but these claims were later withdrawn). The tribunal found that the employers' failure to act on their knowledge of the harassment being suffered by Miss Reed constituted a detriment and Miss Reed's claim was upheld. The employers appealed.
>
> The EAT held that the SDA 1975 should be interpreted consistently with the Equal Treatment Directive which says that 'there shall be no discrimination whatsoever on the grounds of sex'. They concluded that treating someone less favourably on the grounds of a declared intention to undergo gender reassignment was a sex-based act and that there was no requirement for a male/female comparison to be made.
>
> *Chessington World of Adventures v Reed*
[1997] IRLR 556, EAT

This case shows that it may not always be necessary to compare the treatment of one individual with a comparator and that it may be sufficient to show that the treatment is offensive and unwanted. This sort of sex discrimination is akin to discrimination on the grounds of pregnancy where it would, similarly, be difficult to make a direct comparison with someone of the opposite sex.

7.3.3 Proposed legislation

It should be noted that the EOC has published a consultation document containing proposals for a new Sex Equality Act to replace the existing SDA

1975 and Equal Pay Act 1970. The proposed Act would tackle a range of issues that are not satisfactorily addressed by existing legislation such as homosexuality and transsexuality; it would also expressly prohibit sexual harassment, incorporating the definition of sexual harassment contained in the EC Code. The EOC has not yet submitted its proposals to the Secretary of State for Education and Employment but once it has there may be a major overhaul in sex discrimination legislation.

7.4 RACIAL HARASSMENT

7.4.1 Definition of racial harassment

The RRA 1976 has a very similar construction to the SDA 1975. As explained earlier, the RRA 1976 covers those working under a contract for services (self-employed people) and contract workers as well as employees. It legislates against both direct and indirect race discrimination and, as with sexual harassment, racial harassment falls within the definition of direct discrimination.

Claims of racial harassment must make out the three requirements of: less favourable treatment, on the grounds of race and suffering a detriment. These are set out in ss 1(1)(a) and 4(2)(c). As with the SDA 1975, in order to fit racial harassment within the RRA 1976, the relevant parts of the sections must be read together.

> '1(1) A person discriminates against another in any circumstances relevant for the purposes of any provision of this Act if –
>
> (a) on racial grounds he treats that other less favourably than he treats or would treat other persons ...'
>
> '4(2) It is unlawful for a person, in the case of a person employed by him at an establishment in Great Britain, to discriminate against that employee –
>
> ...
>
> (c) by dismissing him, or subjecting him to any other detriment.'

Although the European Commission has issued a code to combat sexual harassment, it has not issued a similar code to combat racial harassment. However the CRE has issued a Code of Practice for the Elimination of Racial Discrimination and the Promotion of Equality of Opportunity in Employment (reproduced at Appendix 3). This does not give specific guidance on racial harassment but is useful in general terms as a guide to the elimination of racial harassment and enhancement of equality of opportunity.

In s 3(1), the RRA 1976 defines racial grounds as 'colour, race, nationality or ethnic or national origins'. It will usually be obvious whether or not a person falls within one of the racial grounds covered by the Act but it may be necessary to go back to the wording of the Act to decide whether or not any harassment was on racial grounds.

Note that the RRA 1976 also includes discrimination against a person on the grounds of someone else's race. If, for example, a white employee suffers a detriment for refusing to carry out a racist instruction – not to allow any black people into a night club, for example – this will also be covered by the RRA 1976.

This was confirmed in *Weathersfield Ltd v Sargent*,[1] where Ms Sargent resigned from her job as a receptionist because she could not bring herself to discriminate against black customers, which she had been instructed to do by her employers. The EAT found that the detriment she had suffered – in the form of constructive dismissal – amounted to unlawful race discrimination on the ground not of her race but of the customers' race.

7.4.2 Less favourable treatment

In order to succeed in a claim of race discrimination the complainant must establish that he or she has been less favourably treated than a comparator in the same or similar circumstances has been, or would have been, treated. If Mr X who is black is paid less then Mr Y who is white, it will be easy to show less favourable treatment (although the less favourable treatment might be based on grounds other than race – seniority for example).

As racial harassment is simply a form of race discrimination, less favourable treatment must be shown in order to succeed in a claim. It may be obviously less favourable – for example the case of *Milovanovic v Hebden Dyeing and Finishing Company Ltd and Others*[2] where an employee of Serbian origin was subjected to racist 'jokes' and remarks which would only have been addressed to someone of foreign origin.

Racial harassment might take more subtle forms such as being deliberately ignored or not being invited on nights out. It might involve being assigned the least pleasant jobs to do. Whatever form it takes, it must amount to less favourable treatment.

7.4.3 On racial grounds

The less favourable treatment must be on racial grounds, ie on the grounds of colour, race, nationality, ethnic or national origins. For example a black worker, who was the newest arrival in the department might always be asked to make the tea. However this less favourable treatment might be based not on the fact that he was black but on the fact that he was the newest arrival, and the newest arrival had always been expected to make the tea – regardless of his or her colour, race, nationality, ethnic or national origins. The test as to whether any particular action is on racial grounds or not is answered by analogy with sex discrimination cases – if a person were not of that racial group, would he or she have been vulnerable to the act in question?

> *Example* Mr Hussain, a Muslim, worked for a small metal castings foundry. The first major incident happened when a pig's head was shoved in his face as he was coming out of the shower while a number of his colleagues stood around laughing. On another occasion, he was in the shower when he turned round to find a colleague urinating on his leg. The colleague said: 'That's all you Pakis are worth: a piece of piss.' The tribunal found unanimously that Mr Hussain had been a victim of racial discrimination.
>
> *Hussain v Westcroft Castings Ltd (1) Scotson (2) & Irivine (3)*
> 1995, IT Case No 21853/94

---

1   [1998] IRLR 14, EAT.
2   1995, IT Case No 29691/94.

7.4.4 Suffering a detriment

As with the SDA 1975, a detriment within the RRA 1976 simply means putting at a disadvantage in some way. However, complaints of racial harassment are likely to centre on the creation of a hostile, threatening or demeaning work environment.

> *Example*   A black employee of British Leyland had been arrested for theft in the plant and had been granted bail. Management thought he might try to return to the plant and that he might use a false name. They therefore issued instructions that every black person entering the plant must be subjected to a thorough identity check. A group of black employees sought to establish that they had suffered a detriment. The EAT held that the circulation of the instructions and the setting up of the identity checks was capable of constituting a detriment within the meaning of the RRA 1976 even though no employees had, by the time of the complaint, been subjected to an identity check.
>
> *British Leyland Cars Ltd v Brown*
> [1983] IRLR 193, EAT

Racial banter exists in many workplaces but this is just the sort of detriment which leads to complaints of race discrimination.

> *Example*   Mr McAuley, an Irishman, worked on the shop floor in Auto Alloys. He was constantly referred to by his colleagues as 'Irish Paddy' or 'typical thick Paddy'. He complained to his line manager but was told to ignore the comments because they were just jokes. Mr McAuley was finally dismissed and the tribunal commented that they thought his dismissal was principally because he was an Irishman who would not take Irish jokes lying down, in other words he did not 'fit in'. The tribunal found that he had been discriminated against on racial grounds, which include grounds of nationality or ethnic origin, and awarded him compensation totalling £8,000.
>
> *McAuley v Auto Alloys Foundry Ltd and Taylor*
> 1994, IT Case No 62824/93

As well as racial banter and racial 'jokes' in the workplace, there are still, unfortunately, examples of extreme cases of detriment suffered by workers on the grounds of their race (such as in the case of *Jones v Tower Boot*[1]). In extreme cases it will be relatively easy to show the detriment so that all that needs to be shown is that the detriment suffered was on racial grounds. Sometimes the detriment will be more difficult to show.

> *Example*   Mrs de Souza was referred to as 'the wog' in a conversation between two managers. She did not overhear this conversation but was told about it by a colleague who did. She brought a claim of race discrimination in the industrial tribunal. Her claim was rejected and eventually went to the Court of Appeal where it was held that she could not:
>
> 'be said to have been treated less favourably by whomsoever used the word, unless he intended her to overhear the conversation in which it was used, or knew or ought

---

1   [1997] IRLR 168, CA.

reasonably to have anticipated that the person he was talking to would pass the insult on or that the appellant would hear of it in some other way.'

The Court of Appeal rejected her claim.

> De Souza v Automobile Association
> [1986] ICR 514

So it seems that the conduct in question must be directed towards the complainant or must be considered reasonably likely for him or her to have become aware of the conduct in order for it to constitute a detriment.

Employers faced with racial harassment claims must be aware of the fact that, as in sexual harassment claims, it is the perception and interpretation of the person who feels harassed that is central to deciding whether or not harassment has occurred.

> **Example** Mr Clarke, who is of Afro-Caribbean origin, had worked at Fatati's, a company making carpets for cars, since March 1989. He was subjected to a good deal of racist banter and, following his dismissal, brought a complaint of race discrimination in the industrial tribunal. The tribunal found that the racial abuse Mr Clarke suffered constituted a detriment under the RRA stating:
>
> > 'It is not what a bystander might consider to be a disadvantage, or anyone else other than the applicant, but what the applicant himself considered ... it was not material that other employees might shrug off being called racist names ... or that things were said without malice [but that] the applicant was upset, and thought he was being singled out.'
>
> The tribunal awarded Mr Clarke a total of £11,350 in compensation.
>
> > Clarke v BTR Fatati Ltd
> > 1992, IT Case Nos 22828/91; 5414/92; 34485/91

The tribunals have been increasingly willing to award substantial sums for injury to feelings, for example in *Armitage, Marsden and HM Prison Service v Johnson* (below).

> **Example** Mr Johnson, of Afro-Caribbean origin, was employed by the Prison Service as an auxiliary prison officer at Brixton Prison. After he complained about the way a black prisoner was treated by other prison officers, he was subjected to a campaign of racist remarks, false accusations and ostracism. The matter was not properly investigated, which resulted in further discrimination. The industrial tribunal awarded him compensation for injury to feelings amounting to £21,000 (and this amount was upheld by the EAT).
>
> > Armitage, Marsden and HM Prison Service v Johnson
> > [1997] IRLR 162, EAT

7.5 DISABILITY HARASSMENT

7.5.1 Definition of disability harassment

For employment purposes, the DDA 1995 is similar to the SDA 1975 and RRA 1976 but some differences do exist. As with the SDA 1975 and RRA 1976, it covers not only employees working under a contract of employment but also those working under a contract for services (self-employed people) and contract workers. Unlike those Acts, however, there is no concept of indirect discrimination (ie applying a condition or requirement which appears to apply to all groups equally, but which has the effect of discriminating against one group of victims). Instead, there is direct discrimination and discrimination for failure to carry out the duty to make adjustments. Harassment falls within the definition of direct discrimination. It should be noted that employers with fewer than 20 employees are exempt from the employment provisions in the Act.

First, it is necessary to define a disabled person so that it is clear who the Act is intended to protect. Section 1 says:

> '(1) Subject to the provisions of Schedule 1, a person has a disability for the purposes of this Act if he has a physical or mental impairment which has a substantial and long-term adverse effect on his ability to carry out normal day-to-day activities.
> (2) In this Act "disabled person" means a person who has a disability.'

Schedule 1 deals in more detail with impairment, long-term effects, normal day-to-day activities and substantial adverse effects.

Section 2 makes it clear that the DDA 1995 not only protects those who have a disability but also those who have had a disability. The DDA 1995 does not, however, protect anyone other than those categories of people (except under the victimisation provisions, as we shall see later). This is unlike the SDA 1975 and the RRA 1976 which afford protection not only to men and women who are discriminated against but also to any individual who suffers a detriment as a result of the discrimination against someone else. For example, if a barman is told not to serve black people and is dismissed for disobeying those instructions, he has suffered a detriment and can bring a claim under the RRA 1976, even though the discrimination is not against him.

The provisions of the DDA 1995 in relation to discrimination by employers are similar to those in SDA 1976 and RRA 1975. Again, there is no definition of harassment and any claim for disability harassment must satisfy the disability discrimination requirements of less favourable treatment against a disabled person by subjecting him to a detriment. However, in the case of the DDA 1995, the discrimination will be lawful if the less favourable treatment is justified, but only if 'the reason for [the justification] is both material to the circumstances of the particular case and substantial' (s 5(3)). The relevant sections are ss 4(2)(d) and 5(1):

> '4(2) It is unlawful for an employer to discriminate against a disabled person whom he employs –
> . . .
> (d) by dismissing him or subjecting him to any other detriment.'
>
> '5(1) For the purposes of this Part, an employer discriminates against a disabled person if –
> (a) for a reason which relates to the disabled person's disability, he treats him less favourably than he treats or would treat others to whom that reason does not or would not apply; and
> (b) he cannot show that the treatment in question is justified.'

7.5.2 Less favourable treatment

As with sex and race discrimination, the concept of disability discrimination calls for a comparative approach. As clearly stated in s 5(1)(a), discrimination occurs if the employer treats a person with a disability less favourably than he treats or would treat others who do not have that disability. A disabled person may not be able to point to other people who were actually treated more favourably but it is still less favourable treatment if the employer would have given better treatment to someone else to whom the disability did not apply. So a disabled complainant could use a hypothetical rather than an actual comparator.

7.5.3 Relating to a disability

In order for the claim to succeed, the less favourable treatment must relate to the disabled person's disability. The employer's intention or motive is not relevant, but there must be a causal connection between the discriminatory treatment and the person's disability. For example, an employer decides to close down a factory and makes all the employees redundant including a disabled person who works there. This is not discrimination as the disabled employee is not being dismissed for a reason which relates to the disability. If, on the other hand, a disabled employee is taunted by his or her colleagues and called offensive names, then this would be less favourable treatment relating to the employee's disability.

7.5.4 Justification

Justification of any disability discrimination must be 'material to the circumstances of the particular case and substantial'. The Code of Practice for the elimination of discrimination in the field of employment against disabled persons or persons who have had a disability (Code of Practice (Employment)) which is issued by the Secretary of State and admissible as evidence in any proceedings under the Act before an employment tribunal, county court or sheriff court, gives various examples of justifiable and non-justifiable treatment at section 4.6 of the Code. One such example is:

> A factory worker with a mental illness is sometimes away from work due to his disability. Because of that he is dismissed. However, the amount of time off is very little more than the employer accepts as sick leave for other employees and so is very unlikely to be a substantial reason.

It is extremely unlikely that any form of harassment will have a justifiable defence and, at present, there is no case-law on this issue.

7.5.5 Suffering a detriment

Section 6.22 of the Employment Code of Practice states:

> 'The Act does not refer to harassment as a separate issue. However, harassing a disabled person on account of a disability will almost always amount to a detriment under the Act.'

As with sexual and racial harassment, there is no limit on the level of compensation which an employment tribunal can award and an award can be made in respect of injury to feelings.

7.6 VICTIMISATION

The SDA 1975, RRA 1976 and DDA 1995 all legislate against 'victimisation'. It occurs when a person victimises another person for bringing a claim or giving evidence in connection with a claim of discrimination. A claim of victimisation can be brought by anyone who is treated less favourably as a result of doing one of the protected acts; this need not necessarily be the person who suffered the original discrimination. Section 4 of the SDA 1975 and s 2 of the RRA 1976 are very similar:

'(1) A person ("the discriminator") discriminates against another person ("the person victimised") in any circumstances relevant for the purposes of any provision of this Act if he treats the person victimised less favourably than in those circumstances he treats or would treat other persons, and does so by reason that the person victimised has –

(a) brought proceedings against the discriminator or any other person under this Act [. . .], or
(b) given evidence or information in connection with proceedings brought by any person against the discriminator or any other person under this Act [. . .], or
(c) otherwise done anything under or by reference to this Act [. . .] in relation to the discriminator or any other person, or
(d) alleged that the discriminator or any other person has committed an act which (whether or not the allegation so states) would amount to a contravention of this Act [. . .],

or by reason that the discriminator knows the person victimised intends to do any of those things, or suspects the person victimised has done, or intends to do, any of them.

(2) Subsection (1) does not apply to treatment of a person by reason of any allegation made by him if the allegation was false and not made in good faith.'

The equivalent section in the DDA 1995 (s 55) reads as follows:

'(1) For the purposes of Part II [Employment] . . . , a person ('A') discriminates against another person ('B') if –

(a) he treats B less favourably than he treats or would treat other persons whose circumstances are the same as B's; and
(b) he does so for a reason mentioned in subsection (2).

(2) The reasons are that –

(a) B has –
    (i) brought proceedings against A or any other person under this Act; or
    (ii) given evidence or information in connection with such proceedings brought by any person; or
    (iii) otherwise done anything under this Act in relation to A or any other person; or
    (iv) alleged that A or any other person has (whether or not the allegation so states) contravened this Act; or
(b) A believes or suspects that B has done or intends to do any of those things.

(3) Where B is a disabled person, or a person who has had a disability, the disability in question shall be disregarded in comparing his circumstances with those of any other person for the purposes of subsection (1)(a).

'(4) Subsection (1) does not apply to treatment of a person because of an allegation made by him if the allegation was false and not made in good faith.'

The purpose of these sections is to deter employers from taking action against employees who have brought proceedings under one of the Acts or given evidence in the course of such proceedings. Although these provisions are complex and it is relatively difficult to succeed in a victimisation claim, employers should be aware of their existence and should prohibit victimisation in any harassment policy.

7.7 BULLYING

7.7.1 Remedies

There is no specific legislation which deals with bullying at work. Victims of bullying must rely on existing legal remedies which, because they do not deal specifically with bullying, are often less than satisfactory. However, it may be possible to bring a claim for constructive dismissal under the ERA 1996. It may be that a bullied employee has a legal remedy under the Public Order Act 1986 or the Protection from Harassment Act 1997, or it may be possible to frame a claim for bullying within the existing health and safety legislation. The most commonly used legal basis for a bullying claim is a constructive dismissal claim under the ERA 1996.

7.7.2 Constructive dismissal

A constructive dismissal takes place when:

'the employee terminates the contract under which he is employed (with or without notice) in circumstances in which he is entitled to terminate it without notice by reason of the employer's conduct.'[1]

In order to be successful in a constructive dismissal claim, an employee must show the existence of the following three elements:

–   that there was a fundamental breach of the employment contract on the part of the employer;
–   that it was the employer's breach which caused the resignation; and
–   that he or she did not delay too long before resigning – a delay may mean the employee has waived the breach.

The question which must be answered is what constitutes a fundamental breach of contract which would entitle an employee to resign and claim constructive dismissal. An employment contract (whether written or not) includes both terms which have been expressly agreed and terms which are implied into the contract. The implied terms are legal duties which are central to the relationship between the employer and the employee. More often than not, a breach of one or more of the implied terms of the employment contract, rather than a breach of the express terms, is relied on as a basis for a constructive dismissal claim. The implied terms relied on in constructive dismissal claims are:

---

1   Employment Rights Act 1996, s 95(1)(c).

the duty of mutual trust and confidence; the duty to provide reasonable support; and the duty to provide a safe workplace.

(a) *Mutual trust and confidence*

This is the term most commonly relied upon by bullied employees as the basis for a constructive dismissal claim. This duty has been set out by the Court of Appeal in *Bliss v South East Thames Regional Health Authority*[1] as:

> '... (the employer shall) not without reasonable cause conduct itself in a manner likely to damage or destroy the relationship of confidence and trust between the parties as employer and employee.'

An example of a breach of this implied term is *Hilton International Hotels (UK) Ltd v Protopapa* (below).

> *Example* An employee had been absent from work for a short time with toothache. When she returned she was subjected to a humiliating, intimidating and degrading rebuke from her superior. The EAT upheld the tribunal's finding that this amounted to a breach of trust and confidence that went to the root of the contract, entitling the employee to resign and claim constructive dismissal.
>
> *Hilton International Hotels (UK) Ltd v Protopapa*
> [1990] IRLR 316

(b) *Reasonable support*

The duty to provide reasonable support may be breached by an employer who fails to suport an employee in his or her work (which might itself be a form of bullying) or it may take the form of bullying by fellow employees, which the employer fails to deal with properly. For example, if an employee is bullied and harassed by colleagues, the employer is under a duty to protect the employee by investigating the harassment and trying to stop it. If the employer fails in this duty, this may amount to a fundamental breach of contract entitling the employee to resign and claim constructive dismissal.

(c) *Safe workplace*

The duty to provide a safe workplace includes the provision of safe systems of working. If an employee is being bullied, the employee's safety is potentially at risk and an employer who fails to deal with the problem may face a claim of unfair dismissal for breach of the implied term of mutual trust and confidence.

7.7.3 Psychological injury

Under the Health and Safety at Work etc Act 1974 employers are under a duty to ensure so far as is reasonably practicable the health, safety and welfare of their employees. This essentially embraces the common law principles that went before it. If the employer acts in breach of this duty, the employee can bring a negligence (ie personal injury) claim against the employer if they can show:

– the employer owed the employee a duty of care;

---

1   [1987] ICR 700.

- the employer was in breach of that duty of care;
- the employee did in fact suffer some form of injury;
- the employer's breach of duty was the cause of the employee's injury; and
- the risk of injury to the employee was reasonably foreseeable.

Employers may be held liable for psychological injury and stress-related illnesses suffered by employees as a result of their working environment. This was demonstrated in the case of *Walker v Northumberland County Council*[1] where Mr Walker suffered a nervous breakdown as a result of pressure of work. He returned to work but did not receive the support he had been promised. He had another nervous breakdown six months later. Mr Walker successfully sued his former employer in the High Court for breaching their duty to ensure his health, safety and welfare. They were not held liable for the first nervous breakdown as this was not reasonably foreseeable but, having suffered one nervous breakdown, it was reasonably forseeable that he could suffer another.

This case establishes the principle that psychiatric damage is an injury and therefore within the employer's duty of care. There is thus no reason why mental injuries suffered as a result of bullying or any other form of harassment should not be actionable.

7.8 PUBLIC ORDER ACT 1986

Bullying or harassment which takes the form of assault, sexual or otherwise, may result in criminal liability. The perpetrators of actual bodily harm, grievous bodily harm, sexual assault or rape, for example, may well be prosecuted through the criminal courts. Criminal liability may also arise under the Public Order Act 1986, as amended by the Criminal Justice and Public Order Act 1994, which creates a criminal offence of intentional harassment. Section 4A of the 1986 Act states:

> '(1) A person is guilty of an offence if, with intent to cause a person harassment, alarm or distress, he –
>
> (a) uses threatening, abusive or insulting words or behaviour, or disorderly behaviour, or
> (b) displays any writing, sign or other visible representation which is threatening, abusive or insulting,
>
> thereby causing that or another person harassment, alarm or distress.'

The harassment must be intentional and the burden of proof will be the criminal standard of 'beyond reasonable doubt'. Although this section of the Act is aimed at racial harassment, race is not specifically mentioned, so there is no need to prove that the harassment was racially motivated. All forms of harassment will be covered. The penalty for intentional harassment under this Act is imprisonment for up to six months and/or a fine not exceeding £5,000.

---

1   [1995] IRLR 35, QBD.

7.9 PROTECTION FROM HARASSMENT ACT 1997

The principal aim of the Protection from Harassment Act 1997 is to deal with stalking. However, harassment in this context could cover any form of harassment in or outside the workplace on the grounds of, for example, a person's sex, race, disability or sexual orientation. The Act prohibits harassment in s 1 as follows:

'(1) A person must not pursue a course of conduct –

(a) which amounts to harassment of another, and
(b) which he knows or ought to know amounts to harassment of the other.

(2) For the purposes of this section, the person whose course of conduct is in question ought to know that it amounts to harassment of another if a reasonable person in possession of the same information would think the course of conduct amounted to harassment of the other.'

Section 7 goes on to explain that:

'(2) References to harassing a person include alarming the person or causing the person distress.
(3) A "course of conduct" must involve conduct on at least two occasions.'

Section 3(1) of the Act makes it clear that harassment under the Act is a civil as well as a criminal offence and that damages for anxiety caused by the harassment are available as well as injunctive relief.

The Act also prohibits putting people in fear of violence:

'4(1) A person whose course of conduct causes another to fear, on at least two occasions, that violence will be used against him is guilty of an offence if he knows or ought to know that his course of conduct will cause the other so to fear on each of those occasions.'

Section 4(2) goes on to give a similar 'reasonable person' test as that in s 1(2).

The offences do not require any intention on the part of the perpetrator to cause the victim to feel harassed or in fear of violence; it only has to be proved that the conduct occurred in circumstances where a 'reasonable person in possession of the same information' would realise that that would be the effect. It therefore goes further than the Public Order Act 1986 which legislates against intentional harassment.

Chapter 8

LIABILITY FOR HARASSMENT

Who is liable? – Vicarious liability – Employer's direct liability – Victimisation – Individual liability

8.1 WHO IS LIABLE?

This chapter considers the question of who is liable when a claim for harassment is successful. This will include the issue of an employer's vicarious liability for the acts of its employees and a principal's liability for the acts of its agent as well as circumstances in which an employer is directly liable for acts of harassment. The issue of victimisation and the circumstances in which an employee is personally liable for acts of harassment are also considered.

It should be remembered that the SDA 1975, the RRA 1976 and the DDA 1995 extend their protection to cover not only employees employed under a contract of employment but also workers under a contract for services (self-employed workers) provided they execute the work personally. Contract workers (for example staff provided by an agency) are also protected by the discrimination legislation. In terms of liability, this means that employers will be potentially liable not only for harassment suffered by their employees but also for harassment suffered by self-employed workers and workers who are provided by an agency if this occurs on their premises.

Also worth bearing in mind in this context is the Court of Appeal case of *Harrods Ltd v Remick and Others* (below) which established a broad construction of contract worker for the purposes of discrimination legislation.

> *Example* Mrs Remick, who is black, was employed by Shaeffer Pens to work in the Harrods pen department where Shaeffer had a sales counter. In order to work for a Harrods concessionaire (as Shaeffer was), staff had to be approved by Harrods and had to observe Harrods' rules regarding dress, deportment and behaviour. They were required to wear a Harrods uniform and would be indistinguishable to the public eye from Harrods' employees. Harrods could withdraw its approval of any such individual at any time.
>
> Eight months after Mrs Remick started work at Harrods, the store withdrew their approval of her as she was considered to have failed to adhere to the Harrods dress code. No details of her alleged failure were given to her. As a consequence of the loss of Harrods' approval of her, she was given notice by Shaeffer Pens and lost her job. She complained to the industrial tribunal of unlawful race discrimination by Harrods. Two other women also complained of unlawful discrimination against Harrods and the three cases were consolidated for hearing in the Court of Appeal.
>
> The question which the Court of Appeal had to decide was whether Harrods could be liable for discrimination under the RRA 1976. They looked at s 7(1) of the RRA 1976 which defines contract work:

'This section applies to any work for a person ('the principal') which is available for doing by individuals ('contract workers') who are employed not by the principal himself but by another person who supplies them under a contract made with the principal.'

and s 7(2) which states that:

'It is unlawful for the principal, in relation to work to which this section applies, to discriminate against a contract worker –

...

(b)   by not allowing him to do it or continue to do it.'

The Court of Appeal held that the work which Mrs Remick was employed to do was work done for Harrods as well as for Shaeffer Pens, and that it therefore fell within the remit of s 7 of the RRA 1976. Harrods could therefore be liable for the discriminatory acts against the employees of its concessionaires.

Remick v Harrods
[1997] IRLR 583

Remick v Harrods is not about harassment but about a different form of race discrimination. Employers should take note that they could be held liable for any discriminatory acts against their contract workers, including racial, sexual, or disability harassment, and that a broad construction of contract worker will be adopted for the purposes of liability under the SDA 1975, RRA 1976 or DDA 1995.

8.2 VICARIOUS LIABILITY

8.2.1 Vicarious liability for employees

The first point to consider is whether the individual is an 'employee' of the employer, thus rendering the employer liable under the vicarious liability rules. The 'general interpretation provisions' of s 82 of the SDA 1975, s 78 of the RRA 1976 and s 68 of the DDA 1995 (which is worded slightly differently) state in effect:

'employment means employment under a contract of service or of apprenticeship or a contract personally to execute any work or labour, and related expressions shall be construed accordingly.'

This means that if there is a contract personally to execute any work or labour between the employer and the worker, that worker will not only be protected against harassment but may render the employer liable if he or she commits an act of harassment. A self-employed person would fall into this category, provided that they have contracted to carry out the work personally. The words 'employment', 'employer' and 'employee' are all to be interpreted as covering this situation.

'Vicarious liability' means liability for an act done by someone for whom you have responsibility. This concept was developed originally in personal injury cases. For example, if an employee suffers an injury through the negligence of a fellow employee who is acting in the course of employment, the employer will be vicariously liable for the wrong-doing of that employee. There is nothing to prevent the injured employee suing the individual who inflicted the harm but, in practice, the employer will be sued either as well as, or instead of, the individual. This is because the employer will be insured against such claims and will therefore be in a better position to pay any sum awarded to the injured employee.

There are many cases where personal injury claims have been made by one employee against another and/or against the mutual employer and there has been much discussion of the words 'in the course of employment'. It is still the case in personal injury claims that, in order for the employee to have acted in the course of employment, and for the employer therefore to be vicariously liable, the employee must have been doing an act authorised by his employees, even if he was doing that act in an unauthorised way. For example, if a fight breaks out in the workplace canteen and Employee A's nose is broken by Employee B, the question of vicarious liability will arise. Was Employee B carrying out an authorised act in an unauthorised way? The employer will no doubt seek to argue that Employee B was not employed to fight in the canteen and that, as this was not an authorised act, the employer is not vicariously liable. This common law test remains the test for vicarious liability in personal injury cases.

Allegations of harassment are also often made by one employee against another. The SDA 1975, the RRA 1976 and the DDA 1995 all provide that an employer will be vicariously liable for the discriminatory behaviour of its employees where those acts are done by the employee in the course of employment. Section 41(1) of the SDA 1975, s 32(1) of the RRA 1976 and s 58(1) of the DDA 1995 (which is very similar but the wording is slightly different) state in effect:

> 'Anything done by a person in the course of his employment shall be treated for the purposes of this Act . . . as done by his employer as well as by him, whether or not it was done with the employer's knowledge or approval.'

There has been much discussion of the term 'in the course of employment' in relation to discrimination legislation. Originally it was thought that the common law meaning of 'in the course of employment' should be adopted in discrimination cases. This would mean that, in order for an employer to be liable for the acts of its employee, the employee must have been carrying out an authorised act (albeit in an unauthorised way); if the act complained of had no connection with the employment other than the fact that it was done at the workplace or during work hours, then the employer would not have been liable.

Example Mr and Mrs Irving were black Jamaicans. They lived next door to a postman whom they did not get on with. One day, while sorting the mail, the postman saw an envelope addressed to the Irvings and he wrote on the back of it, 'Go back to Jamaica Sambo' and added an offensive drawing. The Irvings brought discrimination proceedings against the Post Office. The Court of Appeal held that the Post Office were not liable for the discrimination because the postman was not acting 'in the course of his employment' when he wrote the offensive remark. The writing of the offensive remark formed no part of the postman's duties and could not therefore be regarded as an unauthorised way of performing an authorised act.'

Irving and Irving v The Post Office
[1987] IRLR 289

This decision had the unfortunate effect that the more gross the discriminatory acts of a fellow employee, the less likely the employer was to be liable for those acts, since they were more likely to be viewed as private acts not authorised as part of the employment. Three years later, the EAT case of *Bracebridge Engineering Ltd v Darby* (below) went some way towards addressing the balance. The EAT examined the question of vicarious liability and reached a different conclusion to that reached in the *Irving* case.

> *Example* Mrs Darby had been employed for 13 years by Bracebridge Engineering. At the end of her shift she was grabbed by her chargehand and the works manager and taken to the manager's office. The lights were put out and the works manager picked up her legs and put them around him. She tried to get away but was threatened with a written warning for leaving work early. The chargehand then subjected her to a sexual assault.
>
> Mrs Darby complained to the general manager, and when nothing was done about the incident she resigned and claimed constructive dismissal and sex discrimination. The industrial tribunal upheld both complaints and the employers appealed.
>
> The EAT upheld the decision of the industrial tribunal and, with reference to the vicarious liability of the employers, stated:
>
> 'The two lay members sitting with me with their experience of the workings in industry both on the shop floor and generally, have no doubt that in the picture which they envisage here, this act was perpetrated in the course of the employment of these two men. . . . These men were involved in carrying out their functions as part of their employment.'
>
> The EAT agreed with the industrial tribunal that Bracebridge Engineering was vicariously liable for the acts of the two employees as the acts were done in the course of their employment.
>
> *Bracebridge Engineering Ltd v Darby*
> [1990] IRLR 3

The *Bracebridge* decision led to the rather unsatisfactory situation that only if employees were acting in a supervisory or disciplinary function when they committed the acts of harasssment would they be acting in the course of their employment, and only then would their employers be vicariously liable. The situation was not satisfactorily clarified until *Jones v Tower Boot Co Ltd* (below) where the Court of Appeal scrutinised the concept of vicarious liability.

> *Example* Mr Jones, who is of mixed ethnic parentage, was 16 when he went to work for Tower Boot. This was his first job. He resigned after a month of being physically and verbally tormented by two fellow workers. The incidents consisted of burning his arm with a hot screwdriver, whipping him on the legs with a piece of welt, throwing metal bolts at him, and trying to put his arm in a lasting machine; he was also repeatedly called 'chimp', 'monkey' and 'baboon'. Mr Jones resigned and subsequently brought a claim of race discrimination against his employers.

The main issue for the Court of Appeal to decide was whether the two employees were acting 'in the course of their employment' when they racially harassed Mr Jones, and, therefore, whether the employers were liable for the acts of harassment. The Court of Appeal differentiated between vicarious liability used in the law of tort (ie in personal injury claims) and vicarious liability used in discrimination legislation and stated that a plain and common-sense view should be taken to the meaning of the words 'in the course of employment' for the purposes of the discrimination legislation. The Court of Appeal added that, as industrial juries, tribunals are particularly well placed to interpret this phrase in laymen's terms, and that to do otherwise would seriously undermine the statutory scheme of protection against discrimination.

Jones v Tower Boot Co Ltd
[1997] IRLR 168

Tower Boot Co Ltd was found to be vicariously liable for the discriminatory acts of its employees. Thus in relation to race and sex discrimination (and presumably also in relation to disability discrimination) if employees commit acts of harassment which are within a layman's understanding of 'in the course of employment', employers will be vicariously liable for such harassment unless they can show that they have taken reasonably practicable steps to prevent employees from doing such acts, such as implementing a harassment policy.

Unless the employer has a statutory defence, it will probably be relatively easy to establish the vicarious liability. However, even adopting the broad approach of 'in the course of employment' set out in *Tower Boot*, there are limits to an employer's liability for acts of harassment, as can be seen in the Court of Appeal case *Waters v Commissioner of Police of the Metropolis* (below).

Example Ms Waters was employed as a police constable. She alleged she had been sexually assaulted in her section house by a male police officer while both were off duty. Following an internal inquiry the Commissioner decided that her allegations were unsubstantiated. Subsequently Ms Waters was transferred to a different police station. She alleged that, from the time she reported the sexual assault, she was subjected to harassment, unfair treatment and victimisation by other police officers which led to ill health, including mental illness and post-traumatic stress disorder. She brought a claim in the industrial tribunal for victimisation.

The industrial tribunal had to decide, first, whether the male officer had been acting in the course of his employment when the alleged sexual assault took place. The tribunal noted that the alleged assault took place in the middle of the night when both Ms Waters and the male officer were off duty and the act was not committed at the place of employment.

The industrial tribunal held (the EAT and Court of Appeal agreeing) that the alleged assault was not committed 'in the course of employment' since both parties were off duty at the time and in circumstances which placed them in no different position from that which would have applied if they had been social acquaintances only, with no working connection. Since the alleged sexual assault had not been committed in the course of her colleague's employment, the employer could not be deemed to be vicariously liable. It was also held that, as the allegation of victimisation was not in respect of an act by the employer which 'would amount to a contravention of' the SDA 1975, it must be dismissed.

Waters v Commissioner of Police of the Metropolis
[1997] IRLR 589, CA

8.2.2 Vicarious liability for agents

As well as an employer's vicarious liability for its employees, a principal may be liable for the discriminatory acts of its agent. A relationship of principal and agent arises where one party, the principal, consents that another party, the agent, shall act on the principal's behalf and the agent so acts.[1] Section 41(2) of the SDA 1975, s 32(2) of the RRA 1976 and s 58(2) of the DDA 1995 (which is similar but worded slightly differently) state in effect:

'Anything done by a person as agent for another person with the authority (whether express or implied and whether precedent or subsequent) of that other person shall be treated for the purposes of this Act as done by that other person as well as by him.'

In other words, a principal is liable for the acts of his agent if those acts are done with the authority of the principal, whether that authority was express or implied authority, and whether the authority was given in advance of the act or the act was subsequently ratified. This means that one employee might be vicariously liable for the discriminatory acts of another employee if the employees were in a relationship of principal and agent as defined above.

Example Mr Nagarajan, who is of Indian birth, was employed by London Underground Ltd (LUL) as a station foreman. He complained of racial discrimination and, by agreement, was temporarily moved to another post with London Regional Transport (LRT), the holding company for LUL. This appointment was not successful. Mr Nagarajan went on paid leave and eventually reached a compromise agreement which ended his employment with LUL. Some time later he applied for a post with LRT. Mr Swiggs, the central personnel manager of LRT, asked Mr Nagarajan's previous manager, Mr Agnew, whether re-engagement would be recommended. Mr Agnew said that 'under no circumstances should Mr Nagarajan be considered for re-engagement [as] his attitude to his managers was entirely unacceptable'. Mr Swiggs rejected Mr Nagarajan's job application. Mr Nagarajan brought (among others) a claim against Mr Swiggs and LRT alleging discrimination by way of victimisation.

The basis of his claim against Mr Swiggs was that he was vicariously liable under s 32(2) of the RRA 1976 for the actions of Mr Agnew. Mr Swiggs was not the employer of Mr Agnew and his liability could only be established if it could be shown that he was the principal and Mr Agnew was the agent. The EAT held that they could not accept the submission that a relationship of principal and agent was established by the request for a reference. There was no reason to suppose that s 32(2) was aimed at anything other than the well-known legal relationship of principal and agent. Mr Swiggs was not therefore liable under s 32.

Nagarajan v Agnew
[1994] IRLR 61, EAT

---

1   *Chitty on Contracts* (Sweet & Maxwell, 1995).

What about the situation where self-employed workers, and workers who are provided by an agency themselves commit acts of harassment – will employers potentially be liable for those acts as if those people were employees or will the liability be that of a principal for its agent?

It seems clear from the discrimination legislation that, provided the worker falls within the extended definition of employee, the employer will be liable for any acts of harassment committed by that worker (see above). However, if the worker does not fall within the extended definition of employee (such as a temp or management consultant), the situation needs to be looked at carefully.

The wording of the discrimination legislation in relation to liability of a principal for its agent is different to that of employer for its employee. The wording is not, as it is for employees, 'anything done by a person in the course of his activities acting as an agent for another person'. This is a significant difference and implies that, for a principal to be liable for harassment by an agent, the principal either has to have specifically authorised (expressly or impliedly) the harassment, or the harassment must be integral to a thing which the agent is supposed to be doing.

For example, if a management consultant has been brought in to do some interim management, then liability for the consultant's actions should be very much the same as if the consultant had been an employee of the principal. On the other hand, if the role of the management consultant is mainly to provide advice to the employer, the situation might be different. Such a management consultant might, for instance, be asked to make a presentation to the principal's workers about a proposed new management structure. If the consultant was racist or sexist when making the presentation, there is scope to argue that it was something done as an agent for the employer in that it was bound up with the thing that the consultant was expressly authorised to do by the employer (ie, to make the presentation). On the other hand, if the management consultant were to grope a member of staff on the way to the room in which the presentation was to be made, it could be argued that there should be no liability for that action. Bear in mind, however, that the employer may still be vicariously liable for exposing the employee to harassment (see below).

Thus, with an agent, the key point is to identify what it is that the agent is doing, whether the agent has done that for himself or herself or on behalf of the principal and, if the agent has done it on behalf of the principal, whether the agent has authority, whether express or implied.

In any event, following the cases of *Burton and Rhule v De Vere Hotels* and *Chessington World of Adventures v Reed* (discussed below), employers may be held directly liable as opposed to vicariously liable for discriminatory acts if they are in a position to control whether discrimination occurs.

8.3 EMPLOYER'S DIRECT LIABILITY

8.3.1 Liability for acts of third parties

In addition to an employer's vicarious liability for the acts of its employees, an employer might also be held directly liable for the acts of independent third parties. Two important cases have examined this issue.

Example　Two black waitresses who were employed by De Vere Hotels had volunteered to work overtime clearing tables at an all male dinner where the comedian Bernard Manning was to be guest speaker. During the course of Mr Manning's performance, the waitresses were subjected to direct abuse of a racist and sexual nature by Mr Manning and by a number of the guests.

Ms Burton and Ms Rhule brought claims for race discrimination against the hotel. However the hotel could not be vicariously liable as Mr Manning and the guests were not employed by the hotel. Nor could they be said to have been acting as agents. The question in this case was whether the hotel had 'subjected' Ms Rhule and Ms Burton to a detriment as required by s 4(2)(c) of the RRA 1976. The industrial tribunal's view was that although the women had been subjected to racial harassment and had therefore suffered a detriment, the hotel could not be held liable as it was not the hotel which had subjected them to it.

The EAT overturned the industrial tribunal's decision and held that, where an employer has actual knowledge that racial harassment of an employee is taking place or deliberately or recklessly 'closes his eyes' to it and does not act reasonably to prevent it, the employer will readily be found to have subjected the employees to that harassment. The test is whether the event in question was something which was sufficiently under the employer's 'control' such that the employer could have prevented the harassment or reduced the extent of it.

Burton and Rhule v De Vere Hotels
[1996] IRLR 596

Example　Ms Bourdouane was employed as an organiser of children's parties. She was sexually harassed by a parent of one of the children and complained about the incident to her manager. She was told to return to the party. She duly returned and was again sexually harassed by the same parent. Eventually the situation became so bad that the manager told her to go home.

She brought a claim against her employer for sexual harassment on the basis that the employer knew about the harassment and failed to avoid or limit it by following good employment practice. Go Kidz Go was held directly liable for the harassment suffered by its employee at the hands of a third party.

Go Kidz Co v Bourdouane
(1996) IDS 578

Both of these cases rest on the principle that the statutory duty on employers not to discriminate against their employees includes a duty to protect them from discrimination by any person in circumstances where they are in a position to prevent it. These decisions therefore provide a remedy for employees who are harassed by clients or customers whilst carrying out the job that they have been employed to do. Unless the employer can show that reasonable steps were taken to prevent harassment, it will be liable for acts of harassment by third parties against its employees.

1　[1997] IRLR 566, EAT.

8.3.2 Liability for acts of employees

This principle applies also to known acts of harassment by fellow employees, as demonstrated in *Chessington World of Adventures v Reed*.[1] In this case a transsexual employee was subjected to a campaign of harassment by some of her male colleagues, including defacing her belongings with lipstick and leaving a replica coffin on her workbench inscribed with her name and the letters 'RIP'. The industrial tribunal found that she had been subjected to unlawful sex discrimination by her employer due to its failure to act on its knowledge of a concerted course of harassment to which Ms Reed was being subjected. The industrial tribunal found the employer directly liable to Ms Reed under the SDA. It made no finding as to whether the employer was also vicariously liable for the acts of its employees.

Chessington World of Adventures appealed. Two of the issues raised by the parties for determination in the appeal were:

'...

(2) Whether the industrial tribunal erred in law in finding that the appellant was directly liable to the respondent for unlawful sex discrimination.
(3) Whether the tribunal ought to have found, additionally or in the alternative, that the appellant was vicariously liable for the relevant acts of its employees.

...'

The issues were decided as follows:

'In *Burton v De Vere Hotels* [1996] IRLR 596, this appeal tribunal held, in the context of a race discrimination claim, that an employer subjected an employee to the detriment of racial harassment if he caused or permitted the harassment to occur in circumstances in which he could control whether it happened or not.

In our judgment, similar principles apply in this case of sex discrimination, all the more so where those responsible for the harassment are employees and not a third party.

It is abundantly clear, on the tribunal's findings of fact, that [Chessington World of Adventures] was aware of the campaign of harassment directed towards [Ms Reed], but took no adequate steps to prevent it, although it was plainly something over which it could exercise control.

In these circumstances we can find no grounds for interfering with the tribunal's conclusion that direct liability for the sex discrimination suffered by [Ms Reed] lay with [Chessington World of Adventures].'

The EAT also considered the position on vicarious liability (although it was not strictly necessary to do so) and indicated that:

'If the tribunal was wrong in its finding as to direct liability, the EAT would affirm the result on the ground that the appellant was vicariously liable for the acts of harassment of its employees under s 41(1) of the SDA, the tribunal having also found, permissibly, that on the facts the appellant had failed to make out the statutory defence under s 41(3).'

8.3.3 Considerations for employers

The *Burton and Rhule, Bourdouane* and *Chessington World of Adventures* cases illustrate how an employer can be directly, as opposed to vicariously, liable for the discriminatory acts of a third party or employees. If employers permit harassment to occur in circumstances where they are in a position to control whether it happens or not, they will be directly liable for the harassment.

Employers should think carefully about situations in which employees may be subjected to harassment from third parties and the ways in which this can be prevented. Employers should make clear to any customers, clients or members of the public with whom staff have dealings that they have a commitment to protect their staff from harassment.

The question of whether or not employers were in a position to control a particular situation might well lead to as much legal argument as the question of whether or not acts of harassment were done 'in the course of employment'. One thing, however, is clear: employers are potentially liable for all acts of workplace harassment whether based on sex, race or disability. They will find it increasingly difficult to avoid liability for acts of harassment carried out by their employees and it is therefore more important than ever for organisations to have in place an effective harassment policy (see Chapter 10).

8.3.4 Liability under the Health and Safety at Work etc Act 1974

A breach of an employer's statutory duty to keep its employees safe from harm can give rise to criminal proceedings by the Health & Safety Executive in the employment tribunal or by the Crown Prosecution Service in the magistrates' or Crown Court. A breach under this Act can result in the criminal conviction of the employer in the magistrates' court including a fine of up to £5,000 and/or imprisonment; or, in the Crown Court, an unlimited fine and/or imprisonment of up to two years.

8.4 VICTIMISATION

The legal basis of a victimisation claim is set out in Chapter 7. In short, victimisation is a type of discrimination which takes the form of treating someone less favourably because that person has asserted a right under the SDA 1975 (or the Equal Pay Act 1970), the RRA 1976 or the DDA 1995. The issues of vicarious liability will also apply to victimisation, so that any victimisation perpetrated by a person in the course of employment, or by an agent on behalf of a principal, shall be treated as done by the employer or the principal as well as by the individual.

However, it is relatively difficult to establish liability for victimisation as the provisions in the discrimination legislation are narrowly drawn. There must be a causal link between the victimisation and the assertion of the right.

> *Example*   Mr Aziz was a member of Trinity Street Taxis, which had been set up on a co-operative basis. Mr Aziz was to be charged £1,000 to introduce a third taxi into the system, which he regarded as an unfair imposition. He suspected that the decision to levy such charges was racially motivated and began to consider taking action in the industrial tribunal. Some of the other drivers supported him verbally but Mr Aziz was convinced they would not do so if he took legal action, so he secretly tape-recorded their conversations.
>
> Mr Aziz brought an action in the industrial tribunal for race discrimination and the existence of the tape recordings was revealed during the course of the proceedings. Mr Aziz's claim for race discrimination was dismissed.

Following the hearing, the company members voted to expel Mr Aziz from Trinity Street Taxis on the ground that making such recordings constituted a gross breach of trust and confidence between the members of the company. Mr Aziz brought a further discrimination claim, this time on the ground that he had been victimised. The case went to the Court of Appeal.

The Court of Appeal held that the making of the tape recordings was an act done by reference to the RRA 1976. However the question which had to be decided was whether Mr Aziz was expelled from the company because the tape recordings were made with reference to the RRA 1976, or whether he would have been expelled whatever the purpose of the recordings.

The Court of Appeal found that the members of Trinity Street Taxis would have voted for the expulsion of any member who made such recordings, whatever their purpose, on the ground that this was an underhand action and a breach of trust. Mr Aziz failed to show that his expulsion was because of his action under the RRA 1976 and Trinity Street Taxis was not therefore liable for victimisation.

Aziz v Trinity Street Taxis
[1988] ICR 534

A further illustration of the narrowness of the victimisation provisions is given by *Waters v Commissioner of Police of the Metropolis*[1] discussed earlier in this chapter. This case shows that a complaint of victimisation can only succeed if the original allegation of discrimination would, if verified, amount to an unlawful act on the part of the employer.

The case concerned a woman police constable, Ms Waters, who complained of sexual harassment against a male police officer while both were off duty. Her complaint was investigated but did not lead to any disciplinary action. She was subsequently transferred to a different police station and her name was removed from a list of specialist officers. She brought a claim of victimisation which was dismissed by the industrial tribunal. This dismissal was upheld by the EAT.

In order to have succeeded in her allegation for victimisation, Ms Waters had to show that the original allegation of harassment (following which she was, she says, victimised) was a contravention of the SDA 1975. But because the alleged act of harassment had not occurred in the course of employment, it could not amount to a contravention of the Act. If there was no contravention of the SDA 1975, she could not claim that the police officer victimised her because she alleged that he had done something which would amount to a contravention of the SDA 1975. She did not therefore have the necessary legal basis to make out a claim of victimisation.

8.5 INDIVIDUAL LIABILITY

An employee who has been the victim of harassment in the workplace will generally seek to place either vicarious or direct liability on his or her employer. The discrimination legislation specifically provides for vicarious liability of employers or principals and case-law now provides for direct liability for acts of

---

1   [1997] IRLR 589, CA.

harassment over which the employer had control. The employer is likely to have the financial resources to pay any compensation awarded and thus, in practice, employees will generally bring claims of harassment against their employers. However this does not prevent a claim being brought against the individual harasser and does not prevent the individual harasser being personally liable.

8.5.1 Aiding and abetting

The case of *Read v Tiverton District Council and Bull* (below) examines the issue of individual liability.

> *Example* An assistant in the Council's Land Charges Section, Mrs Read, brought a sex discrimination claim on the grounds that she had been discriminated against in failing to be appointed to the post of Chief Land Charges Clerk. The claim was brought against the solicitor to the Council, Mr Bull, whom she described as her employer. The application was subsequently amended so that the claim was against *Tiverton District Council (1) and Bull (2)*. The industrial tribunal looked at whether or not Mrs Read was entitled to bring a claim not only against her employer but also against any employee of that employer who had allegedly personally discriminated against her.
>
> The industrial tribunal pointed out that Mrs Read had relied strongly on s 41 of the SDA 1975 which states:

'(1) Anything done by a person in the course of his employment shall be treated for the purposes of the Act as done by his employer as well as by him, whether or not it was done with the employer's knowledge or approval.
(2) Anything done by a person as agent for another person with the authority (whether express or implied, and whether precedent or subsequent) of that other person shall be treated for the purposes of this Act as done by that other person as well as by him.'

> The industrial tribunal said they recognised that the prime purpose of both those provisions was to ensure that a principal, such as an employer, would be liable for the act of his agent, such as an employee, who is acting within the scope of his authority. But, they said:

'it does seem to us necessarily implicit from the words 'as well as by him' that Parliament was there recognising that such agent should also himself be personally responsible for an act of discrimination.'

> The industrial tribunal went on to say that s 41 is clarified and confirmed by subsections (1) and (2) of s 42 which read as follows:

'(1) A person who knowingly aids another person to do an act made unlawful by the Act shall be treated for the purpose of this Act as himself doing an unlawful act of the like description.
(2) For the purposes of subsection (1) an employee or agent for whose act the employer or principal is liable under section 41 ... shall be deemed to aid the doing of the act by the employer or principal.'

> The industrial tribunal concluded that it would be open to Mrs Read to contend not only that Tiverton District Council was vicariously liable for the

allegedly discriminatory act of its employee but also that Mr Bull was potentially personally liable.

Read v Tiverton District Council (1) and Bull (2)
[1997] IRLR 203

So a person who aids another person to commit an unlawful act of discrimination is deemed to have committed an unlawful act 'of the like description'. Thus an employee or agent who causes his or her employer or principal to be vicariously liable is deemed to have aided the employer's or principal's discrimination.

Even where an employer is held to be vicariously liable for discrimination on the part of an employee (and is ordered to pay compensation), there is no reason why the individual discriminator should not also be ordered to pay compensation. This issue was examined in the case of *Armitage, Marsden and HM Prison Service v Johnson* (below).

> **Example** This case concerned a prison officer of Afro-Caribbean origin. He was ostracised and subjected to harassment by two of his colleagues after he objected to the manhandling of a black prisoner by other prison officers. He brought a claim of race discrimination against the two perpetrators of the discriminatory acts and against HM Prison Service. The tribunal ordered HM Prison Service to pay £20,000 for injury to feelings and £7,500 aggravated damages. In addition, £500 was awarded against both of the prison officers personally on the grounds they had victimised Mr Johnson and aided the employer to discriminate.
>
> HM Prison Service appealed against the amount awarded but the EAT dismissed the appeal. The employer's barrister accepted that the tribunal was entitled as a matter of law to apportion the damages for injury to feelings between the three appellants but submitted that it should not happen in practice save in exceptional circumstances. The EAT ruled, however, that it was a question for the discretion of the tribunal and that, in deciding whether to make an award, a relevant factor will be whether the errant employee was acting in the best interests of his employer or whether, as in this case, the employee was acting out of malice.
>
> *Armitage, Marsden and HM Prison Service v Johnson*
> [1997] IRLR 162

8.5.2 Public Order Act 1986

As well as personal liability under the discrimination legislation, individuals may also be personally liable under criminal legislation. Criminal liability may arise under the Public Order Act 1986 (as amended by the Criminal Justice and Public Order Act 1994) which creates a criminal offence of 'intentional harassment'.

This offence consists of intentionally causing another individual to be harassed, alarmed or distressed by the use of threatening, abusive or insulting words or behaviour including any writing, sign or other visible representation. For an offence to be committed under this section, the harasser must have intended the individual to be alarmed or distressed. The penalty for intentional harassment is imprisonment for up to six months and/or a fine not exceeding £5,000. There is no vicarious liability under this Act.

The above offence does not mention or require any racial, sexual or other discriminatory ingredient. However the primary aim of the legislation is to address concerns about racial harassment. During the debate on the Criminal Justice and Public Order Bill, which amended the 1986 Act, the House of Lords addressed the question of whether specific mention needed to be made of racial harassment and racial intent. Earl Ferrers took the following view:

> 'Although we set out to address the problems of racial harassment, race is not mentioned in the clause. To have done so would have meant that prosecutors were faced with proving not only the fact of the offence but also that it was racially motivated. Proving motivation beyond reasonable doubt is particularly difficult. . . . The new offence will therefore apply equally to harassment on other grounds, such as being offensive, for instance, to people who are in wheelchairs or who suffer some other form of impediment or disability. It is obviously right that the same punishment should be available for behaviour causing the same distress, whatever the motive may happen to be.'

8.5.3 Protection from Harassment Act 1997

The principal aim of this Act is to deal with stalking. However, an individual will also be liable if he or she subjects someone to racial or sexual harassment or to harassment on grounds of sexual orientation or disability, either at work or outside work. Although the Act does not define harassment, it does identify certain factors which have to be present for an individual to be liable:

–   It must entail a 'course of conduct' which is defined as occurring on at least two occasions.
–   The conduct does not have to be physical and can include verbal conduct.

Whether the action amounts to harassment is not assessed from the viewpoint of the perpetrator or harasser, but the test is whether a reasonable person 'in possession of the same information would think the course of conduct amounted to harassment of the other'. If, for example, the harasser knew that the action was harassing the victim, that behaviour would be caught by the test. The definition also encompasses the prospect that an individual ought to have known the impact of his or her behaviour, because a reasonable person would have formed the conclusion that this behaviour would constitute harassment of the victim.

The criminal offence of harassment under this Act carries a penalty of up to six months in prison and/or a fine of up to £5,000.

The Act also legislates against the more serious offence of putting people in fear of violence. An individual will be liable for this offence if it can be shown that his or her course of conduct caused another to fear, on at least two occasions, that violence would be used against that other person and the harasser knew or ought to have known that the other person would fear violence. An individual found guilty of this offence can be imprisoned for up to five years and a fine, which is not limited, may be imposed.

Harassment under this Act is a civil tort as well as a criminal offence. A harasser can be sued in the county court or High Court and, if found liable, will be ordered to pay damages to the victim including damages for anxiety caused by the harassment. In contrast to proceedings under discrimination legislation, a claim under this Act would be brought against the harasser personally rather than against his or her employer.

8.5.4 Offences Against the Person Act 1861

Another form of criminal offence for which individuals may be liable in a case of harassment is 'assault' or 'battery'. These offences are committed where the acts of harassment are physical in nature. It is not necessary to establish a sexual, racial or other discriminatory intent for an offence of battery or assault to be committed. The following offences exist:

- wounding or inflicting grievous bodily harm (whether with or without a weapon);
- attempting to choke, suffocate or strangle another person;
- common assault, which differs from grievous bodily harm, because the harm which is caused need not be permanent and could include disturbing an individual's comfort or adversely affecting his health.

The penalties for an offence under this Act vary dependent on the seriousness of the offence, but a term of imprisonment of five years, or in serious cases life imprisonment, together with a fine, are possible.

One example of a harassment case brought under this rather dated piece of legislation is *R v Gelder*.[1] An employee of a bank began to harass a female customer, making a number of obscene telephone calls to the customer's home. The calls were of such a nature and so frequent that the customer felt threatened and her health suffered considerably as a consequence.

The employee was charged with grievous bodily harm under s 20 of the 1861 Act. In the Crown Court, having been found guilty, he was sentenced to 18 months' imprisonment. This conviction was subsequently overturned by the Court of Appeal because of a technical difficulty with the original trial and a misdirection on the part of the judge. Nevertheless, it is a useful illustration of the way in which this legislation could operate.

8.5.5 Sexual offences

In addition to cases of assault, acts of sexual harassment could constitute other criminal offences such as indecent assault, and, in the most extreme cases, rape or attempted rape.

8.5.6 Non-physical criminal offences

As we have seen, it is possible for harassment to occur by means other than physical acts or verbal abuse. This is recognised in the criminal context, where the act of harassment must be so serious that it amounts to malicious conduct. The making of malicious telephone calls amounts to a criminal offence contrary to s 43 of the Telecommunications Act 1984. This covers telephone calls which are offensive, obscene or menacing, as well as nuisance calls, ie those which the Act defines as causing 'annoyance, inconvenience or needless anxiety'. Similarly communications by post would be caught by the Malicious Communications Act 1988. This includes indecent and offensive information as well as items which are threatening or knowingly false.

---

1   *R v Gelder* (Crown Court 24594).

Chapter 9

DEFENCES

No 'less favourable treatment' – No detriment suffered – Not in the course of employment – Reasonably practicable steps – Defences to complaints of bullying

The previous chapter set out the circumstances in which an employer or an employee will be liable for acts of harassment in the workplace. This chapter looks at the defences available and the circumstances in which the defences will be successfully made out.

9.1 NO 'LESS FAVOURABLE TREATMENT'

In direct discrimination claims, such as harassment, the complainant must compare the treatment he or she has received to the treatment a comparator received or would have received. The comparator will be, for example, a man where a woman complains of sex discrimination, a white person where a black person complains of race discrimination and a person who does not have a disability where a person with a disability complains of disability discrimination. A defence available to employers, therefore, is that a particular person was not treated less favourably than a comparator was or would have been and that the reason for the particular treatment was not based on sex, race or disability but was because of some other reason.

However, in the case of harassment, the requirement for a comparator has caused some difficulties and it is not always possible to make a comparison. For example, in the case of a transsexual employee who was harassed, *Chessington World of Adventures v Reed*,[1] the employers argued that the SDA 1975 required a comparison to be made between persons of different biological sexes and the Act therefore could not apply to discrimination on the grounds of gender reassignment. However, the EAT held that not every act of discrimination under the SDA 1975 was necessarily based on a comparison between a man and a woman. They cited in support the fact that dismissal on the grounds of pregnancy had been held to be discriminatory even though no direct comparison could be made with a male employee.[2]

The defence that the treatment was not 'less favourable treatment' should therefore be viewed with caution. This defence was put forward in the sexual harassment case of *Porcelli*,[3] where the harassers tried to argue that they would have treated a man they disliked in a similar way and that Ms Porcelli could not establish that she had been treated less favourably than a man. The EAT decided

---

1   [1997] IRLR 566, EAT.
2   *Webb v EMO Cargo (UK) Ltd* [1994] ICR 770.
3   *Porcelli v Strathclyde Regional Council* [1986] ICR 564.

that the less favourable treatment of Mrs Porcelli arose because of the nature of the conduct against her, rather than the motive, and that she was susceptible to the particular action because of her sex. For that reason she was treated less favourably.

9.2 NO DETRIMENT SUFFERED

9.2.1 Workplace banter

An employer's defence that racially or sexually offensive remarks are merely workplace banter is unlikely to succeed.

> *Example*   This case concerned Mr Quaid, whose father is from Yemen. He claimed that throughout his employment he had been subjected to racist insults such as 'black bastard' and 'fucking nigger'. The employers accepted that racist comments were made regularly but that they formed part of the everyday banter of a fish-processing factory, that Mr Quaid 'gave as good as he got' and that he had not objected to the comments.
>
> The tribunal concluded that Mr Quaid had been discriminated against because, although other employees may also have been insulted, Mr Quaid's treatment was clearly 'on racial grounds'. The tribunal thought that he would not have been called 'black bastard' or 'fucking nigger' if there had not been a racial element behind the terms used to him. He was awarded compensation of £8,219 including £5,000 for injury to feelings.
>
> *Quaid v L Williamson (Shetland) Ltd t/a Sheltie*
> 1996, Case No 60642/95

> *Example*   Miss Wintripp, who was employed by Hartlepool Wholesale Bakeries, was subjected to remarks of a sexual nature by one of the owners of the business. Miss Wintripp brought a complaint of sex discrimination to the industrial tribunal.
>
> The employer sought to argue that the type of language used was just workplace banter and that Miss Wintripp could give as good as she got. But the industrial tribunal said that this was not a defence to discrimination under the SDA 1975 especially when the acts of discrimination are perpetrated by an employer. She was awarded £1,670 including £1,000 for injury to feelings.
>
> *Wintripp v Hartlepool Wholesale Bakeries and Others*
> 1995, Case No 61024/94

9.2.2 Character of complainant

Although the robust character of a complainant cannot actually provide a defence to a harassment case, it can go a long way in reducing the potential compensation payable.

> *Example*   This case concerned a female employee who claimed she was subjected to sexual harassment by one of the company's directors. The EAT upheld the industrial tribunal's finding that compensation for injury to feelings should be limited to £50. The EAT said the industrial tribunal was entitled to take into account the fact that on occasion Miss Wileman wore

scanty and provocative clothes to work. It went on to say that remarks of a sexual nature may constitute very great discrimination and cause very great detriment in some cases, while in others they may not cause any detriment or any real detriment. The degree of detriment and the range of awards is for an industrial jury to decide having seen and heard the witnesses.

Wileman v Minilec Engineering Ltd
[1988] IRLR 144, EAT

Example   A catering manager, Mrs Snowball, alleged she had been sexually harassed by her district manager. She claimed he had asked her to make love on the office table and had sent her suggestive underwear and sex magazines, and had pestered her with telephone calls. During the course of the tribunal proceedings, Mrs Snowball was cross-examined about her sexual attitudes in an attempt to show that, if harassment had occurred, she had not suffered any injury to her feelings as a result. It was suggested, for example, that she had described her bed as a 'play pen' to fellow employees and talked about her black satin sheets.

The EAT upheld the industrial tribunal's ruling and said that:

'the industrial tribunal was entitled to rule that evidence as to the complainant's attitude to matters of sexual behaviour was relevant and admissible in law for the purposes of determining her complaint of sexual harassment.'

The EAT went on to say that:

'Compensation for sexual harassment must relate to the degree of detriment and, in that context, there has to be an assessment of the injury to the woman's feelings, which must be looked at both objectively with reference to what any ordinary reasonable female employee would feel and subjectively with reference to her as an individual.'

Snowball v Gardner Merchant
[1987] IRLR 397, EAT

The above two cases appear to contrast with the outcome of a more recent case, *British Telecommunications Plc v Williams* (below).

Example   Miss Williams who was employed as a clerical officer. Her annual appraisal was prepared by Mr Moore, her senior manager. She was given very low marks for her appraisal which led to an interview with Mr Moore. Miss Williams claimed that Mr Moore was sexually aroused during the interview, that he stared at her legs and effectively trapped her in the room. Miss Williams said that this amounted to sexual harassment and brought a sex discrimination claim in the industrial tribunal.

The industrial tribunal accepted Mr Moore's denial that he was sexually aroused but upheld the complaint on the grounds that the atmosphere at the interview was sexually intimidating. Only one copy of the appraisal was taken into the room which meant they had to sit close together and the interview lasted between one and a half and two hours which the tribunal found was excessively long. Moreover, no female manager sat in on the interview.

However, the industrial tribunal's decision was overturned by the EAT. It noted that the industrial tribunal had accepted the evidence that Mr Moore was not sexually aroused at the interview and that therefore the only conclusion the industrial tribunal was entitled to reach was that the complaint of unlawful sex discrimination was not proved. The EAT also rejected the industrial tribunal's conclusion that the lack of a third party rendered the interview sexually intimidating.

British Telecommunications Plc v Williams
[1997] IRLR 668, EAT

The outcome of the *Williams* case appears to turn entirely on whether or not the interviewing manager had an erection! The industrial tribunal (the EAT agreeing) accepted the evidence that he did not, that this meant he was not sexually aroused and that he could therefore not have been behaving badly for sexual reasons. This focuses attention on the alleged perpetrator and moves away from the subjective test of whether the recipient found the behaviour offensive. Arguably, the original decision of the industrial tribunal, that a reasonable person would find the situation sexually intimidating, is the correct one and sits better with the cases of *Wileman* and *Snowball*.

9.3 NOT IN THE COURSE OF EMPLOYMENT

In workplace personal injury cases, an employer will often try to argue that the injury suffered by Employee A at the hands of Employee B did not happen in the course of employment of Employee B and the employer cannot therefore be vicariously liable. (See further Chapter 8.)

The SDA 1975, the RRA 1976 and the DDA 1995 all contain a provision for vicarious liability. Section 41(1) of the SDA 1975, s 32(1) of the RRA 1976 and s 58(1) of the DDA 1995 (which are all slightly differently worded) state in effect:

> 'Anything done by a person in the course of his employment shall be treated for the purposes of this Act as done by his employer as well as by him, whether or not it was done with the employer's knowledge or approval.'

Until recently employers relied heavily on this section as a defence for allegations of discrimination brought by one employee against another: arguing that they were not liable for the discriminatory act of Employee B against Employee A as Employee B was not acting in the course of his employment when the discriminatory act was carried out. But the case of *Jones v Tower Boot Co Ltd*[1] (discussed in the previous chapter) has changed the 'course of employment' test, with the result that this defence is now far more difficult to rely on.

It had previously been thought that an employer would only be liable for the discriminatory acts of its employee if the employee was doing an authorised act, albeit in an unauthorised way. The *Tower Boot* case set a different test for the purposes of discrimination legislation. The relevant part of the judgment in that case reads as follows:

> 'The tribunals are free, and are indeed bound, to interpret the ordinary, and readily understandable, words 'in the course of employment' in the sense in which every layman would understand them. This is not to say that when it comes to applying them to the infinite variety of circumstance which is liable to occur in particular instances – within or without the workplace, in or out of uniform, in or out of

---

1   [1997] IRLR 168, CA.

rest-breaks – all laymen would necessarily agree as to the result. That is what makes their application so well suited to decision by an industrial jury. The application of the phrase will be a question of fact for each industrial tribunal to resolve, in the light of the circumstances presented to it, with a mind unclouded by any parallels sought to be drawn from the law of vicarious liability in tort.'

This judgment makes it difficult for an employer to use this defence successfully. However, it was successfully used in the case of *Waters v Commissioner of Police of the Metropolis* (below).

> *Example* This case concerned a woman police constable, Eileen Waters, who lived in a room in the section house. In the early hours of the morning, while she was off duty, she was visited by a male police constable who was also off duty. They went for a walk together and then returned to the section house. Miss Waters alleged that she was then seriously sexually assaulted in her room by the male police officer. She reported the assault to her superiors but, following an internal inquiry, no action was taken against the male officer. She alleged that from that time she was victimised and, on this basis, brought a complaint of victimisation to the industrial tribunal.
>
> Before looking at the victimisation claim the industrial tribunal had to decide whether the alleged sexual assault had taken place in the course of the male police officer's employment. The industrial tribunal held (the EAT and Court of Appeal agreeing) that the alleged assault was not committed in the course of employment since both parties were off duty at the time and in circumstances which placed them in no different position from that which would have applied if they had been social acquaintances only, with no working connection.
>
> *Waters v Commissioner of Police of the Metropolis*
> [1997] IRLR 589

The facts of this case show that there are limits to an employer's vicarious liability, even under the wide test set out by the Court of Appeal in the *Tower Boot* case. The Court of Appeal's observation that the parties were 'in no different position from that which would have applied if they had been social acquaintances only, with no working connection at all' could prove a useful guide in future cases.

The same defence was also successfully used in *Turville v Wells City Council* (below).

> *Example* Mrs Turville was employed as a clerical assistant. She was asked by a colleague to find out whether a particular bill had been paid. The relevant file was kept in the desk of the town clerk, Mr Donoghue. When she went into his room he was not there, so she looked in his desk and found the file, together with a pornographic magazine. She reported the matter to management but did not bring a tribunal complaint. About 18 months later, Mrs Turville waited for Mr Donoghue to leave the premises and searched his desk. In a drawer underneath a folder she found a magazine which was allegedly pornographic. She again reported the matter and disciplinary proceedings were taken against Mr Donoghue. He gave a written unreserved apology to Mrs Turville but she nevertheless resigned and claimed sex discrimination.

The industrial tribunal dismissed her complaint saying that she:

'acted in an entirely misguided fashion in going through Mr Donoghue's desk. . . . In doing so she was acting outside the course of her duties as an employee and was, in effect, trespassing at that stage into Mr Donoghue's private property.'

Turville v Wells City Council
1997, Case No 41620/96

9.4 REASONABLY PRACTICABLE STEPS

9.4.1 The reasonably practicable steps defence

The above cases show that it is difficult for an employer to make out the defence that the employee was not acting in the course of employment, and it is not reliable to plead that no detriment was suffered by the complainant. Employers are strongly advised, therefore, to ensure that they establish the defence that they took all reasonably practicable steps to prevent the action.

Section 41(3) of the SDA 1975, s 32(3) of the RRA 1976 and s 58(5) of the DDA 1995 (which are all worded slightly differently) state in effect:

'In proceedings brought under this Act against any person in respect of an act alleged to have been done by an employee of his it shall be a defence for that person to prove that he took such steps as were reasonably practicable to prevent the employee from doing that act, or from doing in the course of his employment, acts of that description.'

9.4.2 Discrimination by employees

One of the key cases in which this defence is discussed is *Balgobin and Francis v London Borough of Tower Hamlets* (below).

Example   Mrs Balgobin and Mrs Francis were employed as cleaners in a hostel run by the council. In June 1985 Mr Clarke was appointed as cook in the same hostel. Between June and October 1985 both Mrs Balgobin and Mrs Francis were sexually harassed by Mr Clarke. In October 1985, they complained to the management of the hotel and Mr Clarke was suspended while an inquiry was held. The employers were unable to determine the truth of the matter and Mr Clarke resumed his job as cook. There were no further acts of sexual harassment.

The women complained of sex discrimination to an industrial tribunal. The industrial tribunal found that the women had been sexually harassed between June and October but that there had been no acts of sexual harassment thereafter. The industrial tribunal held that what was done was done in the course of employment but concluded that the employers were not liable because they had established a defence under s 41(3) of the SDA 1975. They said that:

'No one in authority knew what was going on prior to 24th October 1985. Prior to that time [London Borough of Tower Hamlets] were running the hostel with proper and adequate supervision insofar as the staff were concerned. They had made known their policy of equal opportunities. We do not think that there were any other practicable steps which they could have taken to foresee or prevent the acts complained of.'

The women appealed to the EAT but the EAT dismissed their appeal, agreeing with the decision of the industrial tribunal.

Balgobin and Francis v London Borough of Tower Hamlets
[1987] IRLR 401, EAT

So London Borough of Tower Hamlets successfully made out the defence that it had taken all reasonably practicable steps to prevent its employees being harassed. This case should be viewed with caution, however, since it implies that as long as the employers did not know that harassment was occurring, they will not be found liable for it. This conflicts with the wording of s 41(1) of the SDA 1975 which says that an employer will be vicariously liable for acts of its employees 'whether or not it was done with the employer's knowledge or approval'.

Graham v Royal Mail and Nicholson (below) is an example of a racial harassment case in which an employer successfully invoked the 'reasonable steps' defence.

Example The case was brought by Miss Graham, a black woman, who was appointed as a temporary associate postwoman for six months. She complained that she had been racially harassed by a fellow employee, Mr Nicholson. The industrial tribunal found that there were good relations between the two employees and that there was constant banter between them. The incident complained of arose one day when they were leaving work. Miss Graham shouted 'I'll see you later, you white bald-headed bastard', to which Mr Nicholson replied, 'I would prefer to be a white bald-headed bastard than a black bastard'.

Miss Graham took exception to the remark and Mr Nicholson immediately apologised. He also apologised the next day. However, Miss Graham reported the matter to her supervisor and, in accordance with the Royal Mail's procedures for dealing with harassment, Mr Nicholson was immediately transferred to another working area.

The tribunal concluded that Royal Mail had taken 'all reasonable steps to avoid discrimination of this nature' and that it had discharged the burden under s 32(3) of the RRA 1976:

Graham v Royal Mail and Nicholson
1993, Case No 28681/92

The above cases illustrate how this defence can be successfully used. However, there are a number of cases where employers have invoked this defence but have not been successful.

Example Mr Chin was employed at the Post Office's Northampton distribution depot. While he was employed there a black cleaner was frequently taunted and verbally abused by being called names such as 'black bastard', 'Zulu warrior' and 'tribes Mandela'. These remarks were not addressed at Mr Chin, but they offended him nevertheless. He informed his operations manager that he was upset by the racist remarks. His manager outlined the company harassment policy and offered his support if Mr Chin wished to make a formal complaint. Mr Chin did not do so and the racist abuse of the black cleaner continued. Mr Chin brought a race discrimination claim to the industrial tribunal. The tribunal said:

'The [Post Office] can escape liability if they can show that they attempted to prevent the particular act, harassment in this case. The [Post Office] has an equal opportunities policy and a policy on harassment. The policy is prominently displayed and the Post Office took all reasonably practicable steps to bring it to its employees' attention and make employees aware of the serious consequences of such action on their part. When [Mr Chin] complained, he was appraised of the appropriate steps to take. Prior to this complaint, the [Post Office] was unaware of any problems. However, after the complaint was made, the question which arises is whether the [Post Office] took all reasonable steps to protect Mr Chin from further harassment.'

The industrial tribunal concluded that the Post Office failed to do so. The operations manager took the view that the problem was resolved because he heard nothing more about it. No active steps were taken by the Post Office to protect Mr Chin when there was clearly an appreciable risk of the harassment recurring. They found that the Post Office was liable for the abuse of the black employee, which constituted a detriment to Mr Chin.

Chin v The Post Office and Others
1996, Case No 44750/95

Example   An applicant for a job, Claudia Baptiste, who is black, was told during the course of her interview with the display sales manager, Jane Holt, that it was not uncommon for her to use the phrase 'black bastard' and that it was part of the workplace banter in the organisation. Ms Baptiste (who was not offered the job) claimed race discrimination.
The industrial tribunal upheld her claim saying:

'It must be totally unacceptable for a manager interviewing a black person she is seeing for the first time for a post in her department or the organisation, to make such an obvious racist remark. We conclude, without difficulty, that that amounted to race discrimination.'

The tribunal rejected the employer's defence under s 32(3) of the RRA 1976 that it had taken such steps as were reasonable to prevent the manager from making such a remark. The tribunal was shown a copy of the equal opportunities policy, on which the tribunal commented as follows:

'This appears to be a classic example of an employer regarding the preparation of such a document as meeting obligations under the discrimination legislation without providing any supporting advice or instructions to managers to implement or monitor the requirements of the legislation. We find here no recruitment policies or procedures which are designed to take account of those matters.'

Baptiste v Westminister Press Ltd t/a Bradford and District Newspapers
1996, Case No 35945/95

So despite the existence of a harassment policy or an equal opportunities policy in the above two cases, the employer did not make out the reasonable steps defence because of its failure to implement the policy. Advice on drafting and implementing a harassment policy is given in Chapter 10.

It is not clear from the legislation whether the reasonably practicable steps defence applies also to discrimination by an agent in a principal/agent situation.

The safer view is to assume that a principal will be vicariously liable for the acts of its agent in the same way as an employer is liable for the acts of its employee. Thus, in addition to the argument that the acts of the agent were not authorised, it may be appropriate also to use the reasonably practicable steps defence. If a principal is not vicariously liable for the acts of its agent, it will probably be directly liable to the harassed employee in any event, following the *Burton and Rhule v De Vere Hotels* case and the appropriate defence should be pleaded.

9.4.3 Discrimination by third parties

In addition to the drafting and implementation of a harassment policy, there may also be other reasonably practicable steps which employers could take and which, if they fail to do so, may render them liable for the harassment of their employees. These will include situations over which the employer had control, but where the employer failed to take remedial action to prevent harassment occurring.

The key case is *Burton and Rhule v De Vere Hotels*[1] which is extensively discussed in Chapter 8.

In this case, two black waitresses were subjected to racially and sexually explicit remarks by Bernard Manning and some of the guests at an all-male evening function. The EAT held that the waitresses' employer (De Vere Hotels) was liable for the discriminatory acts of the third parties (Bernard Manning and the guests) despite the fact that the discriminators were not employees of the hotel. The employer was liable for the acts of harassment which had occurred in circumstances over which it had control.

What defence could the employer have pleaded? It was clear that the waitresses had suffered a detriment by being referred to in an abusive manner. The industrial tribunal in the original decision ruled that it was not the employer who had subjected them to the detriment (as required by s 4(2)(c) of the RRA 1976) and that the employer could not therefore be liable. The EAT, however, held that the word 'subjecting' in s 4(2)(c) connotes control and that a person 'subjects' another to something if he causes or allows that thing to happen in circumstances where that person can control whether it happens or not.

Whether an employer had control or not will be determined by whether, with the application of good employment practice, the employer could have prevented the harassment or reduced the extent of it.

The only defences available to the employer, therefore, were:

(1) that the event in question was not sufficiently under the employer's control; or
(2) the employer applied good employment practice to prevent or reduce the extent of the harassment.

The employer failed to make out either defence and the EAT said:

> 'In the present case, it would have been good employment practice for the manager to warn his assistants to keep a look out for Mr Manning and withdraw the waitresses if things became unpleasant. Events within the banqueting hall were under the control of the assistants and, if they had been properly instructed, [Ms Burton and Ms Rhule] would not have suffered any harassment. They might possibly have heard

---

1   [1996] IRLR 596.

a few offensive words before they were withdrawn, but that would have been all. Accordingly, the employers 'subjected' [Ms Burton and Ms Rhule] to the racial harassment which they received.'

The EAT also said in the above case that there might be little an employer can do to prevent harassment happening in certain situations. It gave, as an example, the employer of a bus or train conductor, which might recognise the risk of racial harassment, but will not be in a position to control whether or not it happens. In this situation all the employer will be able to do will be to make his attitude to such behaviour known to the public and to offer his employees appropriate support if harassment occurs.

A similar case is the sexual harassment case of *Go Kidz Go v Bourdouane*,[1] where a children's party organiser was sexually harassed by the parent of one of the children attending a party. She reported the harassment to her manager but was encouraged to return to finish the party. She was again sexually harassed by the same parent.

Ms Bourdouane successfully claimed that she had been sexually discriminated against by her employer. The EAT said that it must ask the question whether or not the employer had taken all reasonable steps to prevent the harassment taking place or continuing when it was within the employer's power to prevent it. The EAT held that once the employer knew about the first incident of sexual harassment it could have prevented the second incident by asking the parent to leave or by excusing the employee from attending the rest of the party. By taking neither action, the employer permitted the harassment to continue in circumstances where it could have been prevented.

Both *Burton and Rhule* and *Bourdouane* show that, had the employer followed good employment practices, the harassment could have been prevented or limited, which would have provided a defence for the employer. Employees at all levels should be aware of the possibility of harassment and how to deal with it when it does occur. The implementation of a harassment policy together with the training of the workforce is a key element of good employment practice and could provide a valuable defence to the employer.

9.5 DEFENCES TO COMPLAINTS OF BULLYING

As there is no legislation against bullying, employers will not be able to use the statutory defence of reasonably practicable steps which is available for sex, race or disability harassment. So what defences can employers invoke if employees complain of bullying?

As can be seen in Chapter 7, a bullied employee may bring a constructive dismissal claim, ie a claim that the employer's conduct was such that it caused a fundamental breach of the employment contract. In order to do this the employee must have resigned, and the breach of the contract must be so serious that it goes to the heart of the employment relationship. It will be a defence for the employer if he can show either that there was no breach of contract or that the breach was not sufficiently serious to constitute a fundamental breach. If it was

---

1   (1996) IDS 578.

not a fundamental breach, the employee did not have the right to resign and claim constructive dismissal.

The implied terms relied on for constructive dismissal claims are: (1) loss of mutual trust and confidence between employer and employee; (2) failure of employer to provide reasonable support; and (3) safe workplace. If the employer can show that there was no breach of the implied term of mutual trust and confidence, that the employee was given reasonable support during his employment and that the workplace was safe, then he should be able to defend a claim of constructive dismissal.

In a bullying situation, the best defence for an employer will be to show that a harassment/bullying policy was in place, that this policy was effectively implemented and that any complaint of bullying was taken seriously and was dealt with swiftly and efficiently. In this way, even if there is a bullying incident, the employee would find it difficult to plead that there had been a total lack of mutual trust and confidence, no reasonable support or an unsafe workplace.

> *Example* Ms Hatrick's hair was forcibly cut by a colleague. She reported the incident to management who decided to take no action over what they considered to be a minor act of stupidity. The tribunal thought that employees were entitled to expect protection from this kind of behaviour and that a reasonable employer would have responded immediately to the complaint. The employers' failure to act was a fundamental breach of contract entitling Ms Hatrick to resign and claim constructive dismissal.
> *Hatrick v City Fax*
> COIT 3041/138

Had the employers acted in accordance with a harassment/bullying policy, they might have had a good defence to Ms Hatrick's claim of bullying; the fact that they did not meant that they were held liable for the bullying incident.

A complaint of constructive dismissal may be based on the conduct of a fellow employee even though that employee would not have had the authority to dismiss the complainant; the test is whether the employer is vicariously liable for the conduct complained of. The employer may therefore be able to plead that the act complained of did not occur in the course of employment (see above).

As the law stands at the moment, a person wishing to bring a claim for constructive dismissal must be an employee and must have two years' continuous service. If the complainant is not an employee and/or does not have two years' service, employers should plead this as part of their defence. However the two years' service requirement is under review and is likely to change in the future.

If the bullying results in psychological injury, the employer will need to formulate a defence on the basis that either there was no breach of the employer's duty of care, that the risk of mental injury was not reasonably foreseeable, that the breach was not the cause of the employee's injury or that the employee has not suffered any injury. It is not within the scope of this book to go into detail as to how to defend this type of personal injury claim. Suffice it to say that if this type of personal injury claim is brought, the employer should take great care in formulating a defence in order to try to prevent any similar claims being brought in the future.

Chapter 10

DRAFTING AND IMPLEMENTING A HARASSMENT POLICY

Why have a harassment policy? – How to start – The policy – Responsibilities – Procedure – Implementing the harassment policy – Draft harassment questionnaire – Draft harassment policy

10.1 WHY HAVE A HARASSMENT POLICY?

The reasons for having a harassment policy and for implementing it successfully within an organisation are numerous. A well-drafted and well-implemented policy will help to prevent harassment occurring. When it does occur, a policy will help employees and managers to recognise it and to know what to do about it. It will provide reassurance to employees that their interests are being taken account of. It will go some way to providing a defence to claims of harassment taken to tribunal (see Chapter 9) and the EC Code of Practice on the *Protection of the Dignity of Women and Men at Work* ('the EC Code') recommends that an employer should have such a policy and gives guidance on what it should include.

The Industrial Relations Society has carried out a survey on sexual harassment at work (the results of which are published in IRS Employment Trends Nos 615, 628 and 621) which shows that 72% of organisations operated a policy in 1996, as opposed to 32% recorded in their 1992 survey. A further 9% stated that they had no policy at present but were considering introducing one in future. 18% had no policy and no plans to introduce one. Of the organisations surveyed, 95% of employers with sexual harassment policies cited the need to ensure equal opportunities at work as one of the main reasons for introducing an explicit policy. Other important reasons – reported by around two thirds of those with policies – were to avoid legal action and potential costs, such as increased absenteeism, higher sickness levels and lower productivity. Just under a fifth of respondents (18%) said they had introduced policies in response to EC developments while 14% cited the need to aid recruitment and retention of employees. No organisation reported that union pressure was a factor in introducing their sexual harassment policy.

The results from the survey also confirm that the majority of employers have an equal opportunities policy and most of these also have a separate harassment policy, many of which cover all forms of harassment and not just sexual harassment. Harassment in the workplace is being recognised as a serious and potentially expensive problem – expensive not only in terms of tribunal awards and management time taken to deal with allegations but also in terms of reduced productivity as a result of harassment. Many organisations have realised that it is better to educate than litigate and that the most effective way of doing this is by means of a comprehensive harassment policy and concomitant training of the workforce, from senior management all the way down to the shopfloor.

There has been a substantial amount of case-law on the subject of harassment policies which illustrate the importance which tribunals attach to proper drafting and implementation of policies.

Example Miss Graham, a black woman, was appointed as a temporary associate postwoman for six months. She was dismissed at the end of the period on grounds of unsatisfactory performance. However, she complained that during her employment she had been racially harassed by a fellow employee, Mr Nicholson. Miss Graham took exception to a remark made by Mr Nicholson, for which he immediately apologised, and also apologised the next day. However, Miss Graham reported the matter to her supervisor and, as a result, in accordance with the Royal Mail's procedures for dealing with harassment, Mr Nicholson was immediately transferred to another working area and told that a note would be placed on his file amounting to a warning.

The tribunal noted that Royal Mail's statement on harassment sets out in great detail definitions of harassment and how it is to be dealt with.

'It states that an employee who believes herself to have been harassed should first ask the harasser to stop. If harassment continues, she then has the right to complain. The matter will be dealt with in confidence and where appropriate, the alleged harasser will be transferred to work in another area while an investigation is carried out. The emphasis is on moving the harasser, not the person harassed.'

The tribunal pointed out that the policy:

'gives very detailed guidance to employees and managers, and examples of what constitutes harassment: unwanted verbal conduct or abuse which affects the dignity of an individual. It deals with comments, jokes and banter and the like. It deals with the responsibility of employees.'

The tribunal stated that it was satisfied that:

'the policy is not only detailed, careful, reasonable and in our view, exemplary, but was acted upon. Notices about harassment were posted. [Royal Mail] undertook a questionnaire asking people whether they had been harassed. Out of some 160 people who replied, 16 said they had been harassed: [Royal Mail] investigated every individual case . . . The employees are trained in equal opportunities. Harassment is a live issue, not a dead letter. There is a tight code of conduct.'

The tribunal concluded that Royal Mail had taken 'all reasonable steps to avoid discrimination of this nature' and had therefore taken such steps as were reasonably practicable to prevent the act of discrimination. The tribunal added that:

'we consider that the implementation of the policy – the training, the questionnaire and the notice – has created in the workforce an awareness about discrimination, and how to avoid it, which is unique in our experience. This is a major public employer, which employs many women, and many men and women from ethnic minorities. Such a policy is essential in such an organisation. In our view, the Royal Mail is to be commended for grasping the nettle so effectively.'

The tribunal concluded that there had not been less favourable treatment on the grounds of race.

Graham v Royal Mail and Nicholson
IT, 11 May 1993, Case No 28681/92

It is to be noted that this case was heard in 1993 and, although the chairman of the tribunal said that the level of awareness of the harassment policy was, in his experience, unique, that certainly would not be the case now. Not only are there more harassment policies in place but now there is far better awareness and training of workforces than was previously the case.

Campbell v Datum Engineering Co Ltd (below) illustrates a slightly more recent view taken by an industrial tribunal.

> *Example*   Mr Campbell, a setter/operator of Afro-Caribbean origin, learned that he was being paid 16p per hour less than at least one other person in his section who was employed on the same work. He complained to the production manager about this and later complained that he had been subjected to racial harassment by the production manager. Although the harassment complaint was dismissed, the discrimination claim was upheld and the tribunal awarded compensation of £1,624, including £1,500 for injury to feelings. In the course of the decision the tribunal recommended to the employer that in order to avoid repetition of similar events in the future it should:
>
> 'obtain the Commission for Racial Equality's Code of Practice and give appropriate training to all managers and employees.'
>
>

Campbell v Datum Engineering Co Ltd
20 March 1995, Case No 43749/94

Similarly, in the case of *Dalziel v Muircroft plc*[1] an industrial tribunal recommended, following a finding of sexual harassment, that the employer took steps to contact ACAS (Advisory Conciliation and Arbitration Service) and the Equal Opportunities Commission (EOC):

> 'with a view to obtaining appropriate literature and advice concerning the setting-up of a policy to deal with matters of sexual discrimination and that there should be suitable training and advice given to employees as to how to deal with such situations if they arise and to management as to how to prevent such occurrences in the future.'

The tribunal also awarded compensation of £5,381, including £2,000 for injury to feelings.

The EC Code (which is reproduced at Appendix 1) is sub-titled 'A code of practice on measures to combat sexual harassment'. It sets out in some detail the reasons why organisations should have a sexual harassment policy and what should be included in the policy. It states clearly what is the purpose of a sexual harassment policy and what is the intention of the Code:

> 'The aim is to ensure that sexual harassment does not occur and, if it does occur, to ensure that adequate procedures are readily available to deal with the problem and prevent its recurrence. The Code thus seeks to encourage the development and implementation of policies and practices which establish working environments free of sexual harassment and in which women and men respect one another's human integrity.'

The EC Code relates only to one sort of harassment – sexual harassment – possibly the most prevalent type of harassment and certainly the most publicised.

---

1   11 August 1994, Case No 23842/94.

The Commission for Racial Equality (CRE) has issued a *Code of Practice for the Elimination of Racial Discrimination and the Promotion of Equality of Opportunity in Employment* ('the CRE Code of Practice')[1] which advocates the adoption of an equal opportunities policy but does not mention racial harassment specifically. There is also a Disability Code of Practice (issued by the Secretary of State, as the National Disability Council does not have the power to issue codes of practice) which, similarly, suggests extending any existing policy to cover disability issues but does not mention disability harassment specifically. The EOC has also issued a *Code of Practice for the Elimination of Discrimination on the Grounds of Sex and Marriage and the Promotion of Equality of Opportunity in Employment* ('the EOC Code of Practice')[2] which suggests, quite rightly, that:

> 'an equal opportunities policy will ensure the effective use of human resources in the best interest of both the organisation and its employees.'

While all four Codes of Practice recommend the implementation of a policy, only the EC Code mentions harassment and gives useful guidance on how to draft and implement a harassment policy. There is no reason, however, why the guidelines set out in the EC Code should not be extended to cover any form of harassment including racial and disability harassment and bullying. The CRE leaflet *Racial Harassment – What Employers Can Do* and the EOC leaflets *Sexual Harassment – What You Can Do About It* and *Sexual Harassment – Consider The Cost* all provide useful guidance on implementing policies. Many of the guidelines set out in the 'Policy' section are based on the EC Code and the CRE and EOC leaflets.

10.2 HOW TO START

The starting point is to acknowledge that harassment is a live issue. It is not safe to assume that harassment does not happen. The courage needed to bring a complaint about harassment may mean that individuals would rather resign and move to another job than let it be known that they have been harassed. Employers must not wait for a more vociferous employee to bring a complaint before taking action. The complaint could perhaps be made against a senior member of staff, with the adverse publicity that this would inevitably bring. Anything involving titillating or sensational details is bound to attract the interest of the media and the general public.

It may be appropriate to issue a confidential harassment questionnaire to all employees or to set up a confidential counselling network in order to establish the type and extent of harassment. An example of a harassment questionnaire based on UNISON's draft 'Bullying Survey' is set out at the end of this chapter. Other alternatives would be to conduct a confidential survey of staff through interviews with employees, or to set up a confidential telephone helpline. Whatever the method, all findings should be carefully monitored and collated in order to gauge the extent of the problem.

If it is established that harassment does exist in the workplace to a lesser or greater extent, it must be tackled head on. The aim of a harassment policy is not

---

1   See Appendix 3.
2   See Appendix 2.

only to provide a defence against potential harassment claims, but also to create a climate in which harassment is not tolerated and in which employees feel secure. A harassment policy should not be regarded as just a mechanism to deal with complaints but it should also aim to prevent them happening in the first place.

If the harassment policy is to be successful, it must have the support and be seen to have the support of senior management. It should therefore be made clear from the start that harassment is viewed as a serious issue by senior management and that any questionnaire or counselling service is endorsed by senior management, preferably the managing director (or equivalent).

Having received back the completed questionnaires or having collated the results of the confidential counselling service, consideration should be given to what types of harassment should be included within the policy. It may be that a basic sexual harassment policy is already in existence and this could be extended to include other forms of harassment. This book discusses sexual, racial and disability harassment and bullying, but there is no reason why a harassment policy should not be extended to cover other forms of harassment such as that based on age, sexual orientation, political or religious beliefs.

From a practical point of view, the policy could take a number of forms. It could be included in an Equal Opportunities Policy which could itself be included in an employee handbook. It could be a separate handbook (possibly entitled Harassment at Work) or it could be included in a handbook or section of a handbook covering discrimination issues (possibly entitled Discrimination in the Workplace). It is sensible to produce it in a loose-leaf format so that it can be updated at regular intervals. The draft policy provided in this book would be suitable for inclusion in a loose-leaf employee handbook as a separate section.

Consideration should also be given to the scope of the policy. Should it include all forms of harassment or should it be restricted to the four types of harassment mentioned above? If a new policy is being drafted it may be advisable to include a statement making clear that as well as sexual, racial and disability harassment and bullying, the policy also covers all other types of harassment. A suitable title for a policy to be included in an employee handbook would be 'Harassment Policy'.

The EC Code recognises that the size and structure of organisations vary and that 'it may be particularly relevant for small and medium-sized enterprises to adapt some of the practical steps to their specific needs'. Not all of the following recommendations from the EC Code will be applicable to every organisation and it is for senior management to decide which steps are appropriate to their particular organisation.

10.3 THE POLICY

A suggested draft harassment policy is provided at the end of this chapter, and this will include examples of all the items discussed below.

10.3.1 Policy statement

This should expressly state that all employees have a right to be treated with dignity, that harassment at work will not be permitted or condoned and that employees have a right to complain about it should it occur. It should be a firm unequivocal statement which sends a clear message throughout the organisation.

10.3.2 Definitions

The policy should state what forms of harassment it is intended to cover. The policy should then go on to make clear what constitutes harassment and what is considered inappropriate behaviour at work.

10.3.3 Disciplinary action

It should be made clear in the policy that employees have a right to complain about harassment should it occur and that anyone acting in breach of the policy will be disciplined in accordance with the employer's disciplinary procedure. It should also be made clear that such behaviour may, in certain circumstances, be unlawful.

10.4 RESPONSIBILITIES

The EC Code recommends that the harassment policy sets out a positive duty on managers and supervisors to implement the policy and to take action to ensure compliance with it. It also recommends that a positive duty be placed on all employees to comply with the policy and to ensure that their colleagues are treated with respect and dignity. The responsibilities of employees in general and managers/supervisors particularly, are set out in the EC Code (at section 5A(iii)):

> 'All employees have a responsibility to help ensure a working environment in which the dignity of employees is respected and managers (including supervisors) have a particular duty to ensure that sexual harassment does not occur in work areas for which they are responsible. It is recommended that managers should explain the organisation's policy to their staff and take steps to positively promote the policy. Managers should also be responsive and supportive to any member of staff who complains about sexual harassment; provide full and clear advice on the procedure to be adopted; maintain confidentiality in any cases of sexual harassment; and ensure that there is no further problem of sexual harassment or any victimisation after a complaint has been resolved.'

10.5 PROCEDURE

This is the all-important part of the harassment policy (and is discussed fully in Chapter 11). The EC Code strongly recommends that, because of the issues of sensitivity and confidentiality, the harassment policy should contain a separate grievance procedure consisting of an informal procedure, a formal complaints procedure and a system for advice and assistance.

10.6 IMPLEMENTING THE HARASSMENT POLICY

10.6.1 Ensuring effective implementation

The EC Code recommends that the policy and procedures should be adopted, where appropriate 'after consultation or negotiation with trade unions or employee representatives'. It states:

> 'Experience suggests that strategies to create and maintain a working environment in which the dignity of employees is respected are most likely to be effective when they are jointly agreed.'

Trade unions also have an important role to play in informing their members of the existence of the harassment policy and generally raising awareness of the issues involved. There is a separate section in the EC Code headed 'Recommendations to trade unions' which advises unions to:

> 'raise the issue of sexual harassment with employers and encourage the adoption of adequate policies and procedures to protect the dignity of women and men at work in the organisation.'

Although unions may raise awareness, it is still the responsibility of employers to implement the policy in order to ensure that all employees are aware of it and its contents.

However skilfully drafted the policy, it will have little bearing on the attitudes of the workforce and will provide little defence to a claim of harassment unless it is also fully implemented. Once the policy has been finalised, therefore, it must be implemented in a way which ensures that all employees are aware of and understand the issues covered by it. This will be done by communicating the policy, training the personnel involved in its implementation and monitoring its effectiveness. Management should develop an action plan for implementing the policy, indicating how and when the policy will be communicated to employees, which managers will be responsible for which areas, who the confidential counsellors will be (if any) and who the appropriate officers responsible for investigating allegations of harassment will be. The action plan should also include when and how managers, counsellors and employees will be trained. As the EC Code points out, it is helpful to agree with the trade unions or employee representatives who the confidential counsellors will be as this is likely to enhance their acceptability.

10.6.2 Communication

The importance of successfully communicating the policy is illustrated in the case of *Taylor v (1) Adlam, (2) Adlam & (3) Hanley*.[1] In that case the tribunal found that the employee had suffered a detriment as a result of racist comments and that although the employer had a 'perfectly satisfactory equal opportunities policy' it was not enough:

> 'there has been no evidence of any training courses and there has been no evidence that this equal opportunities policy was pointed out to Mr Hanley on his appointment.'

---

1   2 December 1996, Case No 43213/96.

The EC Code also stresses the importance of communicating the policy:

'Once the policy has been developed, it is important to ensure that it is communicated effectively to all employees, so that they are aware that they have a right to complain and to whom they should complain; that their complaint will be dealt with promptly and fairly; and so that employees are made aware of the likely consequences of engaging in sexual harassment. Such communication will highlight management's commitment to eliminating sexual harassment, thus enhancing a climate in which it will not occur.'

The EOC Code of Practice also has a section on implementing an equal opportunities policy:

'An equal opportunities policy must be seen to have the active support of management at the highest level. To ensure that the policy is fully effective, the following procedure is recommended:

(a) the policy should be clearly stated and, where appropriate, included in a collective agreement;

(b) overall responsibility for implementing the policy should rest with senior management;

(c) the policy should be made known to all employees and, where reasonably practicable, to all job applicants.'

The CRE Code of Practice says:

'This policy should be clearly communicated to all employees – eg through notice boards, circulars, contracts of employment or written notifications to individual employees.'

Taken together, a suitable action plan to communicate the harassment policy would involve some or all of the following steps.

(a) *Distribution to employees*

The policy should be distributed to all employees, preferably with a covering letter from a senior person in the organisation, for example the managing director. The covering letter should reinforce the organisation's stance on harassment, ie that it is committed to creating and maintaining a working environment in which the dignity of employees is respected, that harassment of any sort will not be permitted and that employees have a right to complain about it should it occur. It should state that all complaints will be dealt with promptly and fairly and that anyone found to be in breach of the policy will be disciplined and may be dismissed. An example of a suitable letter is given below.

'A MESSAGE TO ALL EMPLOYEES FROM THE MANAGING DIRECTOR

The Company is committed to a working environment that offers equal treatment and equal opportunities for all its employees. It recognises that all employees have a right to be treated with dignity and respect in order to realise their potential and to achieve the Company's objectives. The Company recognises that any person could be affected by unfair treatment including harassment, bullying or victimisation and is committed to eliminating such behaviour.

For that reason the Company has drawn up a HARASSMENT POLICY which is enclosed for your attention. Please read it – it is for your benefit. If you feel you are being subjected to any of the forms of harassment described in the policy you have the right to complain. You have my assurance that the Company will take any complaint seriously and investigate it as quickly and confidentially as possible. There are a number of trained confidential counsellors you can talk to for any reason connected with the policy who can advise you whether you have a case and the appropriate method of dealing with it.

Anyone found to be in breach of the policy will be disciplined and may be dismissed. Harassment of any form is an issue which will be taken extremely seriously by the Company.

I do not want anyone in this Company to suffer the effects of harassment in silence. You can do something about it and this policy tells you how. Read it.

Yours sincerely

[Managing Director]'

(b) *Incorporation into staff handbook*

The policy could be incorporated into any existing staff handbook and new employees should be specifically directed to this section during their induction and encouraged to read it.

(c) *Reinforcing the message with posters, memos etc*

Awareness of the issue could be increased by the use of posters on staff notice boards, internal memos to all members of staff and articles in company newspapers.

(d) *Reinforcement of the message by managers and supervisors*

Managers/supervisors could be asked to hold meetings with their teams to point to the existence of the policy, the importance of reading it and abiding by it.

(e) *Spot checks*

Occasional spot checks could be carried out to establish whether employees are aware of the policy and if so, whether they know what procedures are in place for dealing with complaints.

(f) *Training sessions*

It might be appropriate to invite trade union representatives to speak at training sessions in order to raise awareness of the policy and the importance of the issues contained in it.

10.6.3 Training

Training has legal implications since an organisation must, in order to avoid liability, have taken reasonably practicable steps to avoid discrimination under the SDA 1975. An employment tribunal is likely to look not only at the policy but also at what steps were taken to implement it. Training is a crucial part of implementation. It must be included as part of an organisation's overall policy with the focus on why the policy is important and how it should be implemented in practice. It should be carried out before the policy is publicised to ensure that procedures are in place before for any complaints are brought.

> *Example*   A tribunal upheld a claim of racial harassment brought by a black American warehouse assistant at Sainsbury's. The company had, the tribunal said:
>
> 'failed to take such steps as were reasonably practicable to prevent the harassment taking place. There was no evidence of formal training in equal opportunities. Apart from the issuing of documents which may or may not have been read, which, in our view, amounts to the most basic of training, nothing was done to ensure that the equal opportunity policy was in any way meaningful. The effect was that the management were just not trained to deal with the situation that arose, either speedily or effectively.'
>
> The tribunal awarded compensation of £17,000.
>
> *Wilson v Sainsbury's Plc*
> DCLD 25

The EC Code states:

> 'An important means of ensuring that sexual harassment does not occur and that, if it does occur the problem is resolved efficiently is through the provision of training for managers and supervisors. Such training should aim to identify the factors which contribute to a working environment free of sexual harassment and to familiarise participants with their responsibilities under the employer's policy and any problems they are likely to encounter.
>
>   In addition, those playing an official role in any formal complaints procedure in respect of sexual harassment should receive specialist training, such as that outlined above.
>
>   It is also good practice to include information as to the organisation's policy on sexual harassment and procedures for dealing with it as part of appropriate induction and training programmes.'

The CRE Code of Practice recommends in relation to its equal opportunities policy:

> 'providing training and guidance for supervisory staff and other relevant decision makers ... to ensure that they understand their position in law and under company policy.'

The method of training is, of course, down to the particular organisation and it is advisable to evaluate the training programme enabling action to be taken to improve the training if appropriate. Training is, however, vital to ensure both that the policy is communicated and that management is committed to creating and maintaining an environment free from harassment.

It is clear from the EC Code that there are three categories of people who should be trained:

(1) managers and supervisors;
(2) those with an official role in the complaints procedure; and

(3) the workforce generally.

(a) *Managers and supervisors*

Good training of managers and supervisors is crucial. It is essential that harassment is seen to be taken seriously from senior management level down. Managers must know what harassment consists of, how to recognise it and what to do about it if they see it happening or are told that it is happening. They must be fully familiar with the harassment policy and be aware of their duty to implement the policy and take corrective action to ensure compliance with it.

Managers and supervisors must:

- know the procedure for dealing with complaints of harassment;
- know what their responsibilities are;
- be aware that complaints must be dealt with promptly and confidentially;
- know who is responsible for other aspects of the harassment complaints procedure; and
- know how to train their team regarding the harassment policy.

(b) *Those with an official role in the complaints procedure*

This will include any confidential counsellors designated to provide advice and assistance to employees subjected to harassment, the officers allocated to carry out the investigation (the harassment investigators) and the human resources officers. Confidential counsellors must have relevant experience in listening to and discussing sensitive issues. They are there to offer emotional support and to discuss the options available to an employee who has suffered harassment. They must be able to maintain strict confidentiality. Specific training must be given to the confidential counsellors on:

- how to handle the initial complaint;
- who to report the complaint to;
- how to explain the harassment policy;
- providing general emotional support for those alleging harassment;
- how to support those accused of harassment; and
- how to assist proven harassers to stop harassing.

The officers allocated to carry out the investigation and the human resources officers will probably be senior personnel with some experience of handling grievances and disciplinary matters. They should have some specific training on how to handle the complaints brought to them. They should also be included in any training specifically related to the harassment policy so that they know exactly who is responsible for which areas of the policy and so that consistency of treatment of complaints is ensured.

(c) *The workforce generally*

All employees must receive awareness training in harassment issues so that everyone knows what constitutes impermissible behaviour and what the consequences of harassing a fellow employee will be. Training of the workforce could take the form of one-off events specifically for learning about the sexual harassment policy, or as part of a general training programme. It could be carried out by the managers or personnel officers who have already been trained or by trade union representatives familiar with the organisation's harassment policy. It should consist of the following:

- acknowledgment of senior management commitment to the policy;
- identifying the forms harassment may take;
- information on who to turn to if harassment occurs;
- reassurance that complaints will be dealt with promptly and fairly and that the importance of confidentiality will be stressed at all times;
- information regarding informal and formal routes and advice on which might be the appropriate route to take;
- clarifying each person's duty towards fellow employees;
- identifying the factors which create a good working environment;
- emphasising the duty to abide by the harassment policy; and clearly stating that failing to do so is a disciplinary offence and may result in dismissal.

10.6.4 Monitoring

The implementation of a new policy or extending the scope of an existing one is bound to be met with some resistance. There will inevitably be teething problems with the implementation of procedures and these may need to be altered accordingly.

The EC Code states:

> 'It is good practice for employers to monitor and review complaints of sexual harassment and how they have been resolved, in order to ensure that their procedures are working effectively.'

In order to monitor a policy effectively, one person should be allocated overall responsibility for the policy. Preferably this will be a member of senior management, perhaps in conjunction with human resources officers. A review date should be decided on and this may be included within the policy itself. A record of all complaints, whether informal or formal, and how they are resolved, should be kept in one place. This information should be used to evaluate the policy and procedures at regular intervals, perhaps in conjunction with trade union representatives if they were involved in the implementation of the policy. Any work areas with a higher than average number of complaints should be identified and appropriate remedial action taken. A central record system and overall responsibility by one person should ensure consistency and proper operation of the policy. Action can then be taken to amend the policy and procedure and deal with any other specific issues, such as continuing training needs in particular areas.

Many cases brought before the employment tribunal are there because employers have ignored or flouted their own policies. It is not sufficient to have a policy if the results of investigations are ignored and no attempts are made to remedy problems. Employers should be able to say how many complaints of harassment have been made in a year, how many were resolved informally (if records of informal complaints are kept), how many were investigated formally, how long each investigation took and the outcome of the investigations. This information should be used to evaluate the policy and procedures at regular intervals, with changes recommended when procedures are shown to be inadequate.

There is a fear among employers that a harassment policy will encourage large numbers of complaints. A channel through which to air genuine complaints of harassment should exist in all organisations and an increase in justified complaints will show that the policy is working successfully. Genuine complaints which do not in fact involve harassment might mistakenly be brought under the harassment policy and these should be re-directed to the normal grievance procedure.

The implementation of a harassment policy might affect existing disciplinary procedures. At the least, the disciplinary procedure should be amended to refer to the harassment policy. For example:

'Anyone found to be in contravention of the Company's Harassment Policy will be subject to the disciplinary procedure. Depending on the nature of the case, harassment may amount to misconduct or gross misconduct and the full range of disciplinary sanctions is available from warning to dismissal. The Company also reserves the right to suspend or relocate anyone accused of harassment either during the investigation or after the investigation has been completed. Anyone found to have brought a claim maliciously will also be subject to the disciplinary procedure.'

DRAFT HARASSMENT QUESTIONNAIRE

Harassment at work can be defined as conduct which is unwanted and offensive which affects the dignity of an individual or group of individuals. It might be based on an individual's sex, sexual orientation, race, political or religious beliefs, age or disability or it might be based on a position of power or authority over an individual. It may take the form of verbal bullying, inappropriate physical contact, distasteful jokes or abusive comments, intimate questions about someone's personal life, exclusion from social events, assumptions based on stereotyping and unfair allocation of work.

Harassment may be intentional or unintentional, overt or covert, explicit or subtle. Whatever form it takes it can be psychologically damaging. Our aim is to eliminate harassment of any form in the workplace. To do this we need your views and experiences on any harassment you have come across at work, either directly or as an observer.

Please help us to help you by answering the following questions. Your replies will be treated as confidential and you will not be asked to provide your name.

Are you: ❑ Male ❑ Female

What is your job? (Give a description if your job title would identify you.)

In which department do you work?

Is harassment/bullying at work: (please tick one)

❑ A very serious problem?
❑ A serious problem?
❑ A minor problem?
❑ A non-existent problem?

Have you ever been harassed or bullied at this place of work? ❑ Yes ❑ No

❑ Are you currently being harassed or bullied? ❑ Yes ❑ No

❑ If yes, when did the harassment or bullying start?

What are the main sources of harassment or bullying? (tick those relevant)

❑ From your line managers
❑ From senior managers
❑ From colleagues
❑ From the public (clients/patients/customers)
❑ From visitors

❑ From contractors' staff
❑ Other (please specify)

What form does the hararssment/bullying take? (tick those relevant)

❑ Shouting
❑ Threats
❑ Intimidation
❑ Humiliation
❑ Excessive criticism
❑ Setting unrealistic targets or deadlines
❑ Unreasonably altering targets or deadlines
❑ Excessive work monitoring
❑ Taking away work or responsibilities
❑ Overruling your decisions
❑ Blocking your promotion
❑ Withholding information or equipment you need for your job
❑ Setting you up to fail in your job
❑ Keeping you out of things
❑ Victimising you
❑ Malicious lies or rumours
❑ Refusing reasonable requests, such as for leave
❑ Asking for sexual favours
❑ Inappropriate touching
❑ Leering
❑ Lewd remarks
❑ Abusive language or racist 'jokes'
❑ Racial name calling
❑ Ridicule of your or someone else's disability
❑ Other (please specify)

How often does the harassment/bullying happen? (please tick one)

❑ Daily
❑ Weekly
❑ Monthly
❑ Less than monthly
❑ Other (please specify)

Have you or other staff in your area had time off work because of harassment or bullying?   ❑ Yes   ❑ No

Have any staff in your area, to your knowledge, left their job because of harassment or bullying at work?   ❑ Yes   ❑ No

If yes, how many?

Do you think harassment or bullying is caused by: (tick those relevant)

- ❏ Excessive workloads
- ❏ Inadequate training for managers
- ❏ Inadequate training for staff
- ❏ Staff shortages
- ❏ Personality clashes
- ❏ Hostile working atmosphere
- ❏ Ignorance
- ❏ Other reasons (please specify)

Can you think of any measures which would reduce harassment or bullying? (Please continue on a separate sheet if necessary.)

Would it help to talk to someone informally about harassment or bullying?

❏ Yes   ❏ No

Would you like to have access to a counselling service?   ❏ Yes   ❏ No

Do you have any other comments or suggestions to make regarding harassment or bullying? (Please continue on a separate sheet if necessary.)

Thank you for completing this questionnaire. Please return it to:

DRAFT HARASSMENT POLICY

POLICY STATEMENT

The Company is committed to a working environment that offers equal treatment and equal opportunities for all its employees. It recognises that all employees have a right to be treated with dignity and respect in order to realise their potential and to achieve the Company's objectives. The Company recognises that any person could be affected by unfair treatment including harassment, bullying or victimisation and is committed to eliminating such behaviour.

The purpose of this policy is to give guidance on what is unacceptable behaviour and the procedures available for dealing with it.

DEFINITIONS

This policy is specifically aimed at sexual, racial and disability harassment and bullying, but also applies to all other forms of workplace harassment including harassment based on age, sexual orientation, political or religious beliefs. Wherever the term harassment is used in this policy, it can be taken to apply to any form of harassment and/or bullying and/or victimisation. Harassment may be intentional or unintentional, overt or covert, explicit or subtle. It is always damaging whether psychologically, personally or professionally. It is the impact on the recipient which determines whether behaviour constitutes harassment and not necessarily the intention of the harasser.

Perpetrators of harassment may be held personally liable for acts of harassment in the event of any legal proceedings. Harassment may also constitute a criminal offence, the penalty for which could be a fine or imprisonment.

Sexual harassment

This is defined as 'unwanted conduct of a sexual nature or conduct based on sex affecting the dignity of women or men at work'. The perception of what constitutes harassment may vary from person to person but consists of conduct of a sexual or sexist nature which is neither invited nor welcome and which causes offence. Such behaviour includes but is not limited to:

— suggestive comments or body language
— unwanted physical contact
— lewd jokes
— leering
— demands for sexual favours and threats of or actual denial of job opportunities if such demands are refused
— verbal threats
— display of pornographic or sexually suggestive pictures

—   offensive comments about appearance or dress.

Racial harassment

Racial harassment can take many forms which may involve hostile or offensive physical, verbal or non-verbal behaviour of a racist nature. Racial harassment includes but is not limited to:

—   abusive language and racist 'jokes'
—   racial name calling
—   display or circulation of racially offensive written or visual material including graffiti
—   physical threats, assault and insulting behaviour or gestures
—   open hostility
—   unfair allocation of work and responsibilities
—   exclusion from normal workplace conversation or social events.

Disability harassment

This consists of undignified treatment, ridicule or exclusion of people with disabilities including people with HIV/AIDS or people with a mental disability.

Bullying

Bullying is where an individual abuses a position of power or authority over another person. It can take many different forms. Bullying includes but is not limited to:

—   shouting at an individual to get things done
—   humiliating an individual in front of his or her colleagues
—   picking on one person when there is a common problem
—   conduct that denigrates, ridicules or humiliates an individual, especially in front of his or her colleagues
—   conduct which is intimidating, physically abusive or threatening
—   consistently undermining someone and his or her ability to do the job

Other forms of harassment

Harassment can take many forms and may be directed towards people because of their age, sexual orientation, transsexuality, political or religious beliefs or for some other reason. It is any behaviour which causes the recipient to feel threatened, humiliated, patronised or embarrassed and which creates an intimidating working environment.

Harassment will often involve repeated forms of unwanted behaviour but a single incident, if it is sufficiently serious, may constitute harassment.

Victimisation

This occurs when a person is treated less favourably because they have asserted their rights (or are believed to have done so) under this policy. This includes both those bringing claims under this policy and any others acting as witnesses in any investigation of a complaint. Employees will be protected from victimisation for bringing a complaint or assisting in an investigation.

DISCIPLINARY ACTION

Disciplinary action will be taken against any employee found to be in breach of this policy. Disciplinary action, which will be taken in accordance with the Company's disciplinary procedure, may include summary dismissal in the case of a serious breach of this policy or in the case of repeated breaches. An employee accused of harassment may be suspended or relocated during the course of an investigation into the matter. Breaches of this policy may also result in the employee responsible being held personally liable in an employment tribunal or other court if legal action is taken. In cases of serious harassment the employee responsible may be prosecuted in the criminal courts. Disciplinary action will also be taken against any employee who victimises or retaliates against an employee for bringing a claim of harassment in good faith, or against an employee who makes malicious or vexatious allegations of harassment.

RESPONSIBILITIES

All employees

All employees have a responsibility to help ensure a working environment in which the dignity of employees is respected. It is your duty:

- to comply with this policy and to ensure that you treat your colleagues with respect and dignity
- to challenge offensive behaviour, whether addressed at you or at a colleague and bring it to the attention of your supervisor/manager
- to support colleagues who suffer such treatment and are considering making a complaint.

Managers and supervisors

As well as your responsibilities as an individual employee, your specific responsibilities as a manager or supervisor are:

- to create a climate at work in which it is clear that harassment of any sort will not be tolerated
- to set a personal example
- to be familiar with the procedure for dealing with complaints
- to explain the Company's policy on harassment to staff for whom you are responsible
- to stress the importance of the policy and the possible consequences of any breach of the policy
- to offer guidance to employees who seek it regarding this policy and the procedure for bringing complaints
- to support and protect employees who bring a complaint of harassment
- to deal with any complaint quickly, sympathetically and confidentially
- to take corrective action if you witness acts of harassment
- to ensure that no employee is victimised for making a complaint of harassment.

PROCEDURE

If you think you are being harassed you are encouraged to do something about it. The purpose of these procedures is to stop any harassment that may be occurring and to produce quick and effective remedies without breaching confidentiality. You have the option of informal or formal action. The use of the informal procedure is encouraged in the first instance unless the harassment is very serious, or unless you wish to go directly to the formal procedure. At any stage of the procedure you may contact a confidential counsellor – see section on ADVICE AND ASSISTANCE. The Company undertakes to deal seriously with all allegations of harassment and to protect any victim of harassment from victimisation or retaliation for bringing a complaint of harassment.

Informal procedure

–   If possible you should attempt to resolve the problem informally; it may be the case that the harasser does not know what effect he or she is having on you.
–   Try speaking to the individual informing him or her that the behaviour in question is unwelcome, that it offends you or makes you feel uncomfortable, or that it interferes with your work, and that it must stop. Instead of speaking to the alleged harasser you may prefer to put this in writing.
–   If you feel unable to do this on your own you could ask a colleague, friend, confidential counsellor or trade union representative to speak or write to the alleged harasser on your behalf.
–   If the conduct continues, before taking action under the formal procedure, you could ask your supervisor/line manager or other senior manager within the department to speak to the harasser and ask him or her to stop.
–   If the conduct still continues you should keep a record of any relevant incidents including date, time, any witnesses present and the way in which the harassment affected you or your work. You should consider taking formal action.

Formal procedure

–   This procedure should be used if you have already approached the harasser and he or she has not stopped the harassment OR if you do not feel the informal procedure is appropriate.
–   You should raise the matter with your supervisor/line manager (or other senior manager if your supervisor/line manager is the alleged harasser). If you would prefer to raise the matter with a person of the same sex or ethnic group, you should speak to one of the confidential counsellors who will discuss with you who to take your complaint to in the first instance.
–   You will be asked to put your complaint in writing and your complaint will then be referred to the harassment investigator who must not have been involved in an advisory capacity.
–   You will receive written confirmation of receipt of your complaint within five working days of the complaint being filed.
–   The matter will be investigated by the harassment investigator in conjunction with a human resources officer as quickly as possible and, if possible, within 15 working days of the complaint being filed. This period may, if necessary, be extended by a further 15 working days.

- The alleged harasser may be relocated or suspended on full pay during the investigation.
- During the investigation the alleged harasser and any witnesses will be interviewed and asked to give statements.
- All investigations will be carried out sensitively and the importance of confidentiality will be stressed at all times.
- The harassment investigator and human resources officer will decide whether or not any further action is appropriate. If the investigation reveals that no further action is appropriate, both the complainant and the alleged harasser will be informed accordingly as soon as possible after completion of the investigation.
- If the investigation reveals that there is a case to be answered then the Company's normal disciplinary procedure will be invoked as soon as possible and both parties will be informed of this in writing. In accordance with the Company's normal disciplinary procedure, the alleged harasser will be told the precise nature of the complaint and will be given sufficient time to prepare his or her case.
- Any employee disciplined for an act of harassment will be subject to the Company's normal disciplinary procedure which may include relocation or dismissal.
- Any employee who victimises or retaliates against another employee for bringing a claim under this policy or for giving evidence in connection with a harassment investigation will also be subject to disciplinary action.
- Any employee found to have brought a claim of harassment maliciously and without foundation of truth will be disciplined.
- If you do not feel that your complaint has been taken seriously or properly investigated you may appeal to [*insert name*] in writing within 10 working days of the decision. Any appeal will be heard within 10 working days of being lodged.
- You should be aware that if you wish to bring a claim in the employment tribunal under the Sex Discrimination Act 1975, the Race Relations Act 1976 or the Disability Discrimination Act 1995 you should do so within three months less one day from the date of the act complained of.

Advice and assistance

- If you would like advice or assistance on harassment at any stage you should contact one of the designated confidential counsellors.
- The counsellor will listen to your query or complaint, support you in any way they can and maintain complete confidence.
- The counsellor will advise you whether informal or formal action is appropriate and will assist you with any action you decide to take, including speaking to the alleged harasser or helping with a written report of the alleged incident(s) of harassment.
- The counsellor will not have a role in the investigation of your complaint nor will anything you say in confidence to the counsellor be used in evidence.
- You may wish to speak to a counsellor of the same sex or same ethnic origin as you.
- A list of counsellors can be found on each staff notice board.

Chapter 11

PROCEDURE FOR DEALING WITH ALLEGATIONS OF HARASSMENT

Why is procedure so important? – Why have a specific harassment procedure? – Setting up the procedure – How to handle allegations – Investigation checklist

This chapter will consider why procedures are important, why it is preferable that a harassment policy should have its own grievance procedure, how to carry out an investigation once an allegation of harassment has been made and what to take into consideration when reaching a decision.

11.1 WHY IS PROCEDURE SO IMPORTANT?

Good internal procedures for dealing with a claim of harassment are vitally important as, without them, an employer will not be seen to have taken reasonably practicable steps to prevent harassment occurring and may therefore render itself liable in a discrimination claim. An illustration of the importance of adequate procedures for dealing with allegations is the EAT case of *Armitage, Marsden and HM Prison Service v Johnson* (below).

> *Example* Mr Johnson, of Afro-Caribbean origin, was employed as an auxiliary prison officer at Brixton Prison. From mid-1991 he was ostracised and subjected to racist remarks by fellow prison officers after he objected to the manhandling of a black prisoner by other prison officers. He brought a discrimination claim and was awarded £28,500 compensation. £7,500 of this was for aggravated damages on the grounds that whenever Mr Johnson tried to complain his complaints were dismissed and put down to defects in his personality. The EAT said:
>
> 'The employers' investigation of the complaints of race discrimination, instead of providing the applicant with a remedy for the wrongs which he had suffered, added to his injury.'
>
> *Armitage, Marsden and HM Prison Service v Johnson*
> [1997] IRLR 162

> *Example* Miss Mullan was employed as a regional fraud investigator in London. She claimed that a male colleague had grabbed her and held her in the air upside down by her ankles while he had simulated oral sex. He had then swung her round and dumped her on the floor. A few days later Miss Mullan handed a detailed report of the incident to her line manager and to the police. The employer did not institute a formal investigation of the complaint but moved the man to another office in London. Miss Mullan later informed the personnel manager that she had agreed with the police to

accept a caution for the man but said that she could no longer work with him. However, the following month, he returned to work in the same building, causing her great distress when they met.

Miss Mullan claimed sex discrimination and the tribunal upheld her claim. The tribunal was amazed at the way the matter had been handled. The Respondent had failed to suspend the man pending inquiries and there had been a delay in dealing with the case after the police involvement was over. The man had been returned to the same building and Miss Mullan was requested to state whether she wanted an inquiry to be held. Then there was a delay in the department obtaining a report from her doctor. Miss Mullan had never been officially told of the result of her complaint and her line manager had expressed regret publicly at the man's transfer.

The tribunal found that Miss Mullan had suffered a severe detriment from the respondent's conduct in the form of anxiety and fear from his non-suspension and return to the workplace, distress caused by the four months' delay and ultimately his non-dismissal.

Mullan v Department of Employment
[1991] IT, Case No 20113
(taken from the EOC Manual 'Towards Equality')

The case of *Insitu Cleaning Co Ltd and Another v Heads* (below) went as far as recommending a separate procedure to deal exclusively with harassment claims. The tribunal recommended an informal first step to enable complaints to be dealt with swiftly before matters got out of hand.

Example Mrs Heads worked as an area supervisor for a contract cleaning firm. One of the firm's managers was the son of two of the firm's directors. He was around half of Mrs Heads' age. On entering a meeting he greeted her with the remark 'Hiya, big tits'. When she complained about this the company invited her to use the normal grievance procedure. She was reluctant to do this and resigned claiming unfair constructive dismissal and sex discrimination. The EAT upheld an industrial tribunal's finding of sex discrimination but dismissed the constructive dismissal claim. Their view was that although the company's existing grievance procedure may not have been the most appropriate way of dealing with a complaint, asking her to use that procedure did not give rise to a constructive dismissal. In the course of their decision the EAT recommended the adoption of a separate harassment procedure to prevent a recurrence of this type of incident.

Insitu Cleaning Co Ltd v Heads
[1995] IRLR 4, EAT

Constructive dismissal claims have, however, been upheld by tribunals because of the lack of adequate internal procedures for dealing with claims of harassment.

Example Ms Powell, who was black, was employed as a head chef at a Nottingham Pizzaland. An assistant manager from another Pizzaland visited Ms Powell at her place of work and asked her who she was working with that day. Ms Powell told him and the assistant manager commented 'There's three niggers working together'. Ms Powell complained on a number of occasions to her manager who took no steps to investigate the complaint. She began to suffer from depression and eventually went off sick.

While on sick leave she made an official complaint to her area manager under the company's grievance procedure. An investigation took place but no formal disciplinary action was taken. The employers refused to give Ms Powell details of the investigation and told her that if she wanted an apology she would have to ask the assistant manager for one herself. Ms Powell resigned and claimed race discrimination and constructive dismissal. She was successful on both counts. The tribunal found that the company's failure to investigate Ms Powell's complaint properly and to tell her what measures had been taken amounted to a fundamental breach of mutual trust and confidence entitling her to resign and claim constructive dismissal.

Powell v Pizzaland International
COIT 2913/29P

What about the rights of the alleged harasser? An employer must also try to avoid unfair dismissal or discrimination claims from employees who have been accused of harassment.

Example Mr Breeze was accused of sexual harassment by two colleagues and was told that he would be subject to the company's disciplinary procedure. He was not given details of the allegations against him prior to the disciplinary hearing nor was he shown copies of the witness statements. The person conducting the hearing had not spoken to the complainants and could not make any judgement on the credibility of their allegations. During the hearing it emerged that Mr Breeze had had a close personal relationship with the first complainant and had recently broken off a relationship with the second complainant's harassment counsellor. The tribunal took the view that this information warranted further investigation and held that the dismissal was unfair as the employer had failed to conduct a reasonable investigation and follow a fair procedure. The tribunal stated:

'While sexual harassment is a serious form of misconduct which must be tackled in the workplace, the rights of potential victims of harassment to a harassment-free working environment must be weighed equally with the rights of alleged harassers to a proper investigation and a fair hearing.'

Breeze v British Railways Board
COIT 2903/206

Example A male firefighter was accused of sexual harassment by a female colleague. He was suspended from duty pending investigation and asked to attend a disciplinary interview. The union initially told Mr Fraser that they would advise and represent him but then informed him that they would support the female firefighter instead. At the disciplinary hearing, seven of the nine allegations against Mr Fraser were dismissed and no action was taken in respect of the other two. The female colleague then withdrew the complaint she had lodged with an industrial tribunal.

Following the withdrawal of the complaint, Mr Fraser applied to the union for assistance with his legal fees, which was refused. He complained to an industrial tribunal that, in refusing to represent him or give him legal assistance, the union had unlawfully discriminated against him on the grounds of his sex. The tribunal inferred that a female in Mr Fraser's position would have received representation and would therefore have been treated more favourably. The tribunal found that Mr Fraser had been unlawfully discriminated against. The union appealed to the EAT, which upheld the finding of the industrial tribunal.

Fire Brigades Union v Fraser
[1997] IRLR 668

This case was subsequently overturned by the Court of Session in Scotland which ruled that Mr Fraser's treatment did not amount to sex discrimination as he was not refused union assistance because he was a man but because he was the alleged harasser. The decision to assist the alleged victim rather than the alleged harasser did not amount to discrimination on the basis of sex as any woman accused of harassment would, equally, not have been represented by the union. It might have been open to Mr Fraser to argue that this amounted to indirect sex discrimination as the union's rule disproportionately affected men, but this was not pleaded. Although now overturned, this case still demonstrates the fact that the alleged harasser also has rights.

We have already seen in Chapter 8 that an employer is under a duty to provide a safe system of work. In *Walker v Northumberland County Council*[1] an employer was held liable for its employee's second nervous breakdown as it had failed in its duty to provide a safe system of work. Being subjected to sexual harassment without adequate procedures in place to complain about such harassment could well constitute a breach of the employer's duty to provide a safe system of work and render the employer guilty of breach of contract. In addition, it is difficult for anyone who feels under pressure from harassment to function effectively at work. Such pressure may result in loss of concentration which could result in mistakes being made and possibly accidents and injuries occurring.

The cases outlined above illustrate that the lack of adequate procedures to deal with allegations of harassment could render the employer liable under anti-discrimination legislation for acts of harassment against its employees. Without adequate procedures, employers might be liable not only for discrimination claims but also for constructive dismissal claims and, without adequate disciplinary procedures, for unfair dismissal claims.

In addition to employer's liability illustrated by the above cases, the provision of effective procedures for complaints to challenge harassment is a critical factor in eliminating it. This is made clear in the EC Code of Practice on the *Protection of the Dignity of Women and Men at Work* ('the EC Code'). This states:

> 'The development of clear and precise procedures to deal with sexual harassment once it has occurred is of great importance. The procedures should ensure the resolution of problems in an efficient and effective manner. Practical guidance for employees on how to deal with sexual harassment when it occurs and with its aftermath will make it more likely that it will be dealt with at an early stage.'

The importance of good procedures is also emphasised:

> 'In addition it is recommended that the [policy] statement explains the procedure which should be followed by employees subjected to sexual harassment at work in order to obtain assistance and to whom they should complain; that it contains an undertaking that allegations of sexual harassment will be dealt with seriously,

---

1   [1995] IRLR 35.

expeditiously and confidentially, and that employees will be protected against victimisation or retaliation for bringing a complaint of sexual harassment.'

Thus the EC Code clearly views procedure as central to the prevention of sexual harassment in the workplace and not simply as a way of dealing with allegations once harassment has happened. Although the EC Code refers specifically to sexual harassment, it is equally applicable to all other forms of harassment. Knowing that there is a sympathetic and confidential procedure that will be followed in instances of harassment of any kind is more likely to encourage someone to bring a claim internally than to air their grievance by taking it directly to an industrial tribunal. The EC Code also recognises that there is a reluctance to complain about harassment:

> 'An absence of complaints about sexual harassment in a particular organisation . . . does not necessarily mean an absence of sexual harassment. It may mean that the recipients of sexual harassment think there is no point in complaining because nothing will be done about it, or because it will be trivialised or the complainant subjected to ridicule, or because they fear reprisals. Implementing the preventative and procedural recommendations outlined below should facilitate the creation of a climate at work in which such concerns have no place.'

A reluctance to complain about any form of harassment will 'sweep the problem under the carpet' which could continue until a serious incident occurs, a claim is brought in the employment tribunal and the organisation receives a lot of adverse publicity. It is far better to deal with the problem in confidence at an early stage than to let it erupt in public.

11.2 WHY HAVE A SPECIFIC HARASSMENT PROCEDURE?

In the section headed 'Procedure' the EC Code gives practical guidance on how to deal with harassment when it occurs. It recommends informal and formal methods of resolving a harassment problem, the provision of advice and assistance for employees who have been harassed, how to investigate complaints and suitable disciplinary sanctions for violating the policy including suspension and dismissal. Most organisations will already have a grievance procedure which employees can turn to if they wish to bring a complaint about some aspect of their work. This is probably fairly simple and will almost certainly not take account of any of the recommendations made by case-law or in the EC Code.

A grievance procedure relating to sexual harassment (and, by extension, all forms of harassment) should, according to the EC Code, include the possibility of an informal approach to the alleged harasser. It should also clearly state how and to whom a complaint should be filed if the person to whom an incident should be reported in the first instance is the alleged harasser. Ideally, it should allow for a sexual harassment claim to be taken in the first instance to someone of the same sex or a racial harassment claim to be taken to someone of the same ethnic origin. It should, if resources allow, include provisions for confidential counsellors and should explain what is expected of both the complainant and the alleged harasser while the procedure is in operation.

It is therefore strongly recommended that a grievance procedure relating specifically to complaints of harassment be included in the harassment policy and followed by management when an allegation of harassment is made. There is no reason, however, why an organisation's existing grievance procedure should not form the formal stage of the procedure, provided the harassment procedure allows for an informal route in the first instance and explains the use of confidential counsellors.

11.3 SETTING UP THE PROCEDURE

11.3.1 Responsibilities

As part of the process of implementing the harassment policy, an organisation must decide who will be responsible for which aspects of the policy. The draft harassment policy uses the term 'harassment investigator'. Depending on the size and resources of the organisation, there may be more than one harassment investigator or a panel of harassment investigators. The person in charge of the investigation may not be called a harassment investigator – some policies refer simply to an 'appropriate officer'. As it is essential that consistency of treatment is maintained, the harassment investigators or panel members or other appropriate officers should meet regularly to discuss the ways in which claims are being handled and investigated and the disciplinary sanctions which are being imposed.

Whatever he, she or they are called, the harassment investigator or investigators will be responsible for investigating allegations of harassment and, possibly, also for disciplining the perpetrators of harassment. They must therefore be senior members of staff with appropriate experience of investigating and handling disciplinary matters. It may be the case that the harassment investigator's full time job will be to investigate claims of harassment and, possibly, also to formulate and monitor the harassment policy. However, that is clearly only possible in large organisations and it is quite acceptable to appoint harassment investigators who also have other duties. It is important that the harassment investigators know what their role is and that they are given adequate time to carry out their duties as a harassment investigator.

The draft harassment policy envisages that the harassment investigator will report the matter to a human resources officer who will assist with the investigation. Wherever possible human resources should be involved but, if this not possible, it is essential that whoever investigates the allegation of harassment has not been in any way involved in the incident and is in no way biased in favour of one or other party. The employee should have the confidence that the matter will be dealt with objectively and should be clear what steps to take if he or she thinks he or she is being harassed at work.

It may be appropriate to hand the actual disciplinary processes and decisions over to the managers who have a more direct responsibility for their staff, such as the harasser's line manager. Whatever the case, it is essential that the organisation's disciplinary procedure is followed and that the alleged harasser has a fair and unbiased hearing. If the act alleged is potentially a criminal offence the police should be contacted at the earliest possible stage. The reason for this is that the police will probably wish to carry out their own investigation and may not wish any other investigation to have taken place which may compromise theirs.

11.3.2 Advice and assistance

The availability and use of confidential counsellors will again depend on the size and resources of the organisation. The EC Code recommends the use of such counsellors to advise and assist in cases of alleged harassment but also recognises that not all organisations will have the resources to provide them. If there are to be confidential counsellors, volunteers should be sought from the workforce to carry out this role which will be carried out in tandem with their normal day-to-day activities. There should, if possible, be at least one woman, one man and at least one counsellor from an ethnic minority. Once they are appointed, appropriate training must be given and the identity of the counsellors must be publicised so that employees know who to turn to for advice and assistance.

Confidential counsellors must be allowed time to carry out their duties and a room must be available for their use, if possible with a telephone so that calls can be received in confidence. Confidential counsellors should be able to take calls or queries at any time but it is also recommended that they be available at a fixed time and location each week. For smaller organisations this may not be feasible and it should therefore be emphasised that confidential counsellors are available at any time.

Confidential counsellors are *confidential* and they should not therefore report incidents of harassment to management unless they have the permission of the person bringing the complaint. An employee must be able to speak to someone without fear of the complaint going any further. However it is sensible for the counsellor to keep a confidential note of the complaint as, if the matter does go to tribunal, this may be useful. In exceptional circumstances a counsellor should be able to report complaints to management in general terms without disclosing the identity of the complainant. Such exceptional circumstances would include criminal acts such as rape or assault or any other act which puts employees in immediate danger.

Confidential counsellors should continue to provide support throughout the investigation and hearing of the matter and afterwards. If counsellors feel unable to deal with any particular issue which arises they should be able to seek the support of other counsellors or arrange for the harassed employee to see a professional counsellor or a medical specialist.

11.3.3 Time-limits

It is also important to consider the time-limits within which each stage of the procedure is to be completed. A point to bear in mind is that immediate action such as suspension or transfer may be required, or it may be necessary to send the harassed employee home for the rest of the working day. This is dealt with in more detail later on in this chapter. The draft harassment policy allows five working days following receipt of the written statement within which to acknowledge receipt of the complaint. It allows 15 working days (with the possibility to extend by another 15 working days) in which to carry out an investigation into the allegation of harassment. Depending on the resources of the organisation and the availability of human resources officers, it may be necessary to make this a longer period, for example 30 working days. The draft policy does not give a specific time within which the complainant and alleged harasser will be informed that no further action needs to be taken but simply states that it will be as soon as possible. If further action is to be taken and the disciplinary procedure invoked, then, again, this is to be done as soon as possible. The time-limit given for appeals against the finding of the investigation is 10 working days (not to be confused with an appeal against a disciplinary sanction imposed which will be contained within the organisation's disciplinary procedure), with the appeal to be heard within 10 working days of being lodged. All of these time-limits are suggestions only and it is up to individual organisations to decide what is right for them. The procedure should be efficient and effective and should not take longer than is necessary.

It should be noted that, overall, the procedure should take less than the three-month time-limit imposed by the employment tribunal. If the internal procedure takes more than three months, individuals wishing to bring a claim in the employment tribunal will need to file their case before internal procedures have been completed, resulting in some cases being taken unnecessarily to the employment tribunal. In the draft harassment policy, it is envisaged that the investigation will take 15 working days (with flexibility to extend by another 15 working days). Ten working days are allowed for an appeal to be lodged and a further 10 working days for the appeal to be heard. This makes 10 weeks (assuming that a 'working day' is Monday to Friday). However there may be some time between the latest incident of harassment and the complaint being brought or between the completion of the investigation and the resultant action being taken. It is therefore best to allow some leeway in the drafting but to keep strictly to the time-limits for the purposes of the procedure.

It should also be borne in mind, however, that a complaint of harassment to an employment tribunal often becomes inextricably linked with the way in which the complaint is handled internally. So, even if three months has passed since the original act of harassment complained of, a complainant may well still be able to bring a discrimination case in the employment tribunal because he or she feels that the discrimination has continued against them in one way or another. Note the case of *Usman v Watford Borough Council*[1] where a tribunal ruled that a local authority which took nine months to publish the findings of an investigation into allegations made by a Pakistani employee under its harassment policy unlawfully discriminated on grounds of race. In that case, Mr Usman made a formal complaint against his line manager consisiting of 27 separate allegations. The procedure stated that the 'investigatory panel should present their findings no later than 21 days after the initial complaint was received'. The decision was notified three months later and the reasons for the decision six months after that. The tribunal found that the delay in the investigation amounted to unlawful race discrimination and awarded Mr Usman £2,160 for injury to feelings.

11.4 HOW TO HANDLE ALLEGATIONS

11.4.1 Informal procedure

The EC Code recognises that 'most recipients of harassment simply want the harassment to stop'. It recommends that employees who are being harassed

---

1   IT, June 1996.

'should attempt to resolve the problem informally in the first instance'. It goes on to say:

> 'In some cases, it may be possible and sufficient for the employee to explain clearly to the person engaging in the unwanted conduct that the behaviour in question is not welcome, that it offends them or makes them uncomfortable, and that it interferes with their work.'

For example, if you worked for a supervisor who kept barking orders at you in front of your colleagues, it might be enough to say: 'I would appreciate it if you didn't speak to me like that, especially in front of my colleagues. I find it intimidating and embarassing'. You would not want to make a formal allegation of bullying and you would not want this to be investigated. You would probably not want to report it and you would probably not feel the need to talk to a confidential counsellor about it. You just want the behaviour to stop and feel that you are quite capable of achieving this on your own.

The EC Code recognises that in some circumstances an employee might need support or assistance to resolve a problem informally:

> 'In circumstances where it is too difficult or embarassing for an individual to do this on their own behalf, an alternative approach would be to seek support from, or for an initial approach to be made by, a sympathetic friend or confidential counsellor.'

For example, a female employee is being harassed by her line manager and has been wondering for some time what she can do about it. She reads the harassment policy which has recently been circulated and sees that there is an informal procedure available which would avoid a big fuss being made but which might resolve the problems she is currently experiencing. Because her line manager is her boss, however, she does not feel that she can talk to him directly about it and, even if she did, she does not think he would take any notice. So she decides to take the next appropriate step described in the harassment policy. She therefore looks on the staff notice board and sees that there are three confidential counsellors, one of whom is a woman. She telephones the counsellor and makes an appointment to see her the next day.

She describes to the counsellor what her line manager has been saying to her and the fact that he keeps putting his arm around her waist. She tells the counsellor that this makes her feel very uncomfortable and that she cannot concentrate on her work for fear that he is going to creep up on her. The counsellor asks whether she has spoken to the line manager about his behaviour. She replies that she hasn't because she thinks he will just laugh at her. The counsellor asks whether she has spoken to anyone else about it. She says she hasn't as she doesn't think anyone else will understand. The counsellor asks whether it would be appropriate for her to speak to the line manager on her behalf to ask him to stop the offensive behaviour. The offer is accepted and the counsellor makes an appointment with the line manager to speak to him.

At the meeting the counsellor shows the line manager a copy of the harassment policy and asks him whether he has seen it. He says he has. She asks him whether he has read it. He says that he has read bits of it but not from cover to cover. The counsellor points to the section on sexual harassment and explains that one of his female members of staff has complained about his behaviour. He becomes defensive and explains that it was only meant to be a bit of fun. The counsellor points out that the behaviour complained of, which is clearly of a sexual nature, is unwelcome and causes offence and that it therefore falls within the definition of sexual harassment. She points out that the company takes any form of harassment very seriously and that, if his offensive behaviour continues, he is likely to be disciplined for it. The line manager says he will apologise to the employee in question now that he realises his behaviour is offensive and will not behave in that way any longer.

The line manager apologises and the offensive behaviour stops. The counsellor speaks to the woman concerned and is reassured that the offensive behaviour has stopped. The counsellor points out that sometimes in this type of situation a person who has brought a claim of harassment is victimised by the harasser who wants to get his own back. The counsellor asks her to be aware of this possibility and to come back if she is treated less favourably by the line manager for no apparent reason as this may be due to the fact that she has complained about him. The counsellor speaks to the woman a month or so later and is again reassured that all is well. The matter is not reported to management but a written and confidential note is kept by the counsellor in a secure place.

Often a word at the right time will nip the problem in the bud and no further action is necessary. However, the EC Code recognises that an informal approach is not always appropriate:

> 'If the conduct continues or it is not appropriate to resolve the problem informally, it should be raised through the formal complaints procedure.'

11.4.2 Formal procedure

A formal complaints procedure should give employees confidence that the organisation will take any allegations of harassment seriously. The EC Code sets out some of the requirements of a formal complaints procedure in relation to complaints of sexual harassment, but these procedures can equally be used for complaints of any form of harassment:

> 'By its nature sexual harassment may make the normal channels of complaint difficult to use because of embarassment, fears of not being taken seriously, fears of damage to reputation, fears of reprisal or the prospect of damaging the working environment. Therefore, a formal procedure should specify to whom the employee should bring a complaint, and it should also provide an alternative if in the particular circumstances the normal grievance procedure may not be suitable, for example because the alleged harasser is the employee's line manager. It is also advisable to make provision for employees to bring a complaint in the first instance to someone of their own sex, should they so choose.'

It is also advisable that, if resources permit, an employee alleging racial harassment should be able to bring the complaint in the first instance to someone of the same ethnic origin. Confidential counsellors should, if possible, be sought from ethnic minorities represented in the workforce.

The draft policy in Chapter 10 sets out the formal steps to be taken by an employee alleging harassment who has either tried the informal route and feels that this has not resolved the situation, or does not feel that the informal route would be appropriate in the circumstances. The following scenario is, infortunately, a realistic possibility in some workplaces.

A young black worker and a relative newcomer to the company is persistently called 'wog' and 'nigger' by his workmates. He is not invited to the pub at the end of the day and feels that he is always given the worst jobs to do. He remembers being given a copy of the company's harassment policy during his induction course and being told that the company takes harassment very seriously. He finds the policy and is fairly sure that the behaviour towards him does consist of racial harassment. He can't face his workmates on his own as there are too many of them. He is unsure of his supervisor's role as the supervisor appears to do nothing to stop the harassment and he is convinced that the supervisor is allocating the worst jobs to him. He decides to seek the advice of a confidential counsellor.

He looks on the notice board and sees that there are six confidential counsellors. He does not know any of them as he is new to the company and does not want to ask any of his colleagues which one to approach. So he decides on a male name and eventually plucks up the courage to telephone him. A meeting is arranged and he tells the counsellor what has been happening. He also tells the counsellor that he thinks his supervisor has done nothing to prevent the harassment although he may not be actively joining in the harassment and always gives him the worst jobs to do. The counsellor listens and tells him that he is happy to help the employee with his problems. He also points out that there is a black harassment counsellor if the employee would prefer to speak to him about the matter. The employee says that he does not feel he needs a black counsellor as long as there is someone to help him. The counsellor offers to speak to the supervisor directly and the worker accepts his offer.

The counsellor makes an appointment to see the supervisor and explains the situation. He tells the supervisor that the employee in question is apparently being harassed by his fellow employees and describes the sort of behaviour he has been subjected to. The counsellor also mentions that the harassed employee believes he has been given the worst jobs to do and that the supervisor has done nothing to stop the harassment. The supervisor explains that it is generally the case that the newest and least experienced worker is given particular jobs to do, that this has been the case with all his members of staff and that it has nothing to do with his colour or ethnic origin. The supervisor says that he has not been aware of any harassment towards the black employee and that he would certainly have stopped it if he had noticed it. The counsellor takes the supervisor to the section in the harassment policy on racial harassment and points to the examples of racial harassment contained in the policy. He asks the supervisor to look out for behaviour which might constitute racial harassment.

The counsellor asks the supervisor to speak to the colleagues in question and tell them that their behaviour towards the newcomer is offensive and that it must stop. The supervisor says he will do this. He speaks to them individually and tells them that a complaint has been made against them about their behaviour. He describes in what way their behaviour is offensive to their fellow employee and asks them to stop. They say it was not intended as racist behaviour and that it was 'just a joke'. At the same time the counsellor speaks to the harassed employee and tells him that the supervisor is speaking to his colleagues and asking them to stop the offensive behaviour. The counsellor says that he hopes the offensive behaviour will now stop but that he must contact him again if it does not.

The harassed employee goes back to his work station and work resumes. His workmates stop calling him 'wog' and 'nigger' but do not answer him when he tries to speak to them. At the end of the week they go out to the pub together but do not invite him and do not tell him where they are going. The next week he finds that his tools have disappeared and, at lunchtime, that there is machine oil in his lunch box. His workmates are angry that he raised a complaint against them and this is their way of retaliating. The supervisor either does not know this is going on or does nothing to prevent it happening.

The harassed employee contacts the counsellor again and tells him what is going on. He says that this is causing him a lot of distress. They meet that day and the harassed employee decides, having talked it through with the counsellor, to make a formal complaint against his colleagues. Together they draft a statement describing what has been happening and the effect this has had on the employee's health. The complainant signs the statement and gives the counsellor permission to speak to the harassment investigator. The counsellor informs the complainant that he should receive confirmation of receipt of his complaint within five days. He also informs him that the matter will be dealt with in confidence as far as possible.

The counsellor then takes the statement to the harassment investigator and hands the matter over to him or her. He has nothing more to do with it other than to support the harassed employee in any way possible. The counsellor is not involved in the investigation.

11.4.3 Investigating complaints

The draft policy in Chapter 10 sets out in the section headed 'Formal Procedure' what steps the harassed employee should take and what the complainant and the alleged harasser should expect in terms of procedure and timescale. How is the allegation actually investigated by management and what factors should be taken into account? Some organisations have an 'Investigators' Guide' which accompanies the harassment policy and which informs the investigators how to handle complaints of harassment and what factors to take into account during the investigation. Included in this chapter is an Investigation Checklist which should serve as an aide memoire during an investigation.

The EC Code says in its section headed 'Investigations':

> 'The investigation should focus on the facts of the complaint and it is advisable for the employer to keep a complete record of all meetings and investigations.'

Although this appears at the end of the section on Investigations, it is really the starting point and should be borne in mind at every stage of the investigation. The only conduct which is relevant to the investigation is conduct relating to the relationship between the complainant and the alleged harasser. An inquiry into a complainant's relations with other workers or their private life is rarely relevant and may deter others from bringing claims. This is perhaps particularly relevant to sexual harassment claims (where it might be tempting to listen to gossip about someone's sex life) but also important to remember when investigating allegations of any form of harassment.

On the subject of sex, the EC Code also states:

> 'It must be recognised that recounting the experience of sexual harassment is difficult and can damage the employee's dignity. Therefore, a complainant should not be required to repeatedly recount the events complained of where this is unnecessary.'

This is particularly true of allegations of sexual harassment as opposed to any other form of harassment. It can be very distressing to recount the details of a sexual incident (especially a serious sexual incident) and victims of sexual harassment should not be made to do this more often than is absolutely essential. Victims of other forms of harassment, such as racial harassment or bullying, might also become distressed at having to recall and recount the incident. A statement should therefore be written down and signed by the victim as soon as possible to avoid unnecessary repetition.

The rest of the Investigations section could refer equally to any form of harassment:

> 'It is important to ensure that internal investigations of any complaints are handled with sensitivity and with due respect for the rights of both the complainant and the alleged harasser. The investigation should be seen to be independent and objective. Those carrying out the investigation should not be connected with the allegation in any way, and every effort should be made to resolve complaints speedily – grievances should be handled promptly and the procedure should set a time limit within which complaints will be processed, with due regard for any time limits set by national legislation for initiating a complaint through the legal system.
>
> It is recommended as good practice that both the complainant and the alleged harasser have the right to be accompanied and/or represented, perhaps by a representative of their trade union or a friend or colleague; that the alleged harasser be given full details of the nature of the complaint and the opportunity to respond; and that strict confidentiality be maintained throughout any investigation into an allegation. Where it is necessary to interview witnesses, the importance of confidentiality should be emphasized.'

The investigator should strongly encourage the complainant to make a written statement detailing the incident or incidents. A written statement serves many purposes: it clarifies the complainant's mind, it avoids the complainant having to recount the experience verbally time after time and it will be useful if the case goes to tribunal in showing that the organisation adopted and followed procedures. The reluctance of an employee to make a written statement should not, however, prevent the procedure continuing. If necessary, the interviewer should be willing to help the complainant with the drafting of a statement, which should be done as soon as possible – preferably immediately.

In order to find out what happened the interviewer may need to prompt the employee by asking questions. The interviewer should be careful not to play the incident down or trivialise the matter. There should be no suggestion that the harassed employee invited the harassment (eg by the clothes he or she was wearing) or that the harassed employee is being over-sensitive; it is the effect the harassment has on the individual and not the intention of the alleged harasser which is important. The questions, which should be asked sensitively and tactfully, should include the following, if the information has not already been given:

–   When did the incident happen, including date and time?
–   What did it consist of?
–   Where did it happen?
–   What effect did it have on you?
–   Were there any witnesses?
–   Has anything similar happened before, if so how often?
–   Have you spoken to anyone else about this?
–   Have you asked the harasser to stop?
–   Repeat the above questions for each alleged incident.

Detailed notes of the interview should be kept and the statement should be written up as soon as possible. Because of the issue of confidentiality it may be easiest for the complainant simply to write out the statement by hand (rather than arranging for it to be typed) and sign it then and there. If the initial interview is carried out by a confidential counsellor, the counsellor should establish whether the complainant wishes to make a formal complaint or whether he or she simply wishes to speak to someone in confidence. If the interviewer is not a confidential counsellor, it should be pointed out (if appropriate) that a confidential counselling service is available if the complainant would like to speak to someone in confidence about the matter.

The complainant should be told that the next step is for the interviewer to pass the matter on to the harassment investigator, who will investigate the matter with the assistance of the personnel department. The complainant should be told that receipt of the complaint will be confirmed in writing within five working days. The complainant should be told that although confidentiality will be stressed to anyone interviewed in the course of the proceedings, confidentiality cannot be guaranteed because of the importance of interviewing anyone involved in any way.

11.4.4 Handover to harassment investigator

Once the statement has been written and signed, the matter should be handed over to the harassment investigator (or investigators). The harassment investigator should not be connected with the allegation in any way. For example, if a woman complaining of sexual harassment is married to one of the harassment investigators that investigator should not have anything to do with the complaint. Or, if one of the harassment investigators is known to dislike either the complainant or the alleged harasser, that investigator should not be involved. If for any reason the harassment investigator allocated to the case feels unable to fulfil the role, he or she should state this clearly to enable another investigator to handle the matter. The investigation must be, and be seen to be, independent and objective.

The draft policy then provides for the harassment investigator to contact the relevant person in the personnel department. Together they should consider what immediate action must be taken.

Should the alleged harasser be relocated during the course of the investigation? The harassment counsellor and/or personnel officer may wish to speak to the initial interviewer to discuss what action is appropriate and feasible, especially if the initial interviewer was the complainant or harasser's line manager or supervisor. Advice can also be sought from the counsellor about the depth of feeling the harassment has provoked: is the individual likely to be able to cope with the present situation during the course of the investigation or should he or she and the alleged harasser be separated during the course of the investigation? If possible, consideration should be given to relocating the alleged harasser rather than the complainant; the complainant should not be penalised for bringing a complaint.

Should the alleged harasser be suspended during the course of the investigation? Suspension on full pay would be appropriate in allegations of serious harassment such as sexual assault or other physical violence. If a suspension is decided on, those concerned should be told clearly that they are suspended, that it will be for as short a period as possible and that they will be called back for interview.

The harassment investigator or personnel officer should write to the complainant as soon as possible acknowledging receipt of the complaint and informing the complainant what the next step in the procedure is, and when he or she can expect to hear from them again. For example:

Dear [ ],

We have received from your line manager/supervisor/other manager/confidential counsellor your statement dated [ ] alleging sexual/racial/other harassment/bullying. This matter will be investigated as quickly as possible. The investigation will involve interviewing the alleged harasser(s) and any witnesses to the harassment. A copy of your statement may be shown to them and statements may be taken from some or all of those interviewed. The importance of confidentiality will be stressed at all times and those interviewed will be told not to discuss the matter.

You are at liberty to contact one of the confidential counsellors at any time and you are strongly urged to do so if there is any repetition of the harassment or if you feel you are being victimised for bringing a claim.

We hope to complete the investigation within three weeks and will contact you at the end of this period.

Yours sincerely
[   ] Harassment Investigator
[   ] Personnel Officer
cc [   ] [initial Interviewer]

The letter should include any other relevant factors such as whether the alleged harasser has been or is to be suspended or relocated during the investigation. If there are many alleged harassers and it would not be feasible to relocate them or suspend them all, it might be appropriate to state this in the letter and ask the complainant whether he or she would like the option of being relocated or, possibly, sent home on full pay during the course of the investigation. If this step is to be taken, the agreement of the complainant should be sought. A copy of the letter should be sent to the initial interviewer.

11.4.5 Interviewing alleged harassers and witnesses

The harassment investigator and/or personnel should, as soon as possible, interview the alleged harasser or harassers. The alleged harasser(s) should be told exactly what the complaint against them is and should be shown the complainant's statement. It should be made clear to the alleged harasser that what is important is not his or her intention towards the complainant but the effect their behaviour has on the complainant. Alleged harassers should be given the opportunity to relate their own account of the incident or incidents. Notes should be taken throughout the interview. The investigators should be careful not to assume that the alleged harasser is guilty and questions should not be phrased in a way which implies guilt. The interviewers should not express their opinion on the matter and should not take any unrelated and irrelevant incidents into account.

Allegations of harassment will often provoke astonishment that the complainant was upset – 'It was only meant as a joke'. In this case, counselling should be offered to the alleged harassers as well as to complainants. A confidential counsellor should be able to explain the effect of such behaviour on other people and that the complainant has a right not to suffer from harassment of any sort and that the behaviour in question must stop.

Sometimes allegations of harassment will provoke a complete denial. If this is the case, it may be appropriate to undertake further investigation to establish whether the complainant was affected by the alleged harassment. Was performance at work affected? Was there a change in attitude? Was the complainant's relationship with the alleged harasser suddenly different?

Whatever the reaction of the alleged harasser, the interviewers must make it clear that a formal complaint has been made and that he or she is required to prepare and sign a written statement in response. He or she must be told that the matter will be fully investigated and that it may result in disciplinary action. Alleged harassers should also be warned that any victimisation or retaliation against the complainant or any other witness may in itself constitute an act of misconduct.

Note that the employment contract may give the alleged harasser the right to be accompanied at the investigatory interview. He or she should, in any event, have the right to be accompanied at any subsequent disciplinary hearing. It should be stressed that this is part of the investigation and does not form part of the disciplinary procedure. If, despite no provision being made for it in the contract, alleged harassers wish to have a representative or colleague with them at the investigatory interview, consideration should be given to this. The EC Code states in its section on Investigations:

> 'It is recommended as good practice that both the complainant and the alleged harasser have the right to be accompanied and/or represented'.

Any witnesses should also be interviewed and, if appropriate, statements taken. Investigators should be aware that it requires courage to act as a witness and that it may be difficult for the witness to recount what he or she has seen. Witnesses should be handled sensitively with an understanding of how upset or shocked they may be. Witnesses should be told the circumstances of the complaint and asked if they are willing to co-operate in the investigation. The witness should be asked to respect the confidentiality of the investigation, whether or not his or her evidence is used in the investigation. Management should consider whether a breach of confidentiality is a disciplinary offence and, if so, the witnesses should be told of this. A note of the meeting with each witness (either typed or hand-written) should be signed by the witness concerned as soon as possible.

11.4.6 Interviewing the complainant

The harassment investigator and/or human resources officer will, by this stage, have interviewed the alleged harasser(s) and any witnesses. Although the initial interviewer will have spoken to the complainant, the investigators may not yet have done so. The purpose of interviewing the complainant is to discuss the alleged harasser's defence with the complainant and to help the investigators to reach a decision on whether to take the matter further. The investigators should meet with the complainant even if they are sure that the matter will necessarily lead to disciplinary action. They must, at the least, inform the complainant of this fact. It should be recognised that this may be a distressing experience for the complainant and the interview should be conducted with sensitivity. The complainant should be told that he or she may be accompanied by a confidential counsellor or colleague or friend.

At the interview the complainant should be introduced to the harassment investigator and the human resources officer (and anyone else present at the interview). The complainant should be told what the purpose of the interview is and should be told who has been interviewed so far and who has seen a copy of his or her statement. The complainant should be shown copies of the statements (if there are a number of statements it might be sensible to provide copies in advance of the meeting) and should be given the chance to comment on them. His or her view should be sought on the best way forward. Having seen the replies to the complainant's statement, does it seem to be just a misunderstanding which could be corrected by counselling the harasser? Does the complainant feel he or she will be able to work with the harasser now that the matter is out in the open? Would an apology be sufficient? Does the complainant feel that disciplinary action should be taken?

It may not be appropriate to ask all of the above questions; it may not be appropriate to ask any. However it is recommended that the investigators meet the complainant and talk about the allegation. It may transpire that a disciplinary hearing is necessary in order to establish whether the alleged harasser is, on a balance of probabilities, guilty of harassment. It may become apparent during the course of the interview that the complainant brought the complaint maliciously, in which case the complainant should be dealt with under the disciplinary procedure. This may require further investigaton.

11.4.7 Reaching a decision

The decision to be reached is whether there is a disciplinary decision to be answered. The harassment investigator and the personnel officer must try to decide whether harassment may have occurred and whether, therefore, a disciplinary hearing is necessary. To do this they must review all the evidence they have gathered during the course of the investigation. They must try to establish what was said or done by whom and whether that constituted harassment, bullying or victimisation as defined in the harassment policy. It may be that the version of events as told by the complainant is in direct contrast to the version of events as told by the alleged harasser. In this case the harassment investigator and personnel officer must decide which is the more credible version.

It may be that the alleged harasser has admitted that the reported incident took place, but denies that this constitutes harassment. In this case the harassment investigator and the personnel officer must reach a decision as to whether the action was capable of constituting harassment. The actual decision well be taken at any subsequent disciplinary hearing.

If it is concluded that there is insufficient evidence to suggest that harassment occurred, the complainant and alleged harasser(s) should be informed of this, and should be told how this decision was reached. They should also be reminded of their right of appeal if they do not feel that the matter has been properly dealt with. Consideration should be given to separating the complainant and the alleged harasser, even if a complaint of harassment is not upheld, rather than making them continue to work together against the wishes of either party. The complainant should be handled very sensitively and reasons for reaching the decision should be explained very carefully. It is best to try to enter into a dialogue with the complainant to help him or her to understand why the complaint was not upheld in order to avoid the complainant bringing a claim of discrimination because of the way the complaint was handled.

If it is concluded that harassment may have occurred, the parties should be told of this conclusion and that the alleged harasser(s) will be subject to a disciplinary hearing under the organisation's disciplinary procedure. The alleged harassers must be told of the time and place for such a hearing and that they are entitled to bring with them a representative, colleague or friend. They should also be offered counselling from a confidential counsellor.

Victims of harassment or bullying may be reluctant to face the alleged harasser as a witness against them at a disciplinary hearing. However, as part of the principle of natural justice, an accused employee should be allowed to cross-examine the evidence of those who make accusations against them. The complainant and witnesses should, therefore, be asked to attend the disciplinary hearing unless they are genuinely in fear of giving evidence in person at the hearing. If so, the following procedure should be adopted:

- The witness must prepare and sign a witness statement.
- The statement should make reference to:
  - the date/time/place of the incident(s);
  - an explanation of the witness's opportunity and ability to observe the incident;
  - why the witness was present or has the knowledge that he or she has (eg why the events were memorable).
- The person taking the statement should ask whether the witness has any reason to lie (eg personal grudge).
- Tactful inquiries into the character of the witness should be made.
- The person conducting the disciplinary hearing should interview the witness personally.
- If the employee wants to cross-examine the witness evidence, the disciplinary hearing should be adjourned and the questions put to the witness personally. Full notes should be taken.

If the outcome of the disciplinary hearing is that harassment probably did occur, the appropriate sanction should be imposed. If the harasser is not dismissed, consideration should be given to relocating him or her. The EC Code says:

> 'Where a complaint is upheld and it is determined that it is necessary to relocate or transfer one party, consideration should be given, wherever practicable, to allowing the complainant to choose whether he or she wishes to remain in their post or be transferred to another location. No element of penalty should be seen to attach to a complainant whose complaint is upheld'.

The wishes of the complainant should be taken into consideration and it may be more appropriate to transfer the complainant than the harasser.

The EC Code also says:

'where a complaint is upheld, the employer should monitor the situation to ensure that the harassment has stopped.'

The monitoring should also ensure that the complainant has not been victimised for bringing a claim. To do this, informal contact should be maintained with the complainant either by a personnel officer or by a confidential counsellor. If the complainant is suffering from victimisation, immediate action should be taken against the perpetrators. If the complainant is suffering from stress and anxiety, further counselling should take place and management should investigate and try to find a solution.

The incident and outcome of any harassment investigation should be recorded centrally and that central record should itself be monitored at regular intervals. Any departments with a higher than average number of incidents of harassment should be carefully looked at and appropriate remedial action taken.

11.4.8 Third-party harassment

Chapter 8 shows how an employer owes a duty of care towards its employees against acts of third parties. In the case of *Burton and Rhule v De Vere Hotels*[1] two waitresses of Caribbean origin were subjected to racially and sexually offensive remarks by the entertainer Bernard Manning and guests at a private hotel while they were clearing the tables after dinner. The EAT decided that the employers were liable for racial harassment of their employees by a third party. Similarly, in the case of *Go Kidz Go v Bourdouane*,[2] the company was held liable for sexual harassment carried out by a third party. In that case, Ms Bourdouane was employed by Go Kidz Go, a company which provided children's parties. Whilst hosting a party for a group of children, Ms Bourdouane was sexually harassed by a parent. She complained to her manager but was told to return to the party, where she was again sexually harassed by the same parent.

What should the employers have done to avoid liability for the actions of these third parties? Clearly following the procedure set out above would not have been appropriate; they could not have disciplined Bernard Manning or the parent at the party as neither of them were employees. Instead, they should have stepped in at the time the incident took place or was reported. When the party hostess at Go Kidz Go came to her manager during the party to complain about the parent, the manager should have gone to the party himself either instead of the female employee or with the female employee in order to monitor the situation and, if necessary, to speak to the parent concerned.

In the De Vere Hotels situation, someone in a position of authority should have been sensitive enough to appreciate the embarassing situation which the two waitresses had been placed in. The waitresses could then have been relieved of their duties of clearing the tables and either transferred to another job in a different room (for example the kitchen) or sent home on full pay. As a general rule, it would be wise to consider beforehand whether an entertainer who may include offensive material in his act is suitable for corporate entertaining.

It is easy to be wise after the event and say what should have happened. It is far more difficult in the heat of the moment to know how to deal with any given situation. However, if an allegation of harassment is brought against a third party,

---

1   [1996] IRLR 596, EAT.
2   (1996) IDS 578, EAT.

action should be taken immediately to separate the complainant and alleged harasser so that the harassment cannot continue. It may then be appropriate to carry out an investigation and possibly report the matter to the police, depending on how serious the incident is. It may be the case that an apology from the alleged harasser is enough. Whatever the appropriate solution, it is essential that the matter is taken seriously and dealt with swiftly and sensitively.

INVESTIGATION CHECKLIST

INVESTIGATING COMPLAINTS

- Focus on the facts of the complaint.
- Keep a written record of all meetings.
- Conduct interviews in a sensitive manner.
- Don't make the complainant recount the experience more often than is necessary.
- Obtain a written statement from the complainant.
- Be ready to ask relevant questions.
- If appropriate, offer counselling to the complainant.
- Stress the importance of confidentiality at all times.

HANDOVER TO HARASSMENT INVESTIGATOR

- Consider whether to relocate or suspend alleged harassers.
- Acknowledge receipt of complaint whithin five days (or other time-limit specified in the harassment policy).
- Copy receipt of complaint to confidential counsellor if appropriate.

INTERVIEWING ALLEGED HARASSERS AND WITNESSES

- Tell the alleged harassers what the complaint against them is.
- Show them the complainant's statement.
- Stress the fact that it is not the intention behind their actions which is important but the effect it has on the complainant.
- Allow them to relate their account of the incident.
- Take notes throughout the interview.
- Do not ask questions which imply guilt.
- Treat alleged harassers and potential witnesses with sensitivity.
- Offer confidential counselling.
- Consider whether any further investigation is necessary.

INTERVIEWING THE COMPLAINANT

- Explain that the purpose of interviewing the complainant is to help him or her to decide whether or not to take the matter further OR to inform the complainant that the matter will be taken further.

- Tell the complainant who has been interviewed so far and who has seen a copy of his or her statement.
- Show the complainant the statements of the alleged harassers and witnesses (if any).
- Ask for his or her views on the statements and discuss the allegation generally.

REACHING A DECISION

- Review all the evidence.
- Decide whether, on a balance of probabilities, harassment occurred.
- If conclusion is that no harassment occurred, inform the parties of this and the reasons for the decision and remind them of their right to appeal.
- Consider separating the complainant and the alleged harasser(s).
- If conclusion is that harassment probably did occur, write to parties informing them of this and asking the alleged harasser(s) to attend a disciplinary hearing.
- Consider relocation or suspension of the alleged harasser(s).
- Consider whether police should be informed.

Chapter 12

WHICH COURT?

The court system – Civil proceedings – Employment tribunal – County court/High Court – Criminal courts

12.1 THE COURT SYSTEM

The legal system in England and Wales has a separate civil and criminal court system, although this distinction is very general because the magistrates' court, which is essentially a division of the criminal court, does in fact deal with some civil issues. The courts available in each system (other than appeals courts, which are examined in Chapter 14) are as follows:

Civil	*Criminal*
Employment tribunal (formerly industrial tribunal)	Magistrates' court
County Court	Crown Court
High Court	

It should be noted that from 1 August 1998, 'industrial tribunals' were renamed 'employment tribunals' by the Employment Rights (Dispute Resolution) Act 1998.[1] Although the new term is generally used in this book, where a case was brought before August 1998 the reference to 'industrial tribunal' is retained.

Harassment at work may take the form of sex or race discrimination under the SDA 1975 or the RRA 1976 (see Chapters 2 and 3). It may take the form of harassment based on a person's disability and will therefore be unlawful under the DDA 1995 (see Chapter 4). Any harassment claims under these Acts can be brought in the employment tribunal. Harassment may take the form of bullying (see Chapter 5) which may result in a fundamental breach of the employment contract entitling the employee to resign and claim constructive dismissal. A constructive dismissal claim will be brought in the employment tribunal. Bullying may result in physical or psychological injury, entitling the victim to bring a personal injury claim in the county court or High Court (see Chapter 7).

Harassment may amount to a criminal offence (see Chapter 8), and in these circumstances it should be reported to the police. The police will investigate the matter and decide whether to hand it over to the Crown Prosecution Service (CPS). The CPS will carry out its own investigation and make a decision as to whether to prosecute the offender. If the offender is prosecuted, the matter will commence in the magistrates' court and the magistrates will decide whether or not it should be committed to the Crown Court. The victim of the harassment

---

1 Employment Rights (Dispute Resolution) Act 1998 (Commencement No 1 and Transitional and Saving Provisions) Order 1998, SI 1998/1658.

will have no say in the decision on which criminal court the hearing will take place.

The harassment may amount to both a civil offence and a criminal offence. In this case the victim may be able to bring a civil complaint in addition to the prosecution of the harasser in the criminal court by the CPS. In some circumstances, it may be possible for the victim to bring a private prosecution against the harasser, but this is rare and is not within the scope of this book.

Having decided whether or not to report the matter to the police, the victim of harassment must then decide whether or not to pursue a civil remedy and, if so, which forum is best for the particular complaint.

12.2 CIVIL PROCEEDINGS

There are certain factors which inevitably will influence any individual who wishes to pursue a legal remedy, after having suffered harassment or bullying at work. The first consideration will be the nature of the harassment itself and whether it amounts to discrimination or personal injury, or whether it justifies resigning and claiming constructive dismissal. The second important consideration will be the costs involved in bringing the case.

12.2.1 Costs

In the county/High Court the general rule is that costs follow the event. In other words the loser usually pays his opponent's costs of the case as well as his own. In the employment tribunal, however, an order for one side to pay the other side's costs is rare; it is generally the case that each party pays only its own costs. The employment tribunal was designed to be user-friendly with less complex rules of evidence and procedure than the county/High Court. It is more readily accessible, without the need for legal representation, and thus cheaper.

There are exceptions to both rules, however. In the county court, matters worth less than £3,000 are generally referred to arbitration rather than a full trial. In this situation, each party will have to bear its own costs and the loser will not have to pay the winner's costs. There is also the mechanism known as 'payment into court' which puts a winning party at risk of paying the losing party's costs. This is where an offer to settle is made by the party defending the claim (the defendant) to the person bringing the claim (the plaintiff). If the offer is rejected, the amount offered may be paid into court and put on deposit awaiting the outcome of the trial. If the trial judge awards the same as or less than the amount paid into court, the plaintiff will be ordered to pay the defendant's costs from the date of the payment into court.

Having been awarded costs (either following a payment into court or otherwise), if the parties cannot agree the amount being paid, the bill will have to go to 'taxation'. This takes the form of a hearing before a taxing master who decides which items of the bill should be recoverable in full and which should be reduced or deleted. This procedure is itself costly in terms of the taxation fee and representation at the hearing.

In the employment tribunal costs are awarded to a successful party only if, in the opinion of the employment tribunal, the other party has acted 'frivolously, vexatiously, abusively, disruptively or otherwise unreasonably in bringing or conducting proceedings'. Costs may also be awarded in the employment tribunal if a hearing has to be postponed or adjourned through the fault of one of the parties.

12.2.2 Time-scales and time-limits

The employment tribunal is quick to hear cases; the aim is that all cases should be listed for hearing within three to six months of commencement. Whether this aim can be achieved in complex discrimination cases is sometimes doubtful. The time-scale is also dependent on the region in which the case is heard – some regions of the country are quicker at listing hearings than others.

An important factor to take into account before deciding which court to take a claim to is the question of time-limits, ie when a claim must be brought:

– for an unfair dismissal, constructive dismissal, or discrimination complaint, the time-limit is three months either from the act of discrimination or from the termination, dependent upon the basis of the complaint;[1]
– in employment tribunal breach of contract claims, the period is three months from the ending of the employment;
– for a breach of contract claim in the county court or High Court, the claim must be brought within six years from the date of the breach;
– in the case of a claim brought in tort or negligence (except for a personal injury claim) the time-limit is six years, for a personal injury claim the time-limit is three years.

In specific circumstances a court or tribunal can extend time to enable a party to proceed, despite the fact that the strict time-limits have passed. However, the ability to extend generally is at the discretion of the court or tribunal and should not be relied on. Parties are well advised to observe these time-scales strictly.

12.3 EMPLOYMENT TRIBUNAL

Case-law has shown that the usual forum for a harassment complaint will be the employment tribunal. We will therefore examine in some detail how a discrimination complaint will be brought and what an employer should do to defend it.

12.3.1 Discrimination

In the employment context, those protected by the discrimination legislation who can bring claims in an employment tribunal include:

– employees;
– workers (ie those carrying out work in a personal capacity); and
– applicants for employment.

The last category might seem unusual at first sight, but individuals who are refused employment or offered employment on less favourable terms due to their

---

1   Limitation Act 1980, Employment Rights Act 1996, Sex Discrimination Act 1975, Race Relations Act 1976, Disability Discrimination Act 1995 and Employment Tribunals Act 1996.

sex, race or disability have been discriminated against and can bring a complaint under the discrimination Acts. It is unlikely that harassment will have occurred; it is more likely that, for example, the employer wants to employ a man rather than a woman. But if, for example, a female applicant is not offered a job because she refuses a sexual proposition which is made to her during the interview, she can argue that due to the harassment based on her sex, she was discriminated against.

Any complaints of harassment based on sex, race or disability can be brought in an employment tribunal under the SDA 1975, RRA 1976 or DDA 1995.

A wide category of individuals are protected; it is not just employees who can claim discrimination but applicants for employment and those carrying out work in a personal capacity. Unlike the unfair constructive dismissal claims, individuals with less than two years' employment can also pursue complaints of discrimination.

The definitions of sexual, racial and disability harassment and the ability to bring a complaint under each corresponding discrimination Act are discussed in Chapters 2, 3 and 4. In essence, an applicant would have to show:

–   they were subject to unwanted conduct of a sexual or racial nature, or an offensive nature, or conduct based on their sex, race or disability;
–   which of itself is inherently offensive or which someone would consider amounts to less favourable treatment of them;
–   as a consequence, they have suffered a detriment.

(a) Procedure

To begin a complaint in an employment tribunal, a form known as an originating application (often called an IT1) must be completed and submitted by the complainant (or 'Applicant'). Unlike the county court or High Court, no fee is payable in order to commence proceedings. The person or organisation against whom the complaint is made (the 'Respondent') must then submit a notice of appearance often known as an IT3, responding to the complaint brought. This must be done within 21 days of receiving the originating application. The notice of appearance should:

–   set out the Respondent's full name and address;
–   state whether or not he intends to resist the application; and
–   if he does intend to resist, state on what grounds , giving sufficient particulars.

If the notice of appearance is not entered in time, the Respondent is not entitled to take any further part in the proceedings. He may, however, apply to the tribunal, either before or after the expiry of the time-limit, for an extension of time for filing the notice. The time-limit was extended to 21 days from 31 July 1998.[1] The increase in the time-limit was accompanied by a much stricter regime for the granting of extensions and it is therefore very important to enter the IT3 within the 21-day limit. The consequences of a late notice of appearance can be very serious.

---

1   Employment Tribunals (Constitution and Rules of Procedure) (Amendment) Regulations 1996, SI 1996/1757.

(b) *Questionnaires*

A person complaining of discrimination may serve on the person against whom the complaint has been made a questionnaire relating to either sex, race or disability discrimination. This can be served either before or after the complaint is presented to the tribunal. The purpose of such a questionnaire is to help a person who thinks that he or she may have been discriminated against to decide whether to institute proceedings and, if proceedings are begun, to formulate and present the case in the most effective manner. The questionnaire is in a form prescribed by the relevant discrimination Act.

The questionnaire and the reply from the employer are admissible as evidence before an employment tribunal provided the time-limits are complied with as follows:

(a) where it has been served before a complaint has been presented to a tribunal (after the IT1 has been issued), within the period of three months beginning when the act complained of was done;

(b) where it is served when a complaint has already been presented to a tribunal, either within the period of 21 days beginning with the day on which the complaint was presented or later within a period specified by a direction of a tribunal.

If it appears to the tribunal that the respondent deliberately and without reasonable excuse omitted to reply within a reasonable period or that the reply given is evasive or equivocal, the tribunal may draw any inference from that fact that it considers just and equitable to draw, including an inference that the respondent committed an unlawful act. It is therefore essential that an employer considers carefully any questionnaire received and that time and care is taken in answering the questionnaire.

(c) *Pre-hearing review*

If the Respondent considers that the case against it has little or no merit, a deposit can be ordered to be paid before the Applicant is permitted to proceed with the complaint. It is open to a party to request that, before the case is listed for a full hearing, the tribunal should consider the merits of the case and give an initial indication of whether the claim is likely to succeed or not. This process and the initial hearing is termed a 'pre-hearing review' and can be applied for under the employment tribunal rules of procedure.[1]

A pre-hearing review may be called by the employment tribunal itself, since it is possible for a tribunal to convene a pre-hearing review of its own motion.

The facts and matters which will be considered by the tribunal at this pre hearing review, are limited. Evidence and witnesses cannot be called and the tribunal will not look at documents and paperwork. It will listen only to arguments and representations put before it either in writing or orally.

Having considered the representations, if the tribunal takes the view that the party against whom the pre-hearing review has been applied has no reasonable prospect of suceeding when and if the matter comes to a full trial, a deposit may be ordered. This means that the tribunal will order that the party can only

---

1   Employment Tribunals Act 1996, s 9 and Employment Tribunals (Constitution and Rules of Procedure) Regulations 1993, SI 1993/2687, Sch 1, r 7.

continue with the case by first paying a deposit into the court office. The amount of the deposit is within the tribunal's discretion but is limited in any event to a maximum currently of £150. This deposit will be forfeited if the case is lost.

It is extremely rare for costs to be awarded against the party who loses a tribunal case. However, if a deposit has been ordered because of the tribunal on its initial assessment considers the case lacks merit, the party who pays the deposit but continues to pursue the case is placed on risk of paying costs.

At the end of the full hearing, which is heard before a different tribunal panel to that which sat at the pre-hearing review, the tribunal, having made its decision, will be notified of the original assessment at the pre-hearing review. The decision of the pre-hearing review tribunal is often contained in a sealed envelope and the second tribunal does not become aware of the first tribunal's view until the end of the case.

If the view of the first tribunal is upheld and the party whose case it was predicted would lose and was warned as to costs is unsuccessful, the tribunal will consider whether to grant costs in accordance with its provisions and whether to allow the deposit which has been paid into court to be paid across to the successful party. Of course, bearing in mind that this deposit will be a maximum of £150, an award of the deposit itself may be somewhat of a hollow victory.

Finally, where a pre-hearing review order for a deposit has been made, the order itself will require payment to the tribunal within 21 days, although the tribunal has a discretion to extend that time period. If the deposit is not paid the tribunal will 'strike out' the originating application or the defence (as appropriate), which effectively means that the action is discontinued and the party cannot continue with their claim or defence.

(d) Conciliation

The Advisory Conciliation and Arbitration Service, commonly known as ACAS, was established to promote the improvement of industrial relations. ACAS appoints conciliation officers to conciliate on matters which are or could be the subject of proceedings before an employment tribunal.

Where a complaint has already been presented to an employment tribunal, a conciliation officer may try to promote a settlement if requested to do so by either party, and *must* try to promote a settlement if he is requested to do so by both parties or if he considers that there is a reasonable prospect of settlement. Information given to the conciliation officer in the performance of his duties is not admissible in evidence before the tribunal except with the consent of the party who has given the information.

Before a complaint is presented to an employment tribunal, a conciliation officer will only take action if requested to do so by a party to the potential complaint. He must conciliate if requested to do so by both parties to the potential complaint, or if he considers that he could conciliate with a reasonable prospect of success.

An agreement to settle an employment tribunal complaint will only normally be binding on the parties if the agreement relates to a complaint or potential complaint where a conciliation officer has taken action in accordance with his statutory powers. The important exception concerns settlements reached after the employee has received independent legal advice from a qualified lawyer (ie compromise agreements). In other cases an agreement to settle a claim or a potential claim is unenforceable, leaving the complainant free to pursue his claim before an employment tribunal. Thus in order to ensure that an agreement to settle a complaint or potential complaint is enforceable, parties should normally seek the assistance of a conciliation officer to promote a settlement and have him record the agreement on the appropriate form.

(e) *Restricted reporting*

One aspect worthy of special mention are rules which have been put in place for the employment tribunal to protect the identity of individuals involved in complaints of sexual or disability harassment. Until these new provisions, there was little protection in an employment tribunal for a complainant, for a victim of harassment or indeed for an individual or organisation accused of harassing an individual. Even so, the powers at present are limited to cases where the harassment is in the nature of sexual harassment or relates to disability. In the case of a racial harassment complaint, the same protection and restricted reporting power does not exist.

There are limited powers given to employment tribunals to hold hearings 'in-camera' thereby excluding the public and the press. However, such a hearing can only be ordered where the tribunal is satisfied that the case will involve:

- matters of national security;
- evidence which, if disclosed, will breach a legal prohibition or law;
- a breach of confidence;
- substantial injury to an undertaking.

Although this last category may seem wide, tribunals are seldom persuaded to make an order under this particular limb.[1] The power to order private hearings is intended to deal only with very limited circumstances.

In 1993, special rules were introduced into the Tribunal Regulations enabling the tribunal to make a restricted reporting order under Sch 1, r 14. It is important to point out that the protection given by a restricted reporting order is not just limited to protecting the complainant or victim. It can also protect the alleged harasser, who is innocent until proven guilty. More recently, it has been confirmed that a restricted reporting order can protect a company and, in particular, an employer organisation.

The scope and protection given by an order of this nature is, never the less, severely limited as Parliament has sought to balance the protection of the individual against the public interest, as was recognised during the course of the debate in the House of Lords on this issue:

> 'Harassment at work can make people's lives a misery and some are unwilling to bring their case before a Tribunal because they fear that evidence given at the Hearing will attract sensational or intrusive media coverage which might identify them. The evidence given at such Hearings may include allegations about either party's private life and character as well as detailed descriptions of the alleged harassment. Bringing such a complaint can be a very distressing experience, and it is in the public interest that reporting restrictions should be available in such cases ...'

---

1   Schedule 1, r 8(3) of the Employment Tribunal (Constitution and Rules of Procedure) Regulations 1993, SI 1993/2687.

However, in a sexual harassment case where an industrial tribunal made a restricted reporting order in respect of both the applicant, her council employer, the chief executive who was her immediate superior and three other employees the order was considered to be far too wide in encompassing virtually everyone connected with the case, including the witnesses. The order itself was challenged by the press, Associated Newspapers Ltd.[1]

The High Court judge took the view that the order was too wide. In particular, he emphasised that in making an order of this nature, it was necessary for the tribunal whilst protecting the parties' identities and considering their rights, to go no further than was necessary to achieve this end. He stressed that it was important to ensure that contemporaneous press reporting of tribunal hearings was allowed to proceed.

Although limited companies and incorporated and unincorporated organisations can also benefit from a restricted reporting order, that definition again is quite tightly defined. The EAT considered this matter in *M v Vincent* (below) and formed the view that an anonymity order can only be extended to a non-individual where identifying the organisation would effectively identify the individuals.

> *Example*   An employee complained that Mr M had discriminated against her and complained of sexual harassment. M was a co-Director in a small family company, and indeed the company was named after his mother. M applied for a restricted reporting order not just for him but for the company itself, on the basis that if the order were limited to himself but company name was disclosed, he would be readily identified. The tribunal agreed and although the matter was taken to the EAT to challenge that view, the EAT accepted that in certain circumstances it may well be appropriate to extend the restriction to the company itself, where the two are so closely identified with each other or the individual and the organisation are likely to be easily associated.
>
> *M v Vincent*
> [1997] ICR 73

The scope of a restricted reporting order applies and is in place so that the parties who are protected cannot be named, only during the course of the tribunal hearing itself. Unless the tribunal revokes or overturns the order at an earlier point, the restriction applies until the decision of the tribunal is delivered, ie when the written decision of the tribunal is provided. Once that is done the parties can be named. In addition to this, even if the case is appealed to the EAT, the original protection granted by the tribunal does not automatically extend to the appeal case and the EAT (somewhat surprisingly) does not have the power to make a restricted reporting order. This point was established relatively recently in a case which was brought by the press: *A v B ex parte News Group Newspapers Ltd* (below).

> *Example*   The case involved allegations of harassment brought by a transsexual employee. The tribunal made a restricted reporting order protecting the identity of both the individual and those against whom she

---

1   *Regina v London (North) Industrial Tribunal ex parte Associated Newspapers Ltd* [1998] TLR 310, QBD.

was complaining, including her company employer. Following the decision, the employer appealed and argued before the EAT that the restricted reporting order made by the tribunal should remain in place during the course of the appeal. The EAT itself identified the limits applicable to restricted reporting orders made under r 14:

(1) The powers as to anonymity could only continue at an appeal level when the appeal is made during the course of the proceedings. Once the decision has been given and issued in writing the protection disappears.

(2) The EAT has not been given the power to make a restricted reporting order (as is made clear in s 31 of the Employment Tribunals Act 1996) and there is no inherent or general power placed upon the EAT itself to grant an order of this nature.

A v B ex parte News Group Newspapers Ltd
[1998] ICR 55

Thus, whilst the ability to apply for a restricting reporting order can be extremely useful, it is important to appreciate its limitations.

12.3.2 Unfair constructive dismissal

Discrimination at work can result in a fundamental breach of the employment contract, entitling an employee to resign and claim constructive dismissal. However, constructive dismissal can also arise where no discrimination has taken place but where, for example, an employee has been bullied to the extent that the bullying has resulted in a fundamental breach of contract (see Chapter 5). A complaint of this nature lies in the Employment Rights Act 1996 (ERA) which deals generally with unfair dismissal complaints.

A constructive dismissal complaint is one type of unfair dismissal complaint. However, unlike the usual unfair dismissal claim where an employee has been dismissed by his employer, a constructive dismissal claim is where an employee resigns as a result of his employer's conduct and is deemed to have been dismissed. This is covered by s 95(1) of the ERA 1996 which states that a dismissal can occur if:

'The employee terminates the contract under which he is employed (with or without notice) in circumstances in which he is entitled to terminate it without notice by reason of the employer's conduct.'

The employee terminates the employment relationship and is entitled to do so, but can still treat himself as having been dismissed by the employer. This is because he has been forced to resign or forced out of the organisation, by the employer's conduct.

There are some important restrictions and limits on who can bring such a claim in the employment tribunal:

– Since this concerns unfair dismissal not discrimination, only employees can claim unfair dismissal rights. Unlike the discrimination legislation, individuals who are self-employed and carrying out work in a personal capacity, cannot gain unfair dismissal rights. Only employees who gain the protection of unfair dismissal who can complain of constructive dismissal.

–   Even within this limited category of employees there are further restrictions. Unfair dismissal rights currently, can only be brought by employees who have two or more years continuous (ie unbroken) employment with an employer. However, at the time of writing the Labour Government has indicated its intention to reduce the two year period to one year.[1] Although the two years' employment generally has to be continuous, there are circumstances where a tribunal will be prepared to allow someone to assume two years' employment even though they have not been carrying out work throughout the entire two years; this is to protect casual workers, temporary workers and those who work on term contracts, particularly in the education field.

–   Unlike discrimination legislation, applicants for employment do not gain any protection whatsoever to complain of unfair dismissal.

12.3.3 Breach of contract

It is possible for an employee to bring a complaint of breach of contract in the county court (see below) if that breach of contract is based on a breach of one of the implied duties examined in Chapter 7 – such as mutual trust and confidence, reasonable care, safe system of work. If the breach of contract occurs at the end of the employment relationship, then as an alternative to the county court, it is possible to bring the claim in the employment tribunal. An important point to note is that if the breach of contract claim is brought whilst the individual remains employed, then it does not arise at the end of the employment and thus at the end of the contract, so that there is no option but to take the case to the county court.

The reason for this distinction is that the powers of the tribunal to deal with breach of contract claims is specifically limited. The detailed rules are contained in two provisions governing this area:

–   Employment Tribunals (Extension of Jurisdiction) (England and Wales) Order 1994;[2]
–   Employment Tribunals (Extension of Jurisdiction) (Scotland) Order 1994.[3]

In reality, because of this limitation to breach of contract claims, complaints of breach of contract – in addition to discrimination – often go hand-in-hand with a complaint of constructive dismissal, where the harassment is of such seriousness that the individual resigns their employment thus ending the contract of employment. A claim of bullying, if it is to be brought in the employment tribunal, would have to be brought under either the unfair dismissal provisions and/or breach of contract.

On its own, the remedy for breach of contract is limited not just as to the circumstances when it can be pursued, but also in value. A tribunal can only order up to £25,000 for the loss which an employee claims, in a breach of contract case. Thus, particularly where an individual can establish that his or her loss is in excess of £25,000, the complaint would be pursued in the county court where the amount which can be recovered is not limited.

---

1   'Fairness at Work' White Paper.
2   SI 1994/1623.
3   SI 1994/1624.

12.4 COUNTY COURT/HIGH COURT

12.5.1 Claims brought in county court or High Court

Although it is envisaged that most harassment claims will be brought in the employment tribunal, there are some claims which cannot. Personal injury claims, breach of contract claims worth more than £25,000 and breach of contract claims which do not occur at the end of the employment relationship, must be brought in the county or High Court.

From the point of view of an individual taking action, the difference between these two courts – apart from detailed procedural rules – is the amount which can be ordered by the court if a claim ultimately is successful. As a general rule, the county court deals with claims of a lesser value than those brought and heard in the High Court. Until very recently, the county court was limited to the amount which it could order, initially to £25,000 and then to £50,000. The general rule now is that, save for exceptional cases where the nature of claim is complex or involves difficult legal argument, the High Court would only hear a claim if potentially the amount to be awarded or being sought is in excess of £50,000.

12.5.2 Personal injury claims

Harassment at work, especially bullying, may result in physical or psychological injury. A personal injury claim is brought under the tort (ie civil claim) of negligence. An employee can bring a claim for personal injury against his employer on the ground of harassment if he or she can show that the employer owed him or her a duty of care, that the employer breached that duty and that the he or she suffered an injury as a result of the employer's breach. The claim can be brought against the harasser personally, or the employer vicariously, or both.

The injury may be such that an employee is incapable of working and any claim will therefore seek to compensate him or her for loss of earnings. The employee will also seek compensation for other quantifiable losses such as medical expenses and travelling expenses. These quantifiable losses are called 'special damages'.

A personal injury claimant will also seek general damages. Unlike special damages these are not capable of precise calculation, but will include compensation for pain and suffering, loss of amenity, loss of future earnings and earning capacity and compensation for the cost of future expenses such as nursing or medical care.

It is also possible in certain circumstances for a victim of harassment to apply to the court for an injunction which requires the harasser to keep out of a particular radius of a location or not to make contact with the victim. Injunctions are examined more fully in Chapter 13.

There are a number of other civil torts which may be relevant to harassment at work, ie assault, battery and false imprisonment. As with negligence, the primary remedies for such actions are financial recompense for any monetary loss suffered plus an amount to reflect injury to feelings and any anxiety and distress caused. If an employee is found liable, his or her employer will also be found liable if the acts were committed in the course of employment. However, 'the course of employment' is much narrower in a tort situation than in a discrimination situation and it will therefore be easier for an employer to argue that the act was not committed in the course of employment. This is discussed in more detail in Chapter 8.

12.5.3 Breach of contract

Until 1993 breach of contract claims could only be brought in the county or High Court as the industrial tribunal (as it then was) did not have the jurisdiction to hear this type of claim. As discussed above, the jurisdiction of the employment tribunal to hear breach of contract claims is limited. This effectively means that any contract claims worth more than £25,000 or any contract claims which arise during the course of employment and not at the end of the employment contract must be brought in the county or High Court.

Every contract of employment contains a number of implied duties, which the law imposes and which is owed by one party to the other. The employers owes a number of implied duties, which could be breached where an employee is exposed to harassment:

- the duty of mutual trust and confidence;
- the duty to provide reasonable support;
- the duty to provide a safe place of work.

The remedy for a breach of contract claim includes damages reflecting financial loss but unlike actions in tort (and indeed actions under the discrimination legislation) the aim of a breach of contract action is to place the individual in the position that they would have been in had the breach not occurred. For this reason, whilst the damages will include lost salary and benefits where the individual resigns the employment because of a breach, the remedy does not cover compensation for any injury to feelings.

12.5 CRIMINAL COURTS

Most instances of harassment or bullying at work will find redress via the employment tribunal or county/High Court. But there are some forms of harassment that will amount to criminal offences and redress may therefore be necessary via the magistrates' court or Crown Court.

In such cases, it is generally not the victim of harassment who brings the complaint (although it is possible to bring a private prosecution in some instances) but the CPS in England and Wales which brings the prosecution on behalf of the Queen – hence case names such as *Regina* (or *R*) *v Joe Bloggs*. The victim of harassment will take the complaint in the first instance to the police, who investigate the matter and then, if appropriate, hand it on to the CPS. The CPS decide whether or not to prosecute and proceedings will generally be commenced in the magistrates' court. Depending on the seriousness of the case, it will either proceed in the magistrates' court or be referred to the Crown Court.

The CPS will only prosecute the alleged harasser if the form of harassment potentially amounts to a criminal offence. The most relevant statutes in this context are the Public Order Act 1986, the Protection from Harassment Act 1997 or the Offences against the Person Act 1861. These are discussed fully in Chapter 8 and cover a wide range of offences from rape to nuisance telephone calls.

Chapter 13

REMEDIES

Employment tribunal remedies – County court/High Court – Criminal court

To a great extent the question of what remedy an individual can obtain for suffering harassment at work is linked to the issues discussed in Chapter 12 'Which Court?' This is because the remedies available to an individual who is subjected to harassment will vary, depending on whether proceedings are issued in the employment tribunal, the county court or High Court, or the criminal court.

The powers of each of these venues vary enormously, both in terms of judgments and orders as well as the financial remedies available.

13.1 EMPLOYMENT TRIBUNAL REMEDIES

13.1.1 Discrimination

There are a range of remedies, including monetary awards, which a tribunal can make if satisfied that an individual has been subjected to harassment which amounts to unlawful discrimination under the SDA 1975, RRA 1976 or DDA 1995. The remedies are effectively threefold:

– a declaration;
– a recommendation; and
– compensation.

(a) Declaration

Generally the declaration will confirm to the individual that he or she was the subject of unlawful discrimination.

A declaration will be made even if no other remedy is granted; for example, when no financial loss is suffered. However, if the declaration confirms that there has been unlawful harassment which amounts to discrimination, it is almost inevitable that some monetary award for injury to feelings will be made.

(b) Recommendation

The aim of a recommendation, according to the discrimination Acts, is:

> 'that the Respondents [Employer], take within a specified period, action appearing to the Tribunal to be reasonable, in all the circumstances of the case, for the purpose of obviating or reducing the adverse effect on the complainant any matter to which the complaint relates.'

The exact terms of a recommendation will inevitably vary according to the nature of the case being brought. It should be borne in mind that the recommendation must be specific to the individual complainant, with the aim of improving matters for him or her. A general recommendation about a particular practice is outside the scope of these provisions.

In harassment cases, the recommendations could cover a variety of aspects:

–   recommendations as to the introduction of particular policies, such as a harassment policy;
–   recommendations on transferring the complainant or taking action against the harasser.

If the employer fails to comply with the recommendation, the individual can apply to the tribunal for additional compensation (in addition to the original compensation ordered by the tribunal at the time when it made the rec-ommendation). Unless the tribunal is satisfied that the employer has a 'reasonable justification' for flouting the orders of the tribunal contained in the recommendation, the amount of compensation to be awarded is at the discretion of the tribunal and must be such an amount as is considered 'just and equitable'.

(c) Compensation

This aspect of discrimination complaints often attracts much publicity. Unlike employment tribunal awards for unfair dismissal which are limited to a maximum of £12,000, the power of the tribunal to award compensation (both for financial loss and injury to feelings) is not constrained.

In fact, the removal of the limit is a relatively recent development, which was introduced in 1993 and 1994 following a decision from the ECJ which emphasised that all EU Member States had to ensure that effective remedies were available to compensate individuals who were subjected to discrimination.[1] The changes were brought about by the Sex Discrimination and Equal Pay (Remedies) Regulations 1993, SI 1993/2798 and the Race Relations (Remedies) Act 1994.

The starting point for the tribunal is to consider the actual loss suffered by the individual and, if it wishes to project future loss, to make an assessment as to what other period it would be appropriate and realistic to project forward, in terms of the Applicant's ongoing loss.

As with the unfair dismissal award, the aspects of loss which could be covered include:

–   lost wages;
–   lost pension;
–   other benefits which have been lost; and
–   expenses incurred in seeking alternative employment.

Any new earnings and State benefits which reduce the financial loss suffered will be offset against the above elements.

(d) Injury to feelings

Of course, the financial loss suffered is easy to quantify in the case of an individual who has actually left the employment as a consequence of the harassment suffered. If, on the other hand, the individual remains employed,

---

1   *Marshall v Southampton and South West Hampshire Area Health Authority (No 2)* [1993] IRLR 445.

then he or she will not have suffered financial loss but will have suffered injury to feelings. The 'injury to feelings' award is in place in order to compensate the individual for the distress, embarrassment and humiliation which is caused in any case of discrimination. However, the amount of injury to feelings is likely to be higher, because the distress and embarrassment may well be higher, where the form of discrimination is harassment. The precise amount is left to the discretion of the tribunal who may award such amount as it considers just and equitable.

In the past, tribunals have used guidance as to certain minimum and maximum amounts which, although not laid down by law, are considered to be useful pointers to the levels of award which are appropriate. Studies are undertaken on a regular basis by a number of organisations and these can provide some indication of what is likely to be awarded in a particular case.

The leading and most recent case in which the court examined how to assess the appropriate level for an injury to feelings award is *Armitage, Marsden and HM Prison Service v Johnson* (below) which itself was a case of racial harassment.

> *Example* Mr Johnson, who is Afro-Caribbean, was employed as a prison officer. He was subjected to a campaign by his work colleagues which included being ostracised, racist remarks, being subjected to unjustified warnings and being reported to management. The tribunal ordered £21,000 as a compensatory award against the Prison Authority for the 'injury to feelings' element and the prison service appealed against this.
>
> In the EAT's view the following guidance had to be borne in mind when considering the appropriate level of awards:
>
> (1) The tribunal must seek a balance to achieve justice between the parties when fixing the level of the injury to feelings: it is compensating the sufferer for indignation but should not at the same time be looking to punish the guilty party.
> (2) 'Injury to feelings' awards should not be so low that they undermine the legislation itself but again there is a balance. If awards are too high, this will not be beneficial either.
> (3) A similarity could and should be drawn with the level of injury to feelings awards made in discrimination cases with those applicable in personal injury cases.
>
> *Armitage, Marsden and HM Prison Service v Johnson*
> [1997] IRLR 162

Although it is difficult to give general guidance on the likely levels of awards, from the statistics available it is possible to identify some general trends and the likely levels of such awards:

– it appears from the studies available that, on average only, injury to feelings awards are higher in race discrimination cases than sex discrimination cases;
– at present, because the disability discrimination provisions are so new, there is insufficient information to make the same comparison. In reality, however, it is highly likely that in disability cases, awards for injury to feelings would be at the higher end;
– the vast majority of awards are in the region of £2,000–£5,000;
– minimum awards would start from £100, but it is more likely that tribunals would look to a realistic amount at the minimum level of £500–£1,000.

The following are examples of the highest awards.

Case name and reference	Injury to feelings awarded
Armitage, Marsden and HM Prison Service v Johnson [1997] IRLR 162	£21,000
Chan v London Borough of Hackney 01359/93	£25,000
Quereshi v Victoria University of Manchester & Brazier EAT/120/97 & 121/93	£25,000
Williams v London Borough of Southwark Case No 47362/92	£20,000

(Note that all of the above are harassment cases.)

We considered liability for harassment in Chapter 8 and outlined the possibility that individuals who are responsible for harassing others at work could be held responsible in their own right, for aiding and abetting an employer. These provisions dovetail with the remedies which a tribunal can award. If an individual is found to have been party personally to harassment and discrimination the tribunal can, in making its compensatory award, order that an element be paid by the individual. More often than not, it is the injury to feelings element, or part of it, which the individual is ordered to pay and for which they are personally liable.

In the *Johnson* case quoted above, two of the prison officers, including the applicant's supervisor, were ordered to pay £500 each of the £21,000 injury to feelings ordered. It is not uncommon for individuals to be ordered to pay £1,000 or £2,000 in recognition of the responsibility which they carry for the discrimination which has occurred.

One remedy which is not available to a person complaining of discrimination, is reinstatement or re-engagement (see below); this only applies in an unfair dismissal case. Only if an individual is eligible to complain of unfair dismissal (as well as discrimination) can they seek a re-employment order. In its recent consultation paper in February 1998 'Equality in the 21st Century' the Equal Opportunities Commission expressed the clear view that this discrepancy should be changed and powers to reinstate extended. Their lobbying in this regard continues.

(f) *Award of interest*

A further advantage to a complainant, which discrimination awards have over unfair dismissal, is the power of the employment tribunal to make an award of interest – which is different from the interest which accrues if any tribunal award is paid 42 days after the decision. This interest of discrimination awards was introduced at the same time as the limits were removed on sex discrimination awards and, also as a result of the *Marshall (No 2)* case referred to above.

The formula on which interest is calculated is quite complex and is calculated differently for the compensation for financial loss and the injury to feelings award, as follows:

–   injury to feelings – interest for the entire period starting with the act of discrimination and ending on the date of the tribunal's decision.
–   financial loss – interest accrues for half of the period (technically known as from mid point) between the act of discrimination and the decision.

The awarding of interest is always a matter for the tribunal's discretion but generally they will follow these guidelines. Although the rate of interest can vary, currently the figure is 8% and it is simple interest not compound interest which applies.[1]

13.1.2 Unfair constructive dismissal

Where the victim pursues a complaint of constructive dismissal, the usual unfair dismissal remedies apply. Under the ERA 1996, there are a number of possible remedies which an individual can seek if it is established that he or she has been unfairly or unfairly constructively dismissed:

(1) reinstatement;
(2) re-engagement; or
(3) compensation.

(a) *Reinstatement*

If an individual has resigned his or her employment because the individual can no longer tolerate his or her work situation, it is highly unlikely that this particular remedy would be sought. A reinstatement order by the tribunal requires the employer to re-employ the individual, compensate the individual for back pay and effectively, treat the employee as if the employee had never been dismissed or had never resigned. All benefits and improvements or increases in pay that would have been given to the employee between the period of dismissal and reinstatement have to be provided.

The intention when the legislation on unfair dismissal was first introduced, was that reinstatement would be the primary remedy. Although in practice reinstatement orders are not regularly made – usually compensation is awarded – the tribunal must first satisfy itself that the applicant does not wish to be reinstated.

It is possible for an employer to resist any request for reinstatement by establishing that it would not be practicable to take the employee back.

When making an order for reinstatement, the tribunal will set out the provisions as to back pay and identify the date by which reinstatement should occur. If, by that date, the employer has not allowed the individual to return to the previous job, the only remedy which the employee is left with is compensation. The compensation may be increased because of the employer's failure to allow him or her to return. Unless the tribunal is convinced that it was not reasonably practicable for the employer to reinstate, it will make the following awards:

- a basic award (see below);
- a compensatory award (see below);
- an additional award (for the failure to comply with the reinstatement order).

If a financial award is made as an alternative to actual reinstatement, there are limits on the amount which can be recovered as a maximum, as follows:

1 Employment Tribunal (Interest on Awards in Discrimination Cases) Regulations 1996, SI 1996/2803.

Unfair dismissal basic award   £6,600
Compensatory award   £12,000
Additional award   £5,720   (between 13 to 26 weeks' pay or 26
                                         to 52 weeks' pay where the dismissal
                                         is race or sex related, ie the
                                         constructive dismissal is because of
                                         racial or sexual harassment).
Total   £24,320

Interest does not accrue automatically to these awards, unless and until the employer fails to make the payment, and comply with the tribunal's order to compensate after the due date. The due date will be 42 days from the date when the tribunal issues its decision. A recent amendment introduced by the Employment Rights (Dispute Resolution) Act 1998 will extend the power to order an additional award to include disability-related dismissals.

(b) Re-engagement

Re-engagement, and the principles which apply to this type of order, is similar to reinstatement. However, instead of reinstating the individual to the old position, the individual returns to the employer (or an associated employer) in a slightly different position or job. Again orders for back pay, all improvements in the intervening period and pension provisions will be made.

The same principles discussed in relation to reinstatement orders will apply in relation to the practicability of complying with the re-engagement order, and the compensatory awards which could be imposed as an alternative for a failure to comply are identical to the reinstatement provisions.

(c) Compensation/financial remedy only

Assuming that the individual has not asked for reinstatement or re-engagement, or that the tribunal has decided that it ought not to make such an order or that the employer convinces the tribunal that it is not reasonably practicable to reinstate or re-engage the individual, the only remedy remaining for the unfair dismissal element is compensation and the basic award.

Basic award

The tribunal will calculate the basic award in broadly the same way as for statutory redundancy. The amount actually payable varies dependent upon the employee's length of service, age at dismissal and salary. The starting point is to calculate an individual's weekly pay; if it is variable, an average is taken counting back the previous 12 weeks. If the week's pay is less than £220, the actual pay is used in the formula. If, however, the week's pay is more than £220, then the figure of £220 is used instead.[1]

The formula is applied as follows:

---

1   Note that the statutory maximum on a week's pay is set by the Secretary of State and is subject to review: the current maximum of £220 was set by the Employment Rights (Increase of Limits) Order 1998, SI 1998/924 from 1 April 1998.

- for each complete year of employment during which the individual was not below 41, one and a half week's pay is awarded;
- for each year of employment under 41 but over 22, one week's pay is awarded; and
- for each complete year of employment when the employee was 21 or under, half a week's pay is awarded.

A maximum of 20 years can be applied to this formula, which means that if the employee has 30 years' employment, the final 20 years are taken for the purposes of the calculation. Because of the limits, the maximum calculation that can apply is as follows:

$$\underset{\text{maximum years}}{20} \times \underset{\text{all over age 41}}{1.5} \times \underset{\text{maximum week's pay}}{£220} = £6,600$$

Compensatory award

On top of the basic award, a compensatory award can be made to reflect the individual's financial loss as a consequence of the unfair dismissal. This amount varies dependent upon a variety of aspects, including whether the individual has found new employment. The tribunal will also consider what efforts the individual has made to actively seek such new employment.

The losses which can be included in this figure range from not just salary, but will also include loss of benefits, lost pension and, to some extent, the costs incurred by the individual in seeking out new employment. The tribunal will also make an award to reflect the fact that the employee, (because he or she needs two years' employment to gain unfair dismissal rights) has lost the security of unfair dismissal rights until the new employment has continued for two years. Generally this element of the award is known as a figure to 'reflect loss of statutory rights' and can range from £200–£500.

Regardless of the actual figure which the tribunal identifies as amounting to the individual loss as a consequence of dismissal – which can run into tens of thousands with senior and higher paid employees – the tribunal can award no more than £12,000 as an absolute maximum.[1] Again interest does not attach to this figure unless payment is delayed.

At present there is some uncertainty about whether the statutory limits on unfair dismissal compensation awards will stay. In its White Paper 'Fairness at Work' the Government outlined a proposal (on which it is seeking views) to remove the limits altogether, thus giving the tribunal unhindered power to award the individuals their loss.[2]

All of the above remedies apply to unfair dismissal complaints made in an employment tribunal and can only be made and ordered against the employer. As seen above, one key distinction between this and the remedies which apply to discrimination complaints, is that it is possible in discrimination complaints for part of the remedy to be ordered against, and therefore payable by, not just the employer but also the individual(s) responsible for the harassment.

---

1   Employment Rights (Increase of Limits) Order 1998, SI 1998/924.
2   Fairness at Work: DTI CM 3968 May 1998.

13.1.3 Breach of contract

The remedy for breach of contract is effectively damages or the recovery of monies. If successful in a claim for breach of contract, the court will seek to put the party who has suffered the breach in the same position financially that they would have been in if the breach had not occurred.

This means that items such as lost salary or benefits can be recovered. Thus there is very little value in an employee who has been harassed and who remains in employment suing for breach of contract. What is the financial loss?

A key distinction between breach of contract damages and other damages for discrimination and in tort, is that there will be no award for injury to feelings.

In terms of the remedy for breach of contract, it should be remembered that a breach of contract claim in the employment tribunal can lead to damages of no more than £25,000. In addition, interest does not attach to breach of contract damages in the tribunal (unlike breach of contract claims in the county court or High Court), which are limited to awards of compensation in discrimination cases except where the date for payment of the tribunal's order for damages has elapsed when, for all tribunal awards, interest begins to accrue after 42 days.

13.2 COUNTY COURT/HIGH COURT

13.2.1 Personal injury

In Chapter 7, we examined the legal basis for a personal injury claim resulting from bullying and/or harassment at work. As with a breach of contract claim, the remedy which a court will order if an individual successfully sues under this head is restoration of financial loss. Again, because there has been a breach of a duty, the aim of compensation will be to place the individual in the position that they would have been in (from a financial perspective) had the breach of duty not occurred.

In addition to the financial loss element, however, there is a further award which can be made in a claim in tort. This is an amount for injury to feelings which is aimed at compensating the individual for the sorts of losses which cannot be 'quantified'; for example, distress, anxiety or consequent ill-health. Even without any compensation for financial loss, the remedy for the injury to feelings could be substantial, particularly in a more serious case where harassment has occurred. Again, as this is a county court remedy, interest will be awarded.

13.2.2 Breach of contract

The remedy for a breach of contract claim in the county court or High Court is as stated above in relation to a breach of contract claim in the employment tribunal. However, in the county court or High Court, the remedy is not limited to £25,000 and interest can be awarded (currently at a rate of 8% per annum) on any damages ordered to be paid, from the date proceedings were issued.

13.2.3 Injunctions

Injunctions are available in the course of civil proceedings, ordinarily breach of contract proceedings. Although available, they are not commonly used. An injunction will commonly be granted in order to prevent a wrong and, in effect, orders a party not to take a particular action which may be in breach. In an employment context, the most common circumstance where injunction proceedings will be granted is to prevent an employee or employer from taking action which would amount to a breach of contract. Although one of the parties could recover damages for the breach of contract, an injunction is often sought in order to prevent further loss or a continued breach of the contract, thereby minimising the damage caused.

Common examples of injunctions granted to prevent breaches of an employment contract include:

–   where the contract contains restrictions preventing the employee from poaching or soliciting customers of the employer, an injunction can be granted to order the employee or ex-employee not to continue the poaching or soliciting of customers;
–   in a dismissal scenario, if the employee is contractually entitled to require the employer to follow the disciplinary procedure and the employer has not done so, the employee can obtain an injunction to require the employer to go through the procedure and meet the terms of the contract.

It must be emphasised that court action is not issued in order to gain an injunction alone; in fact usually the action is for breach of contract, and the injunction is an interim measure which a party can apply for in the course of pursuing his or her damages complaint.

Injunctions are not readily granted by either the High Court or the county court (they cannot be made by an employment tribunal) because there is a need to balance carefully the interests of the parties concerned. A court has to be satisfied that it is in the best interests to order the injunction, on the basis that damages would be insufficient as an overall remedy.[1] By the same token, a court would expect the person seeking the injunction to be in a position, if it transpires that there was no breach of contract and they were not entitled to damages and therefore should not have been granted the injunction in the first place, to compensate their opponent and to right any ultimate wrong. Thus the person bringing the proceedings and asking for the injunction must have sufficient financial standing to be in a position to meet any damages which ultimately may be ordered against them (which may not just be the legal costs of the opponent). The court requires an undertaking to be given concerning the plaintiff's financial status and evidence to be produced to confirm this.

As a further safeguard, the court has to be persuaded that the person asking for the injunction has a sufficiently strong case and that they are likely to be proved right and that the breach has indeed occurred.

Having said all of this, it is extremely unusual for injunction proceedings to be an appropriate remedy when dealing with issues of harassment and the types of breach of contract which arise in these circumstances.

However, injunction proceedings do become relevant if the harassment falls under the Protection from Harassment Act 1997 (see Chapter 7) when the

---

1   *American Cyanamid Co v Ethicon Ltd* [1975] AC 396.

power to grant the restraining order or injunction is somewhat different and is laid out in the Act itself.

Finally it is worth mentioning that where an injunction is made and the individual subject to the injunction breaches its terms, he or she commits a criminal offence. In addition to this, breach of a court order and injunction amounts to contempt of court. The power of the court, and options available to it, to punish a breach of injunction are considerable. They include:

–   committal to prison for contempt for up to two years – although in practice this is rarely used and, if it is imposed, tends to be for lesser periods;[1]
–   a fine;
–   sequestration: ie the seizure of assets – which would be used in the most serious cases;
–   a further injunction to prevent repeating the contempt.

The person guilty of the contempt would be ordered to pay his or her opponent's costs.

13.3 CRIMINAL COURT

The penalties which the law imposes in terms of fines and imprisonment have been discussed under the various criminal offences which could amount to harassment.

In the Crown or magistrates' court there is a general power under the criminal law to make compensation orders for victims. The amount of such an award is based on the defendant's means and, in any event, is subject to a maximum of £5,000 for each offence for which the individual is convicted.[2] Any compensation ordered by the criminal court has to be taken into account in any civil proceedings for damages: for example breach of contract or tort. The reason for this is provided that the order has been complied with and the monies paid. This is because the law will not permit double recovery; ie the complainant cannot recover twice for the same loss. He or she can recover, however, losses in excess of the compensation order.[3]

There are also the remedies, which we again have already identified in Chapter 8, available under the Protection from Harassment Act 1997, including damages and a restraining order.

---

1   Contempt of Court Act 1981, s 14; County Courts (Penalties for Contempt) Act 1983.
2   Magistrates' Courts Act 1980, s 40.
3   Powers of Criminal Courts Act 1973, s 38.

Chapter 14

APPEALS

Tribunal appeals – County court/High Court appeals – Criminal proceedings

If an individual is unhappy with the outcome of the legal process, in limited circumstances, there is a right to take the case further through an appeal process. As we shall see, however, there are severe limitations in place which aim to prevent individuals appealing unnecessarily or simply because they are aggrieved by the outcome of the case. There have to be specific and legitimate grounds for the appeal to be pursued and there are also strict time-limits within which appeals can be taken.

In this chapter we will review the appeal avenues which are available and the court processes, the civil process, highlighting the employment tribunal process as well as the criminal process.

14.1 TRIBUNAL APPEALS

14.1.1 Bringing an appeal

Employment tribunals have a dedicated appeal court to whom cases are referred, which sits in London and Scotland, known as the EAT. In rarer cases, it is also possible for a case to be referred from the employment tribunal to the ECJ, where a point concerning EU law arises. This is less likely to occur in cases of harassment than other forms of discrimination. It would by and large, be related to sex discrimination claims or issues of equal pay, as there is more EU legislation in these areas. Equally, it is less likely in race discrimination claims (which is limited currently under EU law to matters concerning freedom of movement of persons and nationality issues) and very unlikely to occur in disability discrimination cases.

Unlike other appeals in the civil arena, leave does not have to be given by the employment tribunal in order to proceed to appeal. However there are limits on what can form the basis of a legitimate appeal and there are also time-limits which will apply.

14.1.2 Review

Schedule 1, r 11 of the Employment Tribunal (Constitution and Rules of Procedure) Regulations 1993[1] allows an employment tribunal to reconsider or review a decision either because the party has requested that it does so or because the tribunal considers there to be grounds requiring a review. The power to review applies to final judgments and orders which the tribunal may have issued.

The basis upon which a review may be requested and granted are limited. It must be shown either:

– that the decision was an error on the part of the tribunal staff;
– that a party did not receive notice of the proceedings or any hearing leading to the decision;
– that the decision was made in the absence of one party;
– that new evidence has become available which was not available at the hearing and which could not have been reasonably foreseen or known at the time; or
– in the interests of justice.

14.1.3 Of its own motion

The tribunal can review a decision on its own initiative, but it must give notice to the parties of its intention to do so. When giving this notice the tribunal must explain why it is considered appropriate to review the decision in the light of the grounds on which a review can be made (listed above). The notice to the parties must be issued quickly, and whilst it can be issued at any time after the hearing when the decision was given, the latest date by which the notice to the parties of the intention to review can be given is 14 days after the date that the written decision is sent. Whilst the review does not have to take place within that 14-day period, the tribunal has to make a decision and action it by issuing the notice stating that a review is appropriate within those 14 days. There is scope for the tribunal to extend time beyond the 14-day limit.

14.1.4 On request from a party

Any party to proceedings in the tribunal can themselves apply for a review. Whilst it is possible for a request for such a review to be made orally, it is more common for it to be done in writing. The time-limit again runs from the date of the hearing and decision, until, at the latest, 14 days after the decision is sent to the parties. The date the decision is sent is endorsed on the last page of the employment tribunal decision itself.

14.1.5 Process for review

If, in the light of the individual application or the tribunal's notice a review is granted, then in the first instance that review should be undertaken by the tribunal who originally heard the case. If this is not practicable, and the application has been made by one of the parties, then an alternative panel may undertake the review.

The outcome of the review could be one of three options:

---

1   SI 1993/2687.

- the request and the basis for reconsideration could be rejected and the decision confirmed;
- the decision itself could be varied taking into account the further or additional information; or
- the decision could be revoked; however if it is revoked, the tribunal cannot substitute an alternative decision, but must order a rehearing of the case either before the same tribunal panel or a differently constituted tribunal.

14.1.6 Appeal to the EAT

The EAT has jurisdiction to hear appeals referred to it by any party where claims are brought under the SDA 1975, RRA 1976, DDA 1995 and ERA 1996 (for our purposes, unfair dismissal). Until recently, the EAT did not have the power to hear appeals on breach of contract claims brought before an employment tribunal due to an oversight in drafting. This meant that any appeals on breach of contract claims which were brought before the EAT had to be adjourned generally until the appropriate legislation was in force.[1] The relevant part of the Employment Rights (Dispute Resolution) Act 1998 came into force from 8 April 1998 with retrospective effect. This now means that the EAT has the right to hear appeals from the employment tribunal on breach of contract claims.

14.1.7 Time-limits

An appeal to the EAT has to be lodged in a specific format, 42 days from the date that the decision was sent to the parties; as has already been mentioned, this date is notified in the decision itself.

The tribunal is authorised, save in discrimination cases, to issue 'summary' reasons which are a shortened version of the basis of their decision. Having said that, it is obviously in the interests of any party who wishes to appeal to have the fullest rationale for the tribunal's decision. It is essential to make a request for extended reasons where these are not automatically provided (in particular in the types of cases discussed in this book this will be relevant in a bullying constructive dismissal case or a breach of contract claim) because in order to lodge a valid notice of appeal, the rules require a copy of the extended reasons to be attached to the notice of appeal.[2] For this reason, it is advisable to ask for full written reasons or extended written reasons immediately. The 42-day time-limit runs from the date of the extended written reasons being sent.

A request for full written reasons has to be made within 21 days of the date on which the document recording the summary reasons was sent to the parties. In practice, as with leave to appeal in other civil cases, a representative or party should ask for extended reasons at the hearing immediately after the decision is delivered.

If a tribunal rejects a request for full or extended reasons, this can be appealed also.

---

1   *Practice Statement (EAT: Jurisdiction)* [1998] IRLR 22.
2   *Employment Appeal Tribunal Rules 1993*, SI 1993/2854, r 3.

14.1.8 The basis of an appeal

As with civil proceedings, a tribunal decision can only be appealed on a point of law and this is either based on the fact that the tribunal got the law wrong or misdirected itself, or that the decision is wrong in law because, on the evidence, it is 'perverse'. 'Perversity' for these purposes means that a party has to show that the tribunal reached a decision which was not open to it and which was not supported on the evidence, so that no reasonable tribunal would have reached that conclusion. Perversity arguments are inevitably, more difficult to pursue than those arguments based on an error of law.

14.1.9 Preliminary hearing

Since October 1997, due to the number of appeals being referred to it, the EAT has taken the decision to convene a preliminary hearing for every appeal which is launched.

The purpose of the preliminary hearing is to assess the merits of a case and decide whether there is a sufficiently arguable case to proceed to the full hearing. The preliminary hearing will also deal with directions that might be needed in order to dispose of and conclude the appeal. Commonly, for example, if the argument on which the appeal is based is one of perversity, the tribunal chairman's notes of the evidence given at the hearing might be requested – in order to establish exactly what evidence was before the tribunal.

At the preliminary hearing, the party pursuing the appeal is given an opportunity to put forward arguments as to the strength of their case and, although the hearing is in public, the other parties are not given a right of audience. This means they do not have the right to put forward any arguments.

The other step which the EAT may take having heard the arguments for the appellant (the person pursuing the appeal) is to clarify certain of the grounds of the appeal, to decide which points do not stand scrutiny and to require clarification or limits as to the grounds on which that party can proceed to a full appeal.

Of course it is also possible for the party to be informed that they cannot proceed with the appeal on the basis that a reasonable case has not been established and that the appeal will be refused. This is not unlike the process of gaining leave to appeal which operates in the other civil process.

14.1.10 The outcome of appeals to the EAT

There are special rules and procedures which apply to the hearing of the appeal itself, which are outside the scope of this book. However, in order to conclude an appeal, the EAT may take one of a number of actions:

– it may conclude that the appeal has no merit and dismiss the case, in which case the original decision of the tribunal will stand;
– it may allow the appeal and order that the case be returned to the employment tribunal for a rehearing (probably to a different tribunal panel) or it may order that the case be returned to the same tribunal for consideration of particular points;
– it may allow the appeal but, instead of sending the case back to the tribunal, substitute its decision to finally dispose of the case at the appeal stage.

Commonly, if the case is being pursued on a perversity argument so that there are arguments as to the evidence given, the most likely outcome will be that the case is sent back to the tribunal and reheard.

14.1.11 Further appeals

Beyond the EAT, there is scope in harassment cases concerning employment, for a party to take an appeal further to the Court of Appeal (the Court of Session in Scotland). The standard four-week time-limit applies, as in other civil appeals, from the date of the EAT's decision. Leave should be sought for such an appeal from the EAT itself and if refused, an application can be made to the Court of Appeal but this application must be made within seven days.

The case can be taken still further from the Court of Appeal to the House of Lords, and as we have already identified, in rarer cases it may be taken to the ECJ.

One severe limit exists on the EAT's powers: it cannot order anonymity of a party in the same way that an employment tribunal can in cases of sexual harassment or cases involving sexual offences or disability (see Chapter 12).

The other point which is worth making, and which is also mentioned in Chapter 13 (Remedies) is that if an award has been made interest will continue to accrue while the appeal is ongoing. Similarly, even without an award or remedy having been ordered by the tribunal, the period elapsing from the date of the actual discrimination to the appeal and, if the case is lost by an employer or other respondent, by the time the case returns to the remedies hearing, count towards the daily rate of interest and extend the mid point.

Although costs are not automatically awarded in the EAT, which has the same basic cost rules as the employment tribunal, there is still an important financial consideration to be assessed when deciding whether to pursue an appeal. A party must decide whether to risk incurring additional liability because of the interest which will accrue on the award, while also incurring the costs of pursuing the appeal, which costs would not be recovered from the opponents.

14.2 COUNTY COURT/HIGH COURT APPEALS

14.2.1 The right to appeal

Appeals of whatever nature in the civil courts have to be considered carefully, because the law only permits appeals to be brought on limited grounds. A further consideration will be that in civil courts (with the exception of employment tribunal appeals) if the appeal is lost, the costs of the opponent will have to be borne.

The party losing the case will already (except in the case of small claims or arbitration cases) have an order against him to pay his opponent's costs; at any appeal, if unsuccessful, that party will have to be prepared to meet *in addition* both his own and his opponent's legal costs in respect of the appeal itself.

The venue for an appeal varies, dependent upon the court which heard the case and gave the decision which is the subject of the appeal and also depending upon what is actually being appealed. In particular, there is a key distinction between final orders and judgments, ie trial judgments in a case and interim orders, or interlocutory orders, which are orders made during the course of the proceedings but which do not finally determine the action or claim.

14.2.2 Appeal from the county court

If the case was decided by the county court, then any appeal is either to a higher judge or to the Court of Appeal.

An interlocutory order (ie an interim measure such as an injunction), or a decision made by a district judge, can be appealed within the same court venue to a circuit judge. The time-scale is short, however, being only five days from the date of the order or judgment.

If the case was heard via the arbitration route, then there is no appeal although there is a limited right to refer the matter to a circuit judge. This limited right is on very narrow grounds, and only where it can be shown:

- that the arbitrator had no jurisdiction,
- that an error of law occurred,
- that there was some misconduct on the part of the arbitrator.

The time-scale for this type of appeal is 14 days.

Other decisions from the county court, or a decision of the circuit judge, have to be taken to the Court of Appeal and must be lodged within four weeks from the date that judgment was given. That is a relatively short time-scale and, in addition, there is also a prerequisite that an individual obtain 'leave to appeal'. If the original action concerns a claim for less than £5,000, or an amount or remedy which was unquantifiable (for example a non-monetary remedy) then leave to appeal has to be sought before that appeal can proceed. In cases where leave to appeal is required, the common approach and best practice is to ask for leave immediately after the judgment of the court has been given, ie at the time or on the day. In any event, such leave must be sought within the requisite appeal time-limit.

14.2.3 High Court appeals

Again, the appeal route varies dependent upon the subject of the appeal. If the decision was taken by a master or district judge, an appeal can be taken to a high court judge in chambers (ie not in open court); this tends to occur where the claim was heard in chambers and generally in relation to interim orders. The time-limit in such cases is five days if the case was heard in London and seven days elsewhere.

If the decision concerns the outcome of a trial or the remedy and damages awarded, then an appeal lies to the Court of Appeal and a four week time-limit is imposed, although there is no requirement to seek leave first as this applies only to interlocutory orders.

14.2.4 Court of Appeal

A case which is heard in the Court of Appeal can in turn be taken to the House of Lords which, generally speaking, is the highest court in the land. The only exception to this, however, is if the case concerns not just an aspect of UK legislation but also European law when there is the possibility for a reference to be made to the ECJ (see below).

The time-limit for appeal to the House of Lords is one month and leave to appeal must be obtained from either the Court of Appeal itself or the House of Lords.

In less rare circumstances, an appeal may be referred direct from a High Court judge to the House of Lords, thus by-passing the Court of Appeal. This route is known as 'leap-frogging'. However, leap-frogging direct to the House of Lords can occur only if the following is established:

– the parties have consented;
– the trial judge certifies that the appeal concerns an important point of law which is of general public importance and which relates to the construction of particular law;
– the House of Lords agrees by granting leave.[1]

14.2.5 Extension

Extensions of time can be granted for appeals to proceed outside the time-limits, although this will occur only in rare cases and the granting of extensions is entirely at the discretion of the Court. Furthermore, good reasons as to why the time-limit imposed was not met would have to be shown and the Court will look at matters such as the length of any delay, the reasons for the delay, the likelihood of the appeal succeeding and any prejudice caused by the delay to the opponent to the appeal.[2] Similarly, in the case of an appeal from the High Court to the Court of Appeal where leave is required, if a party is close to the four-week time-limit, there is an automatic extension of the time-limit for the appeal by seven days from the date on which leave is granted. This the dead-line becomes the later of four weeks or seven days after leave is granted. Thus will not assist a party who applies for leave which is granted well before the four-week dead-line.

14.2.6 Grounds for appeal

The basis upon which any of the appeals outlined above can be brought is limited. It cannot be brought simply because a party has been unsuccessful and is aggrieved at the outcome. The party must show that the original court and decision fell into error.

14.2.7 Factual appeals/errors

An Appeal Court would guard against changing a decision where a party simply considers that the judge came to the wrong conclusion, based on the evidence before the court. If evidence is disputed, as part or as all of the appeal, it can only be entertained as an appeal case if it can be shown that either:

– in reaching his or her conclusion, the judge had no grounds or evidence on which to base those conclusions;
– the key factors or evidence were not considered;
– new evidence has come to light.

---

1   Administration of Justice Act 1969, ss 12 and 13.
2   *Van Stillevoldt B V v EL Carriers Inc* [1983] 1 WLR 207.

In the latter case, however, it is important to raise the new evidence with the court or judge itself and consider making an application for a review or rehearing, rather than going straight to an appeal.

Understandably, appeals on these grounds are more difficult to pursue both in terms of persuading the Court of Appeal to grant leave and in succeeding at the appeal itself.

14.2.8 Errors of law

The second basis upon which an appeal can be brought, is if the court applied the wrong test, misapplied the test or failed to have due regard to legislation or cases which are binding on it. A court is obliged to follow and apply cases decided by a higher court which clarify the law by providing definitions and tests to be applied.

14.2.9 The outcome of appeals

Once an appeal has been heard, there are generally three options available in order to deal with the appeal and bring it to a conclusion:

– to confirm the original decision so that the appeal fails;
– to set aside the original decision, that is to say confirm that there was some error and return the case to the original court for a re-hearing, often to a different judge;
– for the Appeal Court to substitute its own decision for that of the original court.

14.3 CRIMINAL PROCEEDINGS

14.3.1 The right to appeal

The right to an appeal following the outcome of a criminal case is perhaps less key in the context of harassment because, as has already been outlined in Chapter 12, decisions as to whether to prosecute a claim or to appeal a claim will lie first with the body responsible for prosecution and secondly with the defendant.

The basic options are to appeal from the Crown Court to the Court of Appeal and from the magistrates' court to the Crown Court itself, although, as we shall see, there are variations in particular cases.

Appeals can only be brought on questions of law, ie that the law was applied wrongly in the case, certain aspects were overlooked, or there was some misinterpretation. It is possible to launch appeals on the basis of errors of fact but, ordinarily, leave to appeal must be sought from the Court of Appeal itself in such a case. This means that the Court of Appeal must, at an initial hearing (on the application of the defendant) confirm that it is satisfied that there is sufficient merit in the appeal to allow it to proceed.

Generally speaking, if a defendant is acquitted in the criminal process, the prosecution (the Crown Prosecution Service in England and Wales) does not have the right to appeal. However, if a point of law arises in a particular case, it is open to the Attorney-General to request a view from the Court of Appeal. Such a request does not affect the outcome of the original trial and therefore the defendant's acquittal or conviction is not challenged.

14.3.2 Crown Court proceedings

An appeal in the Crown Court lies with the Court of Appeal and this can be an appeal against the conviction itself, as well as the sentence. As an alternative, however, it is open to a defendant to appeal only on the sentence that is imposed by the Crown Court. The only limit on the power to appeal against sentence applies in respect of criminal offences where the sentence is fixed by law. This does not apply to any of the remedies and actions examined in Chapters 12 and 13 but largely covers very serious offences such as murder, which carries a life sentence.

Leave must be obtained from the Court of Appeal for the appeal itself to proceed, unless the trial judge in the Crown Court confirms that the case is one that is suitable for appeal.

The other variation that exists, when an individual may appeal to the Court of Appeal notwithstanding that he was convicted in a magistrates' court, is where the individual is found guilty in the magistrates' court but the case is referred to the Crown Court for sentencing. This may occur, for example, when in light of the seriousness of the offence and its surrounding circumstances, the magistrates consider that a higher sentence than that which their powers allow them to impose is appropriate.

Where a defendant's conviction has been via this route, there is a right to appeal to the Court of Appeal if the individual sentence involves imprisonment for six months or more, or if the sentence was imposed wrongly because the Court exceeded its power or simply did not have the power to so convict.

As with other Crown Court appeals to the Court of Appeal, leave should be obtained from the Court of Appeal itself, again unless the judge grants a certificate that the case is fit for appeal.

Generally speaking the time-limit in which an appeal should be lodged with the Court of Appeal is 28 days from the date of the conviction.

14.3.3 Magistrates' court convictions

If the criminal case progresses through the magistrates' court, then an appeal lies to the Crown Court, unless the route which we have explored above occurred and the case, following conviction, was referred to the Crown Court for sentencing. The right to appeal is restricted.

- if the defendant pleaded guilty, then he or she can only appeal against the sentence which was imposed and not against the conviction;
- if the defendant pleaded not guilty, then both the conviction and the sentence itself may be subject to an appeal to the Crown Court;
- if found guilty in the magistrates' court and referred to the Crown Court for sentencing, the individual may appeal to the Crown Court itself against the conviction.

The time-limits are slightly shorter in the case of the magistrates' court conviction and run to 21 days after the date of the decision, although it is possible to apply for an extension of time.

14.3.4 Criminal Cases Review Commission

By the Criminal Appeal Act 1995 a body known as the 'Criminal Cases Review Commission' was established. This body has the power to investigate any conviction and may refer a case to the Court of Appeal or the Crown Court, adopting the same process as for an appeal.

The Criminal Cases Review Commission may look into both a conviction itself and the sentence. The Commission can only refer the case on good grounds where it is satisfied either:

– that the conviction would not be upheld.
– that important arguments or evidence were not raised at the original hearing; or
– that a point of law was not raised or certain information was not dealt with in the sentencing; and
– where an appeal has been concluded or leave to appeal refused.

Similarly, the Court of Appeal may refer a matter to the Criminal Cases Review Commission for investigation, with appropriate instructions (known as 'directions') and the Commission will produce a report for the benefit of the Court of Appeal which can then consider the matter.

14.3.5 House of Lords

A final appeal avenue available in the criminal route is from the Court of Appeal to the House of Lords, if the case is such that it raises a matter of public importance. An appeal of this nature can be brought by the defendant or by the prosecutor.

Chapter 15

THE FUTURE

Introduction – The current situation in the United States – Continuing developments – Recommendations for employers – Conclusion

15.1 INTRODUCTION

Complaints of harassment in the UK are increasing, as are the levels of awards which are being made. Employees are becoming more aware of their rights and employers must not allow themselves to be left behind. The aim of this chapter, contributed by the US law firm Preston Gates & Ellis, is to outline the current situation in the United States with regard to discrimination claims generally and harassment specifically, on the basis that the situation in the US is generally three to five years ahead of the UK in terms of litigation. Is this the direction the UK is taking?

15.2 THE CURRENT SITUATION IN THE UNITED STATES

In the United States, employment claims have become in the 1990s what personal injury and product liability were in the 1970s and 1980s – an extremely profitable area for legal practitioners and a nightmare for companies. The following are a selection of examples of legal activity in the US in the Spring and Summer of 1998:

> Mitsubishi Motor Manufacturing of America announced that it will pay $34 million to more than 350 current and former female employees in settlement of their claims of sexual harassment. The $34 million settlement follows a $9.7 million settlement reached last year between Mitsubishi and 27 current and former female employees based on similar claims of a sexually hostile work environment.
> *EEOC v Mitsubishi Motor Manufacturing of America Inc*
> CD Ill No 96-C-1192, settlement announced 11 June 1998

> An insurance company agreed to pay $1.2 million to settle the claims of a handful of current and former female employees who alleged that two corporate officers harassed them, including propositioning them and engaging in verbal and physical sexual conduct.
> *EEOC v BWD Group Ltd*
> EDNY CV 97-2617, settlement reached 28 May 1998

> Holiday Inn will pay $1 million to settle the claims of racial discrimination brought on behalf of more than 1,000 candidates for employment over the last several years. The case alleged that Holiday Inn had refused to hire black

candidates into the most viable positions and coded their applications in order to single them out on the basis of race.

EEOC v Oak Lawn Ltd
ND Ill, No 26 C 0959, settlement reached 29 May 1998

A jury awarded a former employee of McDonnell Douglas Corporation $28 million in damages following a trial in which he alleged that his employment was terminated in retaliation for filing charges of race and age discrimination with the federal agency. The award included $26 million in punitive damages.

Verdine v McDonnell Douglas Corp
Cal Super Ct No BC16826 7 July 1998

A gasoline dealer, Clark Refining & Marketing, will pay $3.3 million to 38 former employees to resolve class action claims for age discrimination. The employees alleged that when they refused to accept offers of early retirement, they were involuntarily dismissed based on their age.

EEOC v Clark Refining & Marketing Inc
ND Ill, No 94-C-2779 15 July 1998

While the size of these verdicts and settlements is impressive, most remarkable is that these cases are far from unique. Whereas 10 years ago, claims of hostile work environment and retaliation were in their infancy and rarely among the 'big dollar' cases, class actions have now become pervasive. Million-dollar verdicts and settlements have become almost commonplace. Small employers are as likely to face a million-dollar demand as the largest corporations.

15.3 CONTINUING DEVELOPMENTS

The trend toward increasing ambit of liability for employers and blanket of protections for employees, which had its origins in the 1960s but languished through the 1970s and much of the 1980s, transformed into an unstoppable train in the 1990s. And the trend continues. The courts and legislatures have been expanding traditional employee protections to include contingent workforces and independent contractors. The US Supreme Court recently expanded the ambit of protection of federal anti-discrimination laws to include same-sex harassment, stating that it relied upon the courts and juries to apply common sense and sensitivity to the social context of fact patterns to place appropriate limits on the scope of liability.[1] During this same term, the Supreme Court also re-examined and clarified the extent to which an employer should be vicariously liable for harassment by its supervisors.[2] Employers have recently been challenged on gender discrimination bases for providing medical insurance coverage for Viagra, a drug designed to aid men to overcome impotence, but not contraception which is available on prescription.

---

1   *Oncale v Sundowner Offshore Services Inc*, US 1998 WL 88039 (3/4/98).
2   *Burlington Industries v Ellerth*; *Faragher v City of Boca Raton*.

15.4 RECOMMENDATIONS FOR EMPLOYERS

If defence employment law attorneys in the United States could turn back the clock for their clients, many of whom are now devoting enormous resources to the defence of discrimination and harassment claims, the following would be included among recommendations for the future.

- *Audit policies and practices* Conduct a full-scale review of the company's employment practices, including documents such as job advertisements and applications, policy manuals, work rules and contracts. Interview selected employees and managers to determine areas of strength and weakness. Identify and address the issues of the disenfranchised and marginalised employees. Hire the best human resources professionals available.
- *Anti-harassment policies* Obtain support for appropriate equal employment and anti-harassment policies from the board of directors, ownership, and upper management of the organisation. Develop comprehensive policies, disseminate them, and enforce them.
- *Employee and manager training* Do it well, do it often, and make sure upper management are included in the training programme. Focus comprehensive training on front-line or first-level supervisors. Assure that anyone who is in a position to hire, fire, discipline, and train employees understands the appropriate standards of behaviour, the company's policies on conduct and behaviour, and knows the steps to take in the event that a problem is identified.
- *Alternative dispute resolution* Explore alternatives to traditional means of pursuing and defending claims by employees. Try to find creative means for addressing employee problems before they become lawsuits or administrative actions. Consider developing internal grievance procedures and engaging the services of a third-party mediator to address issues which are otherwise unresolvable. Contemplate the possibility of mandatory arbitration provisions as a term of employment.

15.5 CONCLUSION

The future arrived too quickly in the United States. Those companies that insisted that there was no reason to alter the status quo and no need to change old patterns of behaviour have found that the cost of this position and attitude is enormous. Those companies that imagined the future and prepared for it have prospered.

APPENDICES

Appendix I

COMMISSION RECOMMENDATION
OF 27 NOVEMBER 1991
ON THE PROTECTION OF THE DIGNITY OF WOMEN
AND MEN AT WORK
(92/131/EEC)

THE COMMISSION OF THE EUROPEAN COMMUNITIES,

Having regard to the Treaty establishing the European Economic Community, and in particular the second indent of Article 155 thereof,

Whereas unwanted conduct of a sexual nature, or other conduct based on sex affecting the dignity of women and men at work, including the conduct of superiors and colleagues, is unacceptable and may, in certain circumstances, be contrary to the principle of equal treatment within the meaning of Articles 3, 4 and 5 of Council Directive 76/207/EEC of 9 February 1976 on the implementation of the principle of equal treatment for men and women as regards access to employment, vocational training and promotion, and working conditions[1], a view supported by case-law in some Member States;

Whereas, in accordance with the Council recommendation of 13 December 1984 on the promotion of positive action for women[2], many Member States have carried out a variety of positive action measures and actions having a bearing, *inter alia*, on respect for the dignity of women at the workplace;

Whereas the European Parliament, in its resolution of 11 June 1986 on violence against women[3], has called upon national governments, equal opportunities committees and trade unions to carry out concerted information campaigns to create a proper awareness of the individual rights of all members of the labour force;

Whereas the Advisory Committee on Equal Opportunities for Women and Men, in its opinion of 20 June 1988, has unanimously recommended that there should be a recommendation and code of conduct on sexual harassment in the workplace covering harassment of both sexes;

Whereas the Commission in its action programme relating to the implementation of the Community Charter of Basic Social Rights for Workers undertook to examine the protection of workers and their dignity at work, having regard to the reports and recommendations prepared on various aspects of implementation of Community law[4];

Whereas the Council, in its resolution of 29 May 1990 on the protection of the dignity of women and men at work[5], affirms that conduct based on sex affecting the dignity of women and men at work, including conduct of superiors and colleagues, constitutes an

---

1   OJ No L 39, 14. 2. 1976, p. 40.
2   OJ No L 331, 19. 12. 1984, p. 34.
3   OJ No C 176, 14. 7. 1986, p. 79.
4   COM(89) 568 final, 29. 11. 1989. For example, 'The dignity of women at work: A report on the problem of sexual harassment in the Member States of the European Communities', October 1987, by Michael Rubenstein (ISBN 92-825-8764-9).
5   OJ No C 157, 27. 6. 1990, p. 3.

intolerable violation of the dignity of workers or trainees, and calls on the Member States and the institutions and organs of the European Communities to develop positive measures designed to create a climate at work in which women and men respect one another's human integrity;

Whereas the Commission, in its third action programme on equal opportunities for women and men, 1991 to 1995, and pursuant to paragraph 3 (2) of the said Council resolution of 29 May 1990, resolved to draw up a code of conduct on the protection of the dignity of women and men at work[1], based on experience and best practice in the Member States, to provide guidance on initiating and pursuing positive measures designed to create a climate at work in which women and men respect one another's human integrity;

Whereas the European Parliament, on 22 October 1991, adopted a resolution on the protection of the dignity of women and men at work[2];

Whereas the Economic and Social Committee, on 30 October 1991, adopted an opinion on the protection of the dignity of women and men at work[3],

RECOMMENDS AS FOLLOWS:

Article 1

It is recommended that the Member States take action to promote awareness that conduct of a sexual nature, or other conduct based on sex affecting the dignity of women and men at work, including conduct of superiors and colleagues, is unacceptable if:

(a) such conduct is unwanted, unreasonable and offensive to the recipient;
(b) a person's rejection of, or submission to, such conduct on the part of employers or workers (including superiors or colleagues) is used explicitly or implicitly as a basis for a decision which affects that person's access to vocational training, access to employment, continued employment, promotion, salary or any other employment decisions;
    and/or
(c) such conduct creates an intimidating, hostile or humiliating work environment for the recipient;

and that such conduct may, in certain circumstances, be contrary to the principle of equal treatment within the meaning of Articles 3, 4 and 5 of Directive 76/207/EEC.

Article 2

It is recommended that Member States take action, in the public sector, to implement the Commission's code of practice on the protection of the dignity of women and men at work, annexed hereto. The action of the Member States, in thus initiating and pursuing positive measures designed to create a climate at work in which women and men respect one another's human integrity, should serve as an example to the private sector.

Article 3

It is recommended that Member States encourage employers and employee representatives to develop measures to implement the Commission's code of practice on the protection of the dignity of women and men at work.

---

1   COM(90) 449 final, 6. 11. 1990.
2   OJ No C 305, 25. 11. 1991.
3   OJ No C 14, 20. 1. 1992.

Article 4

Member States shall inform the Commission within three years of the date of this recommendation of the measures taken to give effect to it, in order to allow the Commission to draw up a report on all such measures. The Commission shall, within this period, ensure the widest possible circulation of the code of practice. The report should examine the degree of awareness of the Code, its perceived effectiveness, its degree of application and the extent of its use in collective bargaining between the social partners.

Article 5

This recommendation is addressed to the Member States.

Done at Brussels, 27 November 1991.

For the Commission
Vasso PAPANDREOU
Member of the Commission

ANNEX
PROTECTING THE DIGNITY OF WOMEN AND MEN AT WORK
A code of practice on measures to combat sexual harassment

I. INTRODUCTION

This code of practice is issued in accordance with the resolution of the Council of Ministers on the protection of the dignity of women and men at work[1], and to accompany the Commission's recommendation on this issue.

Its purpose is to give practical guidance to employers, trade unions, and employees on the protection of the dignity of women and men at work. The code is intended to be applicable in both the public and the private sector and employers are encouraged to follow the recommendations contained in the code in a way which is appropriate to the size and structure of their organization. It may be particularly relevant for small and medium-sized enterprises to adapt some of the practical steps to their specific needs.

The aim is to ensure that sexual harassment does not occur and, if it does occur, to ensure that adequate procedures are readily available to deal with the problem and prevent its recurrence. The code thus seeks to encourage the development and implementation of policies and practices which establish working environments free of sexual harassment and in which women and men respect one another's human integrity.

The expert report carried out on behalf of the Commission found that sexual harassment is a serious problem for many working women in the European Community[2] and research in Member States has proven beyond doubt that sexual harassment at work is not an isolated phenomenon. On the contrary, it is clear that for millions of women in the European Community, sexual harassment is an unpleasant and unavoidable part of their working lives. Men too may suffer sexual harassment and should, of course, have the same rights as women to the protection of their dignity.

Some specific groups are particularly vulnerable to sexual harassment. Research in several Member States, which documents the link between the risk of sexual harassment and the recipient's perceived vulnerability, suggests that divorced and separated women, young women and new entrants to the labour market and those with irregular or precarious employment contracts, women in non-traditional jobs, women with disabilities, lesbians and women from racial minorities are disproportionately at risk. Gay men and young men are also vulnerable to harassment. It is undeniable that harassment on grounds of sexual orientation undermines the dignity at work of those affected and it is impossible to regard such harassment as appropriate workplace behaviour.

---

1   OJ No C 157, 27. 6. 1990, p. 3.
2   'The dignity of women at work: A report on the problem of sexual harassment in the Member States of the European Communities', October 1987, by Michael Rubenstein (ISBN 92-825-8764-9).

Sexual harassment pollutes the working environment and can have a devastating effect upon the health, confidence, morale and performance of those affected by it. The anxiety and stress produced by sexual harassment commonly leads to those subjected to it taking time off work due to sickness, being less efficient at work, or leaving their job to seek work elsewhere. Employees often suffer the adverse consequences of the harassment itself and short- and long-term damage to their employment prospects if they are forced to change jobs. Sexual harassment may also have a damaging impact on employees not themselves the object of unwanted behaviour but who are witness to it or have a knowledge of the unwanted behaviour.

There are also adverse consequences arising from sexual harassment for employers. It has a direct impact on the profitability of the enterprise where staff take sick leave or resign their posts because of sexual harassment, and on the economic efficiency of the enterprise where employees' productivity is reduced by having to work in a climate in which individuals' integrity is not respected.

In general terms, sexual harassment is an obstacle to the proper integration of women into the labour market and the Commission is committed to encouraging the development of comprehensive measures to improve such integration[1].

2. DEFINITION

Sexual harassment means unwanted conduct of a sexual nature, or other conduct based on sex affecting the dignity of women and men at work[2]. This can include unwelcome physical, verbal or non-verbal conduct.

Thus, a range of behaviour may be considered to constitute sexual harassment. It is unacceptable if such conduct is unwanted, unreasonable and offensive to the recipient; a person's rejection of or submission to such conduct on the part of employers or workers (including superiors or colleagues) is used explicitly or implicitly as a basis for a decision which affects that person's access to vocational training or to employment, continued employment, promotion, salary or any other employment decisions; and/or such conduct creates an intimidating, hostile or humiliating working environment for the recipient[2].

The essential characteristic of sexual harassment is that it is unwanted by the recipient, that it is for each individual to determine what behaviour is acceptable to them and what they regard as offensive. Sexual attention becomes sexual harassment if it is persisted in once it has been made clear that it is regarded by the recipient as offensive, although one incident of harassment may constitute sexual harassment if sufficiently serious. It is the unwanted nature of the conduct which distinguishes sexual harassment from friendly behaviour, which is welcome and mutual.

3. THE LAW AND EMPLOYERS' RESPONSIBILITIES

Conduct of a sexual nature or other based on sex affecting the dignity of women and men at work may be contrary to the principle of equal treatment within the meaning of Articles 3, 4 and 5 of Council Directive 76/207/EEC of 9 February 1976 on the implementation of the principle of equal treatment for men and women as regards access to employment, vocational training and promotion, and working conditions[3]. This principle means that there shall be no discrimination whatsoever on grounds of sex either directly or indirectly by reference in particular to marital or family status.

---

1 Third action programme on equal opportunities for women and men, 1991 to 1995, COM(90) 449, 6. 11. 1990.
2 Council resolution on the protection of the dignity of women and men at work (OJ No C 157, 27. 6. 1990, p. 3, point 1).
3 OJ No L 39, 14. 2. 1976, p. 40.

In certain circumstances, and depending upon national law, sexual harassment may also be a criminal offence or may contravene other obligations imposed by the law, such as health and safety duties, or a duty, contractual or otherwise, to be a good employer. Since sexual harassment is a form of employee misconduct, employers have a responsibility to deal with it as they do with any other form of employee misconduct as well as to refrain from harassing employees themselves. Since sexual harassment is a risk to health and safety, employers have a responsibility to take steps to minimize the risk as they do with other hazards. Since sexual harassment often entails an abuse of power, employers may have a responsibility for the misuse of the authority they delegate.

This code, however, focuses on sexual harassment as a problem of sex discrimination. Sexual harassment is sex discrimination because the gender of the recipient is the determining factor in who is harassed. Conduct of a sexual nature or other conduct based on sex affecting the dignity of women and men at work in some Member States already has been found to contravene national equal treatment laws and employers have a responsibility to seek to ensure that the work environment is free from such conduct[1].

As sexual harassment is often a function of women's status in the employment hierarchy, policies to deal with sexual harassment are likely to be most effective where they are linked to a broader policy to promote equal opportunities and to improve the position of women. Advice on steps which can be taken generally to implement an equal opportunities policy is set out in the Commission's guide to positive action[2].

Similarly, a procedure to deal with complaints of sexual harassment should be regarded as only one component of a strategy to deal with the problem. The prime objective should be to change behaviour and attitudes, to seek to ensure the prevention of sexual harassment.

4. COLLECTIVE BARGAINING

The majority of the recommendations contained in this code are for action by employers, since employers have clear responsibilities to ensure the protection of the dignity of women and men at work.

Trade unions also have responsibilities to their members and they can and should play an important role in the prevention of sexual harassment in the workplace. It is recommended that the question of including appropriate clauses in agreements be examined in the context of the collective bargaining process, with the aim of achieving a work environment free from unwanted conduct of a sexual nature or other conduct based on sex affecting the dignity of women and men at work and free from victimization of a complainant or of a person wishing to give, or giving, evidence in the event of a complaint.

5. RECOMMENDATIONS TO EMPLOYERS

The policies and procedures recommended below should be adopted, where appropriate, after consultation or negotiation with trade unions or employee representatives. Experience suggests that strategies to create and maintain a working environment in which the dignity of employees is respected are most likely to be effective where they are jointly agreed.

It should be emphasized that a distinguishing characteristic of sexual harassment is that employees subjected to it often will be reluctant to complain. An absence of complaints about sexual harassment in a particular organization, therefore, does not necessarily mean

---

1   Council resolution on the protection of the dignity of women and men at work (OJ No C 157, 27. 6. 1990, p. 3, point 2 (3) (a)).
2   Positive action: Equal opportunities for women in employment – a guide, Office for Official Publications of the European Communities, 1988.

an absence of sexual harassment. It may mean that the recipients of sexual harassment think that there is no point in complaining because nothing will be done about it, or because it will be trivialized or the complainant subjected to ridicule, or because they fear reprisals. Implementing the preventative and procedural recommendations outlined below should facilitate the creation of a climate at work in which such concerns have no place.

A. Prevention

(i) Policy statements

As a first step in showing senior management's concern and their commitment to dealing with the problem of sexual harassment, employers should issue a policy statement which expressly states that all employees have a right to be treated with dignity, that sexual harassment at work will not be permitted or condoned and that employees have a right to complain about it should it occur.

It is recommended that the policy statement make clear what is considered inappropriate behaviour at work, and explain that such behaviour, in certain circumstances, may be unlawful. It is advisable for the statement to set out a positive duty on managers and supervisors to implement the policy and to take corrective action to ensure compliance with it. It should also place a positive duty on all employees to comply with the policy and to ensure that their colleagues are treated with respect and dignity.

In addition, it is recommended that the statement explain the procedure which should be followed by employees subjected to sexual harassment at work in order to obtain assistance and to whom they should complain; that it contain an undertaking that allegations of sexual harassment will be dealt with seriously, expeditiously and confidentially, and that employees will be protected against victimization or retaliation for bringing a complaint of sexual harassment. It should also specify that appropriate disciplinary measures will be taken against employees found guilty of sexual harassment.

(ii) Communicating the policy

Once the policy has been developed, it is important to ensure that it is communicated effectively to all employees, so that they are aware that they have a right to complain and to whom they should complain; that their complaint will be dealt with promptly and fairly; and that employees are made aware of the likely consequences of engaging in sexual harassment. Such communication will highlight management's commitment to eliminating sexual harassment, thus enhancing a climate in which it will not occur.

(iii) Responsibility

All employees have a responsibility to help to ensure a working environment in which the dignity of employees is respected and managers (including supervisors) have a particular duty to ensure that sexual harassment does not occur in work areas for which they are responsible. It is recommended that managers explain the organization's policy to their staff and take steps to positively promote the policy. Managers should also be responsive and supportive to any member of staff who complains about sexual harassment, provide full and clear advice on the procedure to be adopted, maintain confidentiality in any cases of sexual harassment and ensure that there is no further problem of sexual harassment or any victimization after a complaint has been resolved.

(iv) Training

An important means of ensuring that sexual harassment does not occur and that, if it does occur, the problem is resolved efficiently is through the provision of training for managers and supervisors. Such training should aim to identify the factors which contribute to a working environment free of sexual harassment and to familiarize participants with their responsibilities under the employer's policy and any problems they are likely to encounter.

In addition, those playing an official role in any formal complaints procedure in respect of sexual harassment should receive specialist training, such as that outlined above.

It is also good practice to include information as to the organization's policy on sexual harassment and procedures for dealing with it as part of appropriate induction and training programmes.

B. Procedures

The development of clear and precise procedures to deal with sexual harassment once it has occurred is of great importance. The procedures should ensure the resolution of problems in an efficient and effective manner. Practical guidance for employees on how to deal with sexual harassment when it occurs and with its aftermath will make it more likely that it will be dealt with at an early stage. Such guidance should of course draw attention to an employee's legal rights and to any time limits within which they must be exercised.

(i) Resolving problems informally
Most recipients of harassment simply want the harassment to stop. Both informal and formal methods of resolving problems should be available.

Employees should be advised that, if possible, they should attempt to resolve the problem informally in the first instance. In some cases, it may be possible and sufficient for the employee to explain clearly to the person engaging in the unwanted conduct that the behaviour in question is not welcome, that it offends them or makes them uncomfortable, and that it interferes with their work.

In circumstances where it is too difficult or embarrassing for an individual to do this on their own behalf, an alternative approach would be to seek support from, or for an initial approach to be made by, a sympathetic friend or confidential counsellor.

If the conduct continues or if it is not appropriate to resolve the problem informally, it should be raised through the formal complaints procedure.

(ii) Advice and assistance
It is recommended that employers designate someone to provide advice and assistance to employees subjected to sexual harassment, where possible with responsibilities to assist in the resolution of any problems, whether through informal or formal means. It may be helpful if the officer is designated with the agreement of the trade unions or employees, as this is likely to enhance their acceptability. Such officers could be selected from personnel departments or equal opportunities departments for example. In some organizations they are designated as 'confidential counsellors' or 'sympathetic friends'. Often such a role may be played by someone from the employee's trade union or women's support groups.

Whatever the location of this responsibility in the organization, it is recommended that the designated officer receives appropriate training in the best means of resolving problems and in the detail of the organization's policy and procedures, so that they can perform their role effectively. It is also important that they are given adequate resources to carry out their function, and protection against victimization for assisting any recipient of sexual harassment.

(iii) Complaints procedure
It is recommended that, where the complainant regards attempts at informal resolution as inappropriate, where informal attempts at resolution have been refused, or where the

outcome has been unsatisfactory, a formal procedure for resolving the complaint be provided. The procedure should give employees confidence that the organization will take allegations of sexual harassment seriously.

By its nature sexual harassment may make the normal channels of complaint difficult to use because of embarrassment, fears of not being taken seriously, fears of damage to reputation, fears of reprisal or the prospect of damaging the working environment. Therefore, a formal procedure should specify to whom the employee should bring a complaint, and it should also provide an alternative if in the particular circumstances the normal grievance procedure may not be suitable, for example because the alleged harasser is the employee's line manager. It is also advisable to make provision for employees to bring a complaint in the first instance to someone of their own sex, should they so choose.

It is good practice for employers to monitor and review complaints of sexual harassment and how they have been resolved, in order to ensure that their procedures are working effectively.

(iv) Investigations
It is important to ensure that internal investigations of any complaints are handled with sensitivity and with due respect for the rights of both the complainant and the alleged harasser. The investigation should be seen to be independent and objective. Those carrying out the investigation should not be connected with the allegation in any way, and every effort should be made to resolve complaints speedily – grievances should be handled promptly and the procedure should set a time limit within which complaints will be processed, with due regard for any time limits set by national legislation for initiating a complaint through the legal system.

It is recommended as good practice that both the complainant and the alleged harasser have the right to be accompanied and/or represented, perhaps by a representative of their trade union or a friend or colleague; that the alleged harasser be given full details of the nature of the complaint and the opportunity to respond, and that strict confidentiality be maintained throughout any investigation into an allegation. Where it is necessary to interview witnesses, the importance of confidentiality should be emphasized.

It must be recognized that recounting the experience of sexual harassment is difficult and can damage the employee's dignity. Therefore, a complainant should not be required repeatedly to recount the events complained of where this is unnecessary.

The investigation should focus on the facts of the complaint and it is advisable for the employer to keep a complete record of all meetings and investigations.

(v) Disciplinary offence
It is recommended that violations of the organization's policy protecting the dignity of employees at work should be treated as a disciplinary offence and the disciplinary rules should make clear what is regarded as inappropriate behaviour at work. It is also good practice to ensure that the range of penalties to which offenders will be liable for violating the rule is clearly stated and also to make it clear that it will be considered a disciplinary offence to victimize or retaliate against an employee for bringing a complaint of sexual harassment in good faith.

Where a complaint is upheld and it is determined that it is necessary to relocate or transfer one party, consideration should be given, wherever practicable, to allowing the complainant to choose whether he or she wishes to remain in their post or be transferred to another location. No element of penalty should be seen to attach to a complainant whose complaint is upheld and in addition, where a complaint is upheld, the employer should monitor the situation to ensure that the harassment has stopped.

Even where a complaint is not upheld, for example because the evidence is regarded as inconclusive, consideration should be given to transferring or re-scheduling the work of one of the employees concerned rather than requiring them to continue to work together against the wishes of either party.

6. RECOMMENDATIONS TO TRADE UNIONS

Sexual harassment is a trade union issue as well as an issue for employers. It is recommended as good practice that trade unions formulate and issue clear policy statements on sexual harassment and take steps to raise awareness of the problem of sexual harassment in the workplace, in order to help create a climate in which it is neither condoned or ignored. For example, trade unions could aim to give all officers and representatives training on equality issues, including dealing with sexual harassment, and include such information in union-sponsored or approved training courses, as well as information on the union's policy. Trade unions should consider declaring that sexual harassment is inappropriate behaviour and educating members and officials about its consequences is recommended as good practice.

Trade unions should also raise the issue of sexual harassment with employers and encourage the adoption of adequate policies and procedures to protect the dignity of women and men at work in the organization. It is advisable for trade unions to inform members of their right not to be sexually harassed at work and provide members with clear guidance as to what to do if they are sexually harassed, including guidance on any relevant legal rights.

Where complaints arise, it is important for trade unions to treat them seriously and sympathetically and ensure that the complainant has an opportunity of representation if a complaint is to be pursued. It is important to create an environment in which members feel able to raise such complaints knowing they will receive a sympathetic and supportive response from local union representatives. Trade unions could consider designating specially trained officials to advise and counsel members with complaints of sexual harassment and act on their behalf if required. This will provide a focal point for support. It is also a good idea to ensure that there are sufficient female representatives to support women subjected to sexual harassment.

It is recommended too, where the trade union is representing both the complainant and the alleged harasser for the purpose of the complaints procedure, that it be made clear that the union is not condoning offensive behaviour by providing representation. In any event, the same official should not represent both parties.

It is good practice to advice members that keeping a record of incidents by the harassed worker will assist in bringing any formal or informal action to a more effective conclusion, that the union wishes to be informed of any incident of sexual harassment and that such information will be kept confidential. It is also good practice for the union to monitor and review the union's record in responding to complaints and in representing alleged harassers and the harassed, in order to ensure its responses are effective.

7. EMPLOYEES' RESPONSIBILITIES

Employees have a clear role to play in helping to create a climate at work in which sexual harassment is unacceptable. They can contribute to preventing sexual harassment through an awareness and sensitivity towards the issue and by ensuring that standards of conduct for themselves and for colleagues do not cause offence.

Employees can do much to discourage sexual harassment by making it clear that they find such behaviour unacceptable and by supporting colleagues who suffer such treatment and are considering making a complaint.

Employees who are themselves recipients of harassment should, where practicable, tell the harasser that the behaviour is unwanted and unacceptable. Once the offender understands clearly that the behaviour is unwelcome, this may be enough to put an end to it. If the behaviour is persisted in, employees should inform management and/or their employee representative through the appropriate channels and request assistance in stopping the harassment, whether through informal or formal means.

Appendix 2

EQUAL OPPORTUNITIES COMMISSION CODE OF PRACTICE ON SEX DISCRIMINATION:
EQUAL OPPORTUNITY POLICIES, PROCEDURES AND PRACTICES IN EMPLOYMENT

INTRODUCTION

1. The EOC issues this Code of Practice for the following purposes:

    (a) for the elimination of discrimination in employment;

    (b) to give guidance as to what steps it is reasonably practicable for employers to take to ensure that their employees do not in the course of their employment act unlawfully contrary to the Sex Discrimination Act (SDA);

    (c) for the promotion of equality of opportunity between men and women in employment.

    The SDA prohibits discrimination against men, as well as against women. It also requires that married people should not be treated less favourably than single people of the same sex.

    It should be noted that the provisions of the SDA – and therefore this Code – apply to the UK-based subsidiaries of foreign companies.

2. The Code gives guidance to employers, trade unions and employment agencies on measures which can be taken to achieve equality. The chances of success of any organisation will clearly be improved if it seeks to develop the abilities of all employees, and the Code shows the close link which exists between equal opportunity and good employment practice. In some cases, an initial cost may be involved, but this should be more than compensated for by better relationships and better use of human resources.

Small businesses

3. The Code has to deal in general terms and it will be necessary for employers to adapt it in a way appropriate to the size and structure of their organisations. Small businesses, for example, will require much simpler procedures than organisations with complex structures and it may not always be reasonable for them to carry out all the Code's detailed recommendations. In adapting the Code's recommendations, small firms should, however, ensure that their practices comply with the Sex Discrimination Act.

Employers' responsibility

4. **The primary responsibility at law rests with each employer to ensure that there is no unlawful discrimination.** It is important, however, that measures to eliminate discrimination or promote equality of opportunity should be understood and supported by all employees. Employers are therefore recommended to involve their employees in equal opportunity policies.

Individual employees' responsibility

5. While the main responsibility for eliminating discrimination and providing equal opportunity is that of the employer, individual employees at all levels have, responsibilities too. They must not discriminate or knowingly aid their employer to do so.

Trade union responsibility

6. The full commitment of trade unions is essential for the elimination of discrimination and for the successful operation of an equal opportunities policy. Much can be achieved by collective bargaining and throughout the Code it is assumed that all the normal procedures will be followed.

7. It is recommended that unions should co-operate in the introduction and implementation of equal opportunities policies where employers have decided to introduce them, and should urge that such policies be adopted where they have not yet been introduced.

8. Trade Unions have a responsibility to ensure that their representatives and members do not unlawfully discriminate on grounds of sex or marriage in the admission or treatment of members. The guidance in this Code also applies to trade unions in their role as employers.

Employment agencies

9. Employment agencies have a responsibility as suppliers of job applicants to avoid unlawful discrimination on the grounds of sex or marriage in providing services to clients. The guidance in this Code also applies to employment agencies in their role as employers.

Definitions

10. For case of reference, the main employment provisions of the Sex Discrimination Act, including definitions of direct and indirect sex and marriage discrimination, are provided in a Legal Annex to this Code. (See pages [240–246]).

PART I

THE ROLE OF GOOD EMPLOYMENT PRACTICES IN ELIMINATING SEX AND MARRIAGE DISCRIMINATION

11. This section of the Code describes those good employment practices which will help to eliminate unlawful discrimination. It recommends the establishment and use of consistent criteria for selection, training, promotion, redundancy and dismissal which are made known to all employees. Without this consistency, decisions can be subjective and leave the way open for unlawful discrimination to occur.

RECRUITMENT

12. It is unlawful: UNLESS THE JOB IS COVERED BY AN EXCEPTION:[1] TO DISCRIMINATE DIRECTLY OR INDIRECTLY ON THE GROUNDS OF SEX OR MARRIAGE

---

1   There are a number of exceptions to the requirements of the SDA, that employers must not discriminate against their employees or against potential employees. The main exceptions are mentioned on pages [241–242] of the Legal Annex.

- IN THE ARRANGEMENTS MADE FOR DECIDING WHO SHOULD BE OFFERED A JOB
- IN ANY TERMS OF EMPLOYMENT
- BY REFUSING OR OMITTING TO OFFER A PERSON EMPLOY-MENT.
  [Section 6(1)(a); 6(1)(b); 6(1)(c)][1]

13. It is therefore recommended that:

(a) each individual should be assessed according to his or her personal capability to carry out a given job. It should not be assumed that men only or women only will be able to perform certain kinds of work;

(b) any qualifications or requirements applied to a job which effectively inhibit applications from one sex or from married people should be retained only if they are justifiable in terms of the job to be done;
[Section 6(1)(a), together with section 1(1)(b) or 3(1)(b)]

(c) any age limits should be retained only if they are necessary for the job. An unjustifiable age limit could constitute unlawful indirect discrimination, for example, against women who have taken time out of employment for child-rearing;

(d) where trade unions uphold such qualification or requirements as union policy, they should amend that policy in the light of any potentially unlawful effect.

Genuine occupational qualifications (GOQs)

14. It is unlawful: EXCEPT FOR CERTAIN JOBS WHEN A PERSON'S SEX IS A GENUINE OCCUPATIONAL QUALIFICATION (GOQ) FOR THAT JOB to select candidates on the ground of sex.
[Section 7(2); 7(3) and 7(4)]

15. There are very few instances in which a job will qualify for a GOQ on the ground of sex. However, exceptions may arise[2], for example, where considerations of privacy and decency or authenticity are involved. The SDA expressly states that the need of the job for strength and stamina does not justify restricting it to men. When a GOQ exists for a job, it applies also to promotion, transfer, or training for that job, but cannot be used to justify a dismissal.

16. In some instances, the GOQ will apply to some of the duties only. A GOQ will not be valid, however, where members of the appropriate sex are already employed in sufficient numbers to meet the employer's likely requirements without undue inconvenience. For example, in a job where sales assistants may be required to undertake changing room duties, it might not be lawful to claim a GOQ in respect of *all* the assistants on the grounds that any of them might be required to undertake changing room duties from time to time.

17. It is therefore recommended that:
   - A job for which a GOQ was used in the past should be re-examined if the post falls vacant to see whether the GOQ still applies. Circumstances may well have changed, rendering the GOQ inapplicable.

---

1 For the full text of section 6 or other sections of the Sex Discrimination Act referred to in this Code, Readers are advised to consult a copy of the Act which is available from Her Majesty's Stationery Office.

2 See page [241] of Legal Annex.

Sources of recruitment

18. It is unlawful: UNLESS THE JOB IS COVERED BY AN EXCEPTION:

  – TO DISCRIMINATE ON GROUNDS OF SEX OR MARRIAGE IN THE ARRANGEMENTS MADE FOR DETERMINING WHO SHOULD BE OFFERED EMPLOYMENT WHETHER RECRUITING BY ADVERTISEMENTS, THROUGH EMPLOYMENT AGENCIES, JOBCENTRES, OR CAREER OFFICES.
  – TO IMPLY THAT APPLICATIONS FROM ONE SEX OR FROM MARRIED PEOPLE WILL NOT BE CONSIDERED.
    [Section 6(1)(a)]
  – TO INSTRUCT OR PUT PRESSURE ON OTHERS TO OMIT TO REFER FOR EMPLOYMENT PEOPLE OF ONE SEX OR MARRIED PEOPLE UNLESS THE JOB IS COVERED BY AN EXCEPTION.
    [Sections 39 and 40]

  It is also unlawful WHEN ADVERTISING JOB VACANCIES,

  – TO PUBLISH OR CAUSE TO BE PUBLISHED AN ADVERTISEMENT WHICH INDICATES OR MIGHT REASONABLY BE UNDERSTOOD AS INDICATING AN INTENTION TO DISCRIMINATE UNLAWFULLY ON GROUNDS OF SEX OR MARRIAGE.

19. It is therefore recommended that:

Advertising

  (a) job advertising should be carried out in such a way as to encourage applications from suitable candidates of both sexes. This can be achieved both by wording of the advertisements and, for example, by placing advertisements in publications likely to reach both sexes. All advertising material and accompanying literature relating to employment or training issues should be reviewed to ensure that it avoids presenting men and women in stereotyped roles. Such stereotyping tends to perpetuate sex segregation in jobs and can also lead people of the opposite sex to believe that they would be unsuccessful in applying for particular jobs;
  (b) where vacancies are filled by promotion or transfer, they should be published to all eligible employees in such a way that they do not restrict applications from either sex;
  (c) recruitment solely or primarily by word of mouth may unnecessarily restrict the choice of applicants available. The method should be avoided in a workforce predominantly of one sex, if in practice it prevents members of the opposite sex from applying;
  (d) where applicants are supplied through trade unions and members of one sex only come forward, this should be discussed with the unions and an alternative approach adopted.

Careers service/schools

20. When notifying vacancies to the Careers Service, employers should specify that these are open to both boys and girls. This is especially important when a job has traditionally been done exclusively or mainly by one sex. If dealing with single sex schools, they should ensure, where possible, that both boys' and girls' schools are approached: it is also a good idea to remind mixed schools that jobs are open to boys and girls.

Selection methods

Tests

21. (a) If selection tests are used, they should be specifically related to job and or career requirements and should measure an individual's actual or inherent ability to do or train for the work or career;

(b) Tests should be reviewed regularly to ensure that they remain relevant and free from any unjustifiable bias, either in content or in scoring mechanism.

Applications and interviewing

22. It is unlawful: UNLESS THE JOB IS COVERED BY AN EXCEPTION:

TO DISCRIMINATE ON GROUNDS OF SEX OR MARRIAGE BY REFUS-ING OR DELIBERATELY OMITTING TO OFFER EMPLOYMENT.
[Section 6(1)(c)]

23. It is therefore recommended that:

(a) employers should ensure that personnel staff, line managers and all other employees who may come into contact with job applicants, should be trained in the provisions of the SDA, including the fact that it is unlawful to instruct or put pressure on others to discriminate;

(b) applications from men and women should be processed in exactly the same way. For example, there should not be separate lists of male and female or married and single applicants. All those handling applications and conducting interviews should be trained in the avoidance of unlawful discrimination and records of interviews kept, where practicable, showing why applicants were or were not appointed;

(c) questions should relate to the requirements of the job. Where it is necessary to assess whether personal circumstances will affect performance of the job (for example, where it involves unsocial hours or extensive travel) this should be discussed objectively without detailed questions based on assumptions about marital status, children and domestic obligations. Questions about marriage plans or family intentions should not be asked, as they could be construed as showing bias against women. Information necessary for personnel records can be collected after a job offer has been made.

Promotion, transfer and training

24. It is unlawful: UNLESS THE JOB IS COVERED BY AN EXCEPTION,

FOR EMPLOYERS TO DISCRIMINATE DIRECTLY OR INDIRECTLY ON THE GROUNDS OF SEX OR MARRIAGE IN THE WAY THEY AFFORD ACCESS TO OPPORTUNITIES FOR PROMOTION, TRANSFER OR TRAINING.
[Section 6(2)(a)]

25. It is therefore recommended that:

(a) where an appraisal system is in operation, the assessment criteria should be examined to ensure that they are not unlawfully discriminatory and the scheme monitored to assess how it is working in practice;

(b) when a group of workers predominantly of one sex is excluded from an appraisal scheme, access to promotion, transfer and training and to other benefits should be reviewed, to ensure that there is no unlawful indirect discrimination;

(c)   promotion and career development patterns are reviewed to ensure that the traditional qualifications are justifiable requirements for the job to be done. In some circumstances, for example, promotion on the basis of length of service could amount to unlawful indirect discrimination, as it may unjustifiably affect more women than men;

(d)   when general ability and personal qualities are the main requirements for promotion to a post, care should be taken to consider favourably candidates of both sexes with differing career patterns and general experience;

(e)   rules which restrict or preclude transfer between certain jobs should be questioned and changed if they are found to be unlawfully discriminatory. Employees of one sex may be concentrated in sections from which transfers are traditionally restricted without real justification;

(f)   policies and practices regarding selection for training, day release and personal development should be examined for unlawful direct and indirect discrimination. Where there is found to be an imbalance in training as between sexes, the cause should be identified to ensure that it is not discriminatory;

(g)   age limits for access to training and promotion should be questioned.

Health and safety legislation

26.   Equal treatment of men and women may be limited by statutory provisions which require men and women to be treated differently. For example, the Factories Act 1961 places restrictions on the hours of work of female manual employees, although the Health and Safety Executive can exempt employers from these restrictions, subject to certain conditions. The Mines and Quarries Act 1954 imposes limitations on women's work and there are restrictions where there is special concern for the unborn child (e.g. lead and ionising radiation). However the broad duties placed on employers by the Health and Safety at Work, etc., Act, 1974 makes no distinctions between men and women. Section 2(1) requires employers to ensure, so far as is reasonably practicable, the health and safety and welfare at work of all employees.

SPECIFIC HEALTH AND SAFETY REQUIREMENTS UNDER EARLIER LEGISLATION ARE UNAFFECTED BY THE ACT.

It is therefore recommended that:

–   company policy should be reviewed and serious consideration given to any significant differences in treatment between men and women, and there should be well-founded reasons if such differences are maintained or introduced.

Note. Some statutory restrictions placed on adult women's hours of work were repealed in February 1987 and others in February 1988. They now no longer apply. Paragraph 26 of the code is still relevant, however, to other health and safety legislation which requires men and women to be treated differently, and which has not been repealed.

Terms of employment, benefits, facilities and services

27.   It is unlawful: UNLESS THE JOB IS COVERED BY AN EXCEPTION:

TO DISCRIMINATE ON THE GROUNDS OF SEX OR MARRIAGE, DIRECTLY OR INDIRECTLY, IN THE TERMS ON WHICH EMPLOYMENT IS OFFERED OR IN AFFORDING ACCESS TO ANY BENEFITS[1], FACILITIES OR SERVICES.
[Sections 6(1)(b); 6(2)(a); 29]

28.   It is therefore recomended that:

---

1   Certain provisions relating to death and retirement are exempt from the Act.

(a) all terms of employment, benefits, facilities and services are reviewed to ensure that there is no unlawful discrimination on grounds of sex or marriage. For example, part-time work, domestic leave, company cars and benefits for dependants should be available to both male and female employees in the same or not materially different circumstances.

29. In an establishment where part-timers are solely or mainly women, unlawful indirect discrimination may arise if, as a group, they are treated less favourably than other employees without justification.

It is therefore recommended that:

(b) where part-time workers do not enjoy pro-rata pay or benefits with full-time workers, the arrangements should be reviewed to ensure that they are justified without regard to sex.

Grievances, disciplinary procedures and victimisation

It is unlawful: TO VICTIMISE AN INDIVIDUAL FOR A COMPLAINT MADE IN GOOD FAITH ABOUT SEX OR MARRIAGE DISCRIMINATION OR FOR GIVING EVIDENCE ABOUT SUCH A COMPLAINT.
[Section 4(1); 4(2) and 4(3)]

31. It is therefore recommended that:

(a) particular care is taken to ensure that an employee who has in good faith taken action under the Sex Discrimination Act or the Equal Pay Act does not receive less favourable treatment than other employees, for example by being disciplined or dismissed;

(b) employees should be advised to use the internal procedures, where appropriate, but this is without prejudice to the individual's right to apply to an industrial tribunal within the statutory time limit, i.e. before the end of the period of three months beginning when the act complained of was done, (there is no time limit if the victimisation is continuing);

(c) particular care is taken to deal effectively with all complaints of discrimination, victimisation or harassment. It should not be assumed that they are made by those who are over-sensitive.

Dismissals, redundancies and other unfavourable treatment of employees

32. It is unlawful: TO DISCRIMINATE DIRECTLY OR INDIRECTLY ON GROUNDS OF SEX OR MARRIAGE IN DISMISSALS OR BY TREATING AN EMPLOYEE UNFAVOURABLY IN ANY OTHER WAY.
[Section 6(2)(b)]

It is therefore recommended that:

(a) care is taken that members of one sex are not disciplined or dismissed for performance or behaviour which would be overlooked or condoned in the other sex;

(b) redundancy procedures affecting a group of employees predominantly of one sex should be reviewed, so as to remove any effects which could be disproportionate and unjustifiable;

(c) conditions of access to voluntary redundancy benefit[1] should be made available on equal terms to male and female employees in the same or not materially different circumstances;

(d) where there is down-grading or short-time working (for example, owing to a change in the nature or volume of an employer's business) the arrangements should not unlawfully discriminate on the ground of sex;

(e) all reasonably practical steps should be taken to ensure that a standard of conduct or behaviour is observed which prevents members of either sex from being intimidated, harassed or otherwise subjected to unfavourable treatment on the ground of their sex.

PART 2

THE ROLE OF GOOD EMPLOYMENT PRACTICES IN PROMOTING EQUALITY OF OPPORTUNITY

33. This section of the Code describes those employment practices which help to promote equality of opportunity. It gives information about the formulation and implementation of equal opportunities policies. While such policies are not required by law, their value has been recognised by a number of employers who have voluntarily adopted them. Others may wish to follow this example.

Formulating an equal opportunities policy

34. An equal opportunities policy will ensure the effective use of human resources in the best interests of both the organisation and its employees. It is a commitment by an employer to the development and use of employment procedures and practices which do not discriminate on grounds of sex or marriage and which provide genuine equality of opportunity for all employees. The detail of the policy will vary according to size of the organisation.

Implementing the policy

35. An equal opportunities policy must be seen to have the active support of management at the highest level. To ensure that the policy is fully effective, the following procedure is recommended:

(a) the policy should be clearly stated and where appropriate, included in a collective agreement;

(b) overall responsibility for implementing the policy should rest with senior management;

(c) the policy should be made known to all employees and, where reasonably practicable, to all job applicants.

36. Trade unions have a very important part to play in implementing genuine equality of opportunity and they will obviously be involved in the review of established procedures to ensure that these are consistent with the law.

Monitoring

37. It is recommended that the policy is monitored regularly to ensure that it is working in practice. Consideration could be given to setting up a joint Management/Trade Union Review Committee.

---

1   Certain provisions relating to death and retirement are exempt from the Act.

38. In a small firm with a simple structure it may be quite adequate to assess the distribution and payment of employees from personal knowledge.

39. In a large and complex organisation a more formal analysis will be necessary, for example, by sex, grade and payment in each unit. This may need to be introduced by stages as resources permit. Any formal analysis should be regularly updated and available to Management and Trade Unions to enable any necessary action to be taken.

40. Sensible monitoring will show, for example, whether members of one sex:

   (a) do not apply for employment or promotion, or that fewer apply than might be expected;
   (b) are not recruited, promoted or selected for training and development or are appointed/selected in a significantly lower proportion than their rate of application;
   (c) are concentrated in certain jobs, sections or departments.

Positive action

Recruitment, training and promotion

41. Selection for recruitment or promotion must be on merit, irrespective of sex. However, the Sex Discrimination Act does allow certain steps to redress the effects of previous unequal opportunities. Where there have been few or no members of one sex in particular work in their employment for the previous 12 months, the Act allows employers to give special encouragement to and provide specific training for, the minority sex. Such measures are usually described as Positive Action. *[Section 48]*

42. Employers may wish to consider positive measures such as:

   (a) training their own employees (male or female) for work which is traditionally the preserve of the other sex, for example, training women for skilled manual or technical work;*
   (b) positive encouragement to women to apply for management posts – special courses may be needed;
   (c) advertisements which encourage applications from the minority sex, but make it clear that selection will be on merit without reference to sex;
   (d) notifying job agencies, as part of a Positive Action Programme that they wish to encourage members of one sex to apply for vacancies, where few or no members of that sex are doing the work in question. In these circumstances, job agencies should tell both men and women about the posts and, in addition, let the under-represented sex know that applications from them are particularly welcome. Withholding information from one sex in an attempt to encourage applications from the opposite sex would be unlawful.

*Note. Section 47 of the SDA 1975 allowed training bodies to run single-sex courses. Since November 1986, this has applied also to other persons including employers. Single-sex training need therefore no longer be confined to an organisation's own employees, as indicated in paragraph 42(a) of the Code, but may be extended to other groups – for example, job applicants or school leavers. Positive Action in recruitment for employment, however, is still not allowed.

Other working arrangements

43. There are other forms of action which could assist both employer and employee by helping to provide continuity of employment to working parents, many of whom will have valuable experience or skills.

Employers may wish to consider with their employees whether:

(a) certain jobs can be carried out on a part-time or flexi-time basis;
(b) personal leave arrangements are adequate and available to both sexes. It should not be assumed that men may not need to undertake domestic responsibilities on occasion, especially at the time of childbirth;
(c) childcare facilities are available locally or whether it would be feasible to establish nursery facilities on the premises or combine with other employers to provide them;
(d) residential training could be facilitated for employees with young children. For example, where this type of training is necessary, by informing staff who are selected well in advance to enable them to make childcare and other personal arrangements; employers with their own residential training centres could also consider whether childcare facilities might be provided;
(e) the statutory maternity leave provisions could be enhanced, for example, by reducing the qualifying service period, extending the leave period, or giving access to part-time arrangements on return.

These arrangements, and others, are helpful to both sexes but are of particular benefit to women in helping them to remain in gainful employment during the years of child-rearing.

ANNEX

LEGAL BACKGROUND

This section gives general guidance only and should not be regarded as a complete or definitive statement of law.

The relationship between the Equal Pay Act and the Sex Discrimination Act

The Sex Discrimination Act 1975 (as amended) (the SDA) covers a wide range of non-contractual benefits, in addition to covering practices and procedures relating to recruitment, training, promotion and dismissal. A claim relating to a contractual benefit may also be brought under the SDA provided the benefit does not consist of the payment of money.

The Equal Pay Act 1970 (as amended) (the EPA) provides for an individual to be treated not less favourably than a person of the opposite sex who works for the same employer, as regards pay and other terms of the contract of employment where they are employed on like work (i.e. the same work or work which is broadly similar) or on work which has been rated as equivalent under a job evaluation scheme or on work which is of equal value.

There is no overlap between an individual's rights under the Equal Pay Act and those under the Sex Discrimination Act. All complaints of discrimination in the circumstances covered by the EPA are dealt with under that Act. All complaints of discrimination about access to jobs and matters not included in a contract of employment and about contractual matters (other than those relating to the payment of money) in situations not covered by the EPA are dealt with under the SPA.

Who is covered by the SDA?

The provisions of the SDA apply to both men and women. It is unlawful to discriminate, directly or indirectly, against a person on the grounds of sex or marriage, unless the situation is covered by one of the Exceptions. It is also unlawful to instruct or bring pressure to bear on others to discriminate.

EXCEPTIONS FROM THE ACT

Geographical scope
Section 10(1)

The SDA does not relate to employment which is wholly or mainly outside Great Britain.

Private household or small employer
Section 6(3)(a); Section 6(3)(b)

These exceptions made it lawful under the Sex Discrimination Act to discriminate in relation to existing or potential employment in a private household, or an organisation which employed five people or fewer. These exceptions did not apply to matters covered by the Equal Pay Act. These exceptions were, however, repealed in February 1987.

Small employer
Note: Small employers, as all other employers, are now covered by the SDA. This means that there is now no distinction between small employers and any other employer. There are, however, still certain exclusions which apply to all employers relating to, for example (i) death or retirement, and (ii) Genuine Occupational Qualifications, in accordance with sections 6(4) and 7 of the SDA. Paragraph 3 of the Code, which states that it will be necessary for employers to adapt the Code in a way appropriate to the size and structure of their organisations, has not been superseded.

Private household
Note: There is no longer any distinction between employment in a private household and any other employment for the purposes of the SDA. There can no longer be any sex or marriage discrimination in choosing someone to work in your home except that, in order to respect personal privacy, discrimination on the basis of a person's sex may still be allowed if the job involves physical or social contact with someone in the family, or having knowledge of intimate details of someone's life.

Death or retirement
Section 6(4)

Certain provisions relating to death or retirement are exempt from the SDA. However, retirement ages for male and female employees should be equal.

Pregnancy or childbirth
Section 2(2)s

Special treatment (i e more favourable treatment) may lawfully be afforded to women in connection with pregnancy or childbirth.

Genuine Occupational Qualifications
Section 7

A person's sex may be a Genuine Occupational Qualification (GOQ) for a job, in which case discrimination in recruitment, opportunities for promotion or transfer to, or training for such employment would not be unlawful. A GOQ cannot, however, apply to the treatment of employees once they are in post, nor to discrimination on grounds of marriage, nor to victimisation.

The GOQ is not an automatic exception for general categories of jobs. In every case it will be necessary for an employer to show that the criteria detailed in the SDA apply to the job or part of the job in question.

A GOQ may be claimed only because of:

(a) physiology (excluding physical strength and stamina) or authenticity – for example, a model or an actor;

(b) decency or privacy – for example, some changing room attendants;

 Note: The job being likely to involve the holder of the job doing work, or living, in a private home and needs to be held by a member of one sex because objection might reasonably be taken to allowing a member of the other sex –

 (i)   the degree of physical of social contact with a person living within the home, or

 (ii) the knowledge of intimate details of such a person's life,

 which is likely because of the nature or circumstances of the job or of the home, to be allowed to, or available to, the holder of the job;

(c) the nature or location of the establishment which makes it impracticable for the jobholder to live in premises other than those provided by the employer (e.g. if the job is in a shop or on a remote site) and the only available premises for persons doing that kind of job do not provide both separate sleeping accommodation for each sex, and sanitary facilities which can be used in privacy from the other. In such a case, the employer may discriminate by choosing for the job only persons of the same sex as those who are already living, or normally live, in these premises. However, the exception does not apply if the employer could reasonably be expected either to equip the premises with the necessary separate sleeping accommodation and private sanitary facilities, or to provide other premises, for a jobholder of the opposite sex;

(d) the fact that the establishment, or part of it, provides special care, supervision or attention to people of one sex only – for example, some jobs in a single-sex hospital;

(e) the fact that the job involves the provision of personal services, promoting welfare or education, that are most effectively provided by men (or by women) – for example, some probation officers or wardens of residential hostels;

(f) laws regulating the employment of women;

(g) the laws and customs of the country in which part of the job is to be carried out – for example, a job involving driving in a country where women are forbidden to drive;

(h) the fact that the job is one of two to be held by a married couple.

Definition of 'employment'

Section 82

'Employment' is defined in the SDA as meaning employment under a contract of service or of apprenticeship or a contract personally to carry out any work or labour.

Direct sex discrimination

Section 1(1)(a)

This occurs where a person of one sex is treated less favourably, on the ground of sex, than a person of the other sex would be in the same or not materially different circumstances.

Indirect sex discrimination

Section 1(1)(b)

Indirect sex discrimination occurs when an unjustifiable requirement or condition is applied equally to both sexes, but has a disproportionately adverse effect on one sex, because the proportion of one sex which can comply with it is much smaller than the proportion of the other sex which can comply with it. For example, a requirement to be mobile might bar more women than men. A complainant would have to show that fewer women than men could comply with such a requirement and that it is to her detriment that she cannot comply. Where the employer can justify such a requirement without regard to sex there will be no unlawful act. A finding of unlawful discrimination may be made even though the employer has no intention to discriminate.

Marriage discrimination

Section 3(1)(a); Section 3(1)(b)

Direct discrimination against a married person occurs where a married person is treated less favourably on the grounds of marital status, than an unmarried person of the same sex would be in the same or not materially different circumstances. Indirect discrimination against a married person is similar in concept to indirect sex discrimination and may arise when a condition or requirement is applied equally to married and unmarried persons of the same sex but which is in fact discriminatory in its effect on married persons. For example, a requirement to be mobile might bar more married than single women.

Discrimination by way of victimisation

Section 4

This occurs where a person is treated less favourably than other persons would be treated because he/she has done something by reference to the EPA or the SDA, for example, brought proceedings or given evidence or information in a case under either of those Acts or alleged (expressly or otherwise) that anyone has committed an act which could constitute a breach of those Acts. Victimisation is not unlawful if the allegation was false and not made in good faith.

Discrimination in recruitment

Section 6(1)

This section makes it unlawful for an employer to discriminate when recruiting employees in the following ways:

Section 6(1)(a)

in the arrangements made for deciding who should be offered a job. (One example might be the instructions given to a Personnel Officer or to an Employment Agency. Another example might be advertising a job in a place where only one sex would have the opportunity of seeing the advertisement.);

Section 6(1)(b)

in relation to any terms offered (for instance, in respect of pay or holidays). It is, for instance, unlawful to offer a job (whether or not the candidate accepts), where the terms would be a breach of the EPA should an employment contract be entered into;

Section 6(1)(c)

by refusing or deliberately omitting to offer a person employment (for example, by rejecting an application or deliberately refusing consideration of an application).

Discrimination in the treatment of present employees

Section 6(2)

This section makes it unlawful for an employer to discriminate in the following ways:

Section 6(2)(a)

in the way access is afforded to opportunities for promotion, transfer or training, or to any other benefits[1], facilities or services, or by refusing or deliberately omitting to afford access to them; or

Section 6(2)(b)

by dismissal or the subjection to any other unfavourable treatment.

Section 9

Discrimination against contract workers

Section 9(1)

This section covers contract workers, i.e. workers who are sent to work for an organisation by another organisation which employs them.

Section 9(2)

It is unlawful for the principal firm to discriminate on grounds of sex or marriage:

(a)   in the terms on which it allows the contract worker to do the work; or
(b)   by not allowing the contract worker to do it or continue to do it; or
(c)   in the way the contract worker is afforded access to any benefits, facilities or services or by refusing or deliberately omitting to afford access to any of them; or
(d)   by subjecting the contract worker to any other unfavourable treatment.

Section 9(3)

A principal may rely upon the GOQ exception, where it is applicable, to refuse to allow a contract worker to do, or to continue to do the contract work.

Section 9(4)

Where a principal provides his contract workers with benefits, facilities or services not materially different from those he provides to the public, a complaint relating to the discriminatory provision of such benefits, etc. would not fall under section 9, but under section 29 of the SDA.

Discrimination by trade unions and employers' organisations, etc.

Section 12(1) and 12(2)

It is unlawful, for an organisation of workers or of employers or any other organisation whose members carry on a particular profession or trade for the purposes of which the organisation exists, to discriminate on grounds of sex or marriage against anyone applying for membership:

(a)   in the terms on which it is prepared to admit the person to membership; or
(b)   by refusing or deliberately omitting to accept an application for membership.

Section 12(3)

It is unlawful for such an organisation to discriminate on grounds of sex or marriage against a member:

(a)   in the way it affords access to any benefits, facilities or services or by refusing or deliberately omitting to afford access to them; or
(b)   by depriving a person of membership or varying the terms of membership; or
(c)   subjecting to any other unfavourable treatment.

---

1   Other than the payment of money provided under a contract of employment.

Discrimination by employment agencies

Section 15(1)

It is unlawful for an employment agency to discriminate on grounds of sex or marriage:

(a) in the terms on which they offer to provide any of their services; or
(b) by refusing or deliberately omitting to provide them; or
(e) in the way in which they provide any of them.

Section 15(4)

Section 15(1) will not apply if the discrimination only concerns employment which an employer could lawfully refuse to offer to a woman (or a man).

Section 15(5) and 15(6)

Where an employment agency has the employer's assurance that a vacancy is covered by one of the exceptions and this turns out not to be the case, the agency has a defence if it can prove both that it acted in reliance on a statement by the employer that its action would not be unlawful and that it was reasonable for it to rely on the statement. It is a summary offence punishable by a fine not exceeding £5,000, knowingly or recklessly to make such a statement which in a material respect is false or misleading.

Section 38

Discriminatory advertisements

Section 38(1) and 38(2)

The SDA makes it unlawful to publish or cause to be published an advertisement which indicates, or might reasonably be taken to indicate, an intention to discriminate unlawfully. An advertisement would not be unlawful if it dealt with a job which was covered by an exception.

Section 38(3)

An advertisement which uses a job description with a sexual connotation (for example, 'waiter', 'salesgirl' or 'stewardess') is taken as an intention to commit an unlawful discriminatory act, unless the advertisement states that the job is open to men and women or uses descriptions applying to both sexes (e.g. 'waiter' or 'waitress').

Section 38(4)

There will be cases where a publisher may not know whether a particular advertisement is lawful. A publisher will not be held liable if:

(a) he or she relied on a statement by the person placing the advertisement that the publication would not be unlawful, for example because the vacancy was covered by an exception; and
(b) it was reasonable for the publisher to rely on the statement.

Section 38(5)

It is an offence punishable on summary conviction with a fine not exceeding £5,000, for anyone placing an advertisement knowingly or recklessly to make a materially false or misleading statement to the publisher as to its lawfulness.

Instructions to discriminate

Section 39

It is unlawful for a person who has authority over another person or whose wishes are normally carried out by that other person to instruct or attempt to procure another person (e.g. a member of staff) to carry out an act of unlawful discrimination, e.g. an instruction to an employment agency to discriminate.

Pressure to discriminate

Section 40

It is unlawful for a person to bring pressure to bear on another person to carry out an act of unlawful discrimination, by providing or offering any benefit or threatening any detriment; for example, by a threat of industrial action to persuade an employer to discriminate.

Liability of employers and principals

Section 41

An employer is liable for any act done by an employee in the course of the employment with or without the employer's knowledge or approval, unless the employer can show that such steps were taken as were reasonably practicable to prevent the employee doing the act in question. Similarly, a principal is liable for any act done by an agent with the principal's authority.

Section 42

A person (for example, an employee or agent) who knowingly aids another to do an unlawful act is also to be treated as having done that act, unless it can be shown that he or she acted in reliance on a statement that the act would not be unlawful and that it was reasonable to rely on such a statement.

Positive action by training bodies

Section 47

Training bodies may apply to the Secretary of State for Employment to become designated for the purpose of providing:

(a) training or encouragement for particular work where in the previous 12 months one sex had been substantially under-represented; or
(b) special training for persons following absence from employment because of domestic or family responsibilities.

Note: Until February 1987, training bodies which wished to run single-sex courses needed special designation by the Secretary of State. This is no longer required. Positive Action is, however, confined to training and is still not allowed in recruitment. Section 47 of the Act now applies to any person, not just to training bodies.

Positive action by employers

Section 48

This section of the SDA allows for positive action by employers to overcome the effects of past discrimination, it allows for training and encouragement where few or no members of one sex have been doing particular work in the preceding 12 months. It does not cover recruitment or promotion.

Advice on the promotion of equality of opportunity in employment is available from the EOC. All EOC publications referred to are available from the EOC offices in Manchester.

Other Publications.
Many Policy Statements will cover race as well as sex discrimination. For advice on racial discrimination refer to the Code of Practice issued by the Commission for Racial Equality.

Examples of equal opportunities policy statements are the Trade Union Congress Model Clause and the Confederation of British Industry's Statement Guide.

England
Equal Opportunities Commission
Overseas House
Quay Street
Manchester M3 3HN
E-Mail: info@eoc.org.uk
Web site: www.eoc.org.uk
Fax: 0161 835 1657
Tel & Minicom: 0161 833 9244

Scotland
Equal Opportunities Commission
Stock Exchange House
7 Nelson Mandela Place
Glasgow G2 1QW
E-Mail: scotland@eoc.org.uk
Web site: www.eoc.org.uk
Fax: 0141 248 5834
Tel: 0141 248 5833

Wales
Equal Opportunities Commission
Windsor House
Windsor Lane
Cardiff CF1 3DE
E-Mail: wales@eoc.org.uk
Web site: www.eoc.org.uk
Fax: 01222 641079
Tel: 01222 343552

Appendix 3

COMMISSION FOR RACIAL EQUALITY CODE OF PRACTICE
FOR THE ELIMINATION OF RACIAL DISCRIMINATION AND THE PROMOTION OF EQUALITY OF OPPORTUNITY IN EMPLOYMENT

INTRODUCTION

Purpose and status of the Code

This Code aims to give practical guidance which will help employers, trade unions, employment agencies and employees to understand not only the provisions of the Race Relations Act and their implications, but also how best they can implement policies to eliminate racial discrimination and to enhance equality of opportunity.

The Code does not impose any legal obligations itself, nor is it an authoritative statement of the law – that can only be provided by the courts and tribunals. If, however, its recommendations are not observed this may result in breaches of the law where the act or omission falls within any of the specific prohibitions of the Act. Moreover its provisions are admissible in evidence in any proceedings under the Race Relations Act before an industrial tribunal and if any provision appears to the tribunal to be relevant to a question arising in the proceedings it must be taken into account in determining that question. If employers take the steps that are set out in the Code to prevent their employees from doing acts of unlawful discrimination they may avoid liability for such acts in any legal proceedings brought against them. References to the appropriate sections of the Race Relations Act 1976 are given in the margin to the Code.

Employees of all racial groups have a right to equal opportunity. Employers ought to provide it. To do so is likely to involve some expenditure, at least in staff time and effort. But if a coherent and effective programme of equal opportunity is developed it will help industry to make full use of the abilities of its entire workforce. It is therefore particularly important for all those concerned – employers, trade unions and employees alike – to cooperate with goodwill in adopting and giving effect to measures for securing such equality. We welcome the commitment already made by the CBI and TUC to the principle of equal opportunity. The TUC has recommended a model equal opportunity clause for inclusion in collective agreements and the CBI has published a statement favouring the application by companies of constructive equal opportunity policies.

A concerted policy to eliminate both race and sex discrimination often provides the best approach. Guidance on equal opportunity between men and women is the responsibility of the Equal Opportunities Commission.

Application of the Code

The Race Relations Act applies to all employers. The Code itself is not restricted to what is required by law, but contains recommendations as well. Some of its detailed provisions may need to be adapted to suit particular circumstances. Any adaptations that are made, however, should be fully consistent with the Code's general intentions.

Small firms

In many small firms employers have close contact with their staff and there will therefore be less need for formality in assessing whether equal opportunity is being achieved, for example, in such matters as arrangements for monitoring. Moreover it may not be reasonable to expect small firms to have the resources and administrative systems to carry out the Code's detailed recommendations. In complying with the Race Relations Act, small firms should, however, ensure that their practices are consistent with the Code's general intentions.

Unlawful discrimination

The Race Relations Act 1976 makes it unlawful to discriminate against a person, directly or indirectly, in the field of employment.

Direct discrimination consists of treating a person, on racial grounds,[1] less favourably than others are or would be treated in the same or similar circumstances.

Segregating a person from others on racial grounds constitutes less favourable treatment.

Indirect discrimination consists of applying in any circumstances covered by the Act a requirement or condition which, although applied equally to persons of all racial groups, is such that a considerably smaller proportion of a particular racial group can comply with it and it cannot be shown to be justifiable on other than racial grounds. Possible examples are:

- A rule about clothing or uniforms which disproportionately disadvantages a racial group and cannot be justified.
- An employer who requires higher language standards than are needed for safe and effective performance of the job.

The definition of indirect discrimination is complex, and it will not be spelt out in full in every relevant section of the Code. Reference will be only to the terms 'indirect discrimination' or 'discriminate indirectly'.

Discrimination by *victimisation* is also unlawful under the Act. For example, a person is victimised if he or she is given less favourable treatment than others in the same circumstances because it is suspected or known that he or she has brought proceedings under the Act, or given evidence or information relating to such proceedings, or alleged that discrimination has occurred.

The Code and good employment practice

Many of the Code's provisions show the close link between equal opportunity and good employment practice. For example, selection criteria which are relevant to job requirements and carefully observed selection procedures not only help to ensure that individuals are appointed according to their suitability for the job and without regard to racial group; they are also part of good employment practice. In the absence of consistent selection procedures and criteria, decisions are often too subjective and racial discrimination can easily occur.

---

1   Racial grounds are the grounds of race, colour, nationality – including citizenship – or ethnic or national origins, and groups defined by reference to these grounds are referred to as racial groups.

Positive action

Opportunities for employees to develop their potential through encouragement, training and careful assessment are also part of good employment practice. Many employees from the racial minorities have potential which, perhaps because of previous discrimination and other causes of disadvantage, they have not been able to realise, and which is not reflected in their qualifications and experience. Where members of particular racial groups have been underrepresented over the previous twelve months in particular work, employers and specified training bodies[1] are allowed under the Act to encourage them to take advantage of opportunities for doing that work and to provide training to enable them to attain the skills needed for it. In the case of employers, such training can be provided for persons currently in their employment (as defined by the Act) and in certain circumstances for others too, for example if they have been designated as training bodies.[1] This Code encourages employers to make use of these provisions, which are covered in detail in paragraphs 1.44 and 1.45.

Guides

The guidance papers referred to in the footnotes contain additional guidance on specific issues but do not form part of the statutory Code.

PART I
THE RESPONSIBILITIES OF EMPLOYERS

1.1 Responsibility for providing equal opportunity for all job applicants and employees rests primarily with employers. To this end it is recommended that they should adopt, implement and monitor an equal opportunity policy to ensure that there is no unlawful discrimination and that equal opportunity is genuinely available.[2]

1.2 This policy should be clearly communicated to all employees – eg through notice boards, circulars, contracts of employment or written notifications to individual employees.

Equal opportunity policies

1.3 An equal opportunity policy aims to ensure that:

(a) No job applicant or employee receives less favourable treatment than another on racial grounds.
(b) No applicant or employee is placed at a disadvantage by requirements or conditions which have a disproportionately adverse effect on his or her racial group and which cannot be shown to be justifiable on other than racial grounds.
(c) Where appropriate, and where permissible under the Race Relations Act, employees of underrepresented racial groups are given training and encouragement to achieve equal opportunity within the organisation.

1.4 In order to ensure that an equal opportunity policy is fully effective, the following action by employers is recommended:

(a) Allocating overall responsibility for the policy to a member of senior management.

---

1   Section 7(3) of the Employment Act 1989 has amended section 37 of the Race Relations Act with effect from 16.1.90. Section 7(3) now allows any person including employers (not just training bodies) to provide positive action training without the need for any designation as long as the criteria of underrepresentation are met.
2   The CRE has issued guides on equal opportunity policies: *Equal Opportunity in Employment* and *Monitoring an Equal Opportunity Policy*.

(b) Discussing and, where appropriate, agreeing with trade union or employee representatives the policy's contents and implementation.

(c) Ensuring that the policy is known to all employees and if possible, to all job applicants.

(d) Providing training and guidance for supervisory staff and other relevant decision makers (such as personnel and line managers, foremen, gatekeepers and receptionists), to ensure that they understand their position in law and under company policy.

(e) Examining and regularly reviewing existing procedures and criteria and changing them where they find that they are actually or potentially unlawfully discriminatory.

(f) Making an initial analysis of the workforce and regularly monitoring the application of the policy with the aid of analyses of the ethnic origins of the workforce and of job applicants in accordance with the guidance in paragraphs 1.34–1.35.

Sources of recruitment

Advertisements

1.5   When advertising job vacancies, it **is unlawful** for employers to publish an advertisement which indicates, or could reasonably be understood as indicating, an intention to discriminate against applicants from a particular racial group. (For exceptions see the Race Relations Act.)

1.6   It is therefore recommended that:

(a) Employers should not confine advertisements unjustifiably to those areas or publications which would exclude or disproportionately reduce the numbers of applicants of a particular racial group:

(b) Employers should avoid prescribing requirements such as length of residence or experience in the UK and where a particular qualification is required it should be made clear that a fully comparable qualification obtained overseas is as acceptable as a UK qualification.

1.7   In order to demonstrate their commitment to equality of opportunity it is recommended that where employers send literature to applicants, this should include a statement that they are equal opportunity employers.

Employment agencies

1.8   When recruiting through employment agencies, job centres, careers offices and schools, **it is unlawful** for employers:

(a) To give instructions to discriminate, for example by indicating that certain groups will or will not be preferred. (For exceptions see the Race Relations Act.)

(b) To bring pressure on them to discriminate against members of a particular racial group. (For exceptions, see the Race Relations Act.)

1.9   In order to avoid indirect discrimination it is recommended that employers should not confine recruitment unjustifiably to those agencies, job centres, careers offices and schools which, because of their particular source of applicants, provide only or mainly applicants of a particular racial group.

1.10   **It is unlawful** to use recruitment methods which exclude or disproportionately reduce the numbers of applicants of a particular racial group and which cannot be shown to be justifiable. It is therefore recommended that employers should **not** recruit through the following methods:

(a) Recruitment, solely or in the first instance, through the recommendations of existing employees where the workforce concerned is wholly or predominantly white or black and the labour market is multi-racial.

(b) Procedures by which applicants are mainly or wholly supplied through trade unions where this means that only members of a particular racial group, or a disproportionately high number of them, come forward.

Sources for promotion and training

1.11 It is unlawful for employers to restrict access to opportunities for promotion or training in a way which is discriminatory. It is therefore recommended that:

(a) Job and training vacancies and the application procedure should be made known to all eligible employees, and not in such a way as to exclude or disproportionately reduce the numbers of applicants from a particular racial group.

Selection processes

1.12 It is unlawful to discriminate,[1] not only in recruitment, promotion, transfer and training, but also in the arrangements made for recruitment and in the ways of affording access to opportunities for promotion, transfer or training.

Selection criteria and tests

1.13 In order to avoid direct or indirect discrimination, it is recommended that selection criteria and tests are examined to ensure that they are related to job requirements and are not unlawfully discriminatory. (See also p [250].) For example:

(a) A standard of English higher than that needed for the safe and effective performance of the job or clearly demonstrable career pattern should not be required, or a higher level of education qualification than is needed.
(b) In particular, employers should not disqualify applicants because they are unable to complete an application form unassisted unless personal completion of the form is a valid test of the standard of English required for safe and effective performance of the job.
(c) Overseas degrees, diplomas and other qualifications which are comparable with UK qualifications should be accepted as equivalents, and not simply be assumed to be of an inferior quality.
(d) Selection tests which contain irrelevant questions or exercises on matters which may be unfamiliar to racial minority applicants should not be used (for example, general knowledge questions on matters more likely to be familiar to indigenous applicants.)
(e) Selection tests should be checked to ensure that they are related to the job's requirements, i.e. an individual's test marking should measure ability to do or train for the job in question.

Treatment of applicants

Shortlisting, interviewing and selection

1.14 In order to avoid direct or indirect discrimination it is recommended that:

(a) Gate, reception and personnel staff should be instructed not to treat casual or formal applicants from particular racial groups less favourably than others. These instructions should be confirmed in writing.
(b) In addition, staff responsible for shortlisting, interviewing and selecting candidates should be:

---

1   It should be noted that discrimination in selection to achieve 'racial balance' is not allowed. The clause in the 1968 Race Relations Act which allowed such discrimination for the purpose of securing or preserving a reasonable balance of persons of different racial groups in the establishment is not included in the 1976 Race Relations Act.

- clearly informed of selection criteria and of the need for their consistent application;
- given guidance or training on the effects which generalised assumptions and prejudices about race can have on selection decisions;
- made aware of the possible misunderstandings that can occur in interviews between persons of different cultural background.

(c) Wherever possible, shortlisting and interviewing should not be done by one person alone but should at least be checked at a more senior level.

Genuine occupational qualification

1.15   Selection on racial grounds is allowed in certain jobs where being of a particular racial group is a genuine occupational qualification for that job. An example is where the holder of a particular job provides persons of a racial group with personal services promoting their welfare, and those services can most effectively be provided by a person of that group.

Transfers and training

1.16   In order to avoid direct or indirect discrimination it is recommended that:

(a) Staff responsible for selecting employees for transfer to other jobs should be instructed to apply selection criteria without unlawful discrimination.
(b) Industry or company agreements and arrangements of custom and practice on job transfers should be examined and amended if they are found to contain requirements or conditions which appear to be indirectly discriminatory. For example, if employees of a particular racial group are concentrated in particular sections, the transfer arrangements should be examined to see if they are unjustifiably and unlawfully restrictive and amended if necessary.
(c) Staff responsible for selecting employees for training, whether induction, promotion or skill training should be instructed not to discriminate on racial grounds.
(d) Selection criteria for training opportunities should be examined to ensure that they are not indirectly discriminatory.

Dismissal (including redundancy) and other detriment

1.17   **It is unlawful** to discriminate on racial grounds in dismissal, or other detriment to an employee.

It is therefore recommended that:

(a) Staff responsible for selecting employees for dismissal, including redundancy, should be instructed not to discriminate on racial grounds.
(b) Selection criteria for redundancies should be examined to ensure that they are not indirectly discriminatory.

Performance appraisals

1.18   **It is unlawful** to discriminate on racial grounds in appraisals of employee performance.

1.19   It is recommended that:

(a) Staff responsible for performance appraisals should be instructed not to discriminate on racial grounds.
(b) Assessment criteria should be examined to ensure that they are not unlawfully discriminatory.

Terms of employment, benefits, facilities and services

1.20 It is unlawful to discriminate on racial grounds in affording terms of employment and providing benefits, facilities and services for employees. It is therefore recommended that:

(a) All staff concerned with these aspects of employment should be instructed accordingly.
(b) The criteria governing eligibility should be examined to ensure that they are not unlawfully discriminatory.

1.21 In addition, employees may request extended leave from time to time in order to visit relations in their countries of origin or who have emigrated to other countries. Many employers have policies which allow annual leave entitlement to be accumulated, or extra unpaid leave to be taken to meet these circumstances. Employers should take care to apply such policies consistently and without unlawful discrimination.

Grievance, disputes and disciplinary procedures

1.22 It is unlawful to discriminate in the operation of grievance, disputes and disciplinary procedures, for example by victimising an individual through disciplinary measures because he or she has complained about racial discrimination, or given evidence about such a complaint. Employers should not ignore or treat lightly grievances from members of particular racial groups on the assumption that they are over-sensitive about discrimination.

1.23 It is recommended that in applying disciplinary procedures consideration should be given to the possible effect on an employee's behaviour of the following:

- Racial abuse or other racial provocation.
- Communication and comprehension difficulties.
- Differences in cultural background or behaviour.

Cultural and religious needs

1.24 Where employees have particular cultural and religious needs which conflict with existing work requirements, it is recommended that employers should consider whether it is reasonably practicable to vary or adapt these requirements to enable such needs to be met. For example, it is recommended that they should not refuse employment to a turbanned Sikh because he could not comply with unjustifiable uniform requirements.[1]

Other examples of such needs are:

(a) Observance of prayer times and religious holidays.[2]
(b) Wearing of dress such as sarees and the trousers worn by Asian women.

1.25 Although the Act does not specifically cover religious discrimination, work requirements would generally be unlawful if they have a disproportionately adverse effect on particular racial groups and cannot be shown to be justifiable.[3]

---

1 S.11 of the Employment Act 1989 exempts turban wearing Sikhs from any requirements to wear safety helmets on a construction site. Where a turban wearing Sikh is injured on a construction site liability for injuries is restricted to the injuries that would have been sustained if the Sikh had been wearing a safety helmet.
   S.12 of the Employment Act provides that if, despite S.11, an employer requires a turban wearing Sikh to wear other protective headgear such as a safety helmet on a construction site, the employer will not be able to argue that this is a justifiable requirement in any proceedings under the Race Relations Act to determine whether or not it constitutes indirect racial discrimination.
2 The CRE has issued a guide entitled *Religious Observance by Muslim Employees*.
3 Genuinely necessary safety requirements may not constitute unlawful discrimination.

Communications and language training for employees

1.26   Although there is no legal requirement to provide language training, difficulties in communication can endanger equal opportunity in the workforce. In addition, good communications can improve efficiency, promotion prospects and safety and health and create a better understanding between employers, employees and unions. Where the workforce includes current employees whose English is limited it is recommended that steps are taken to ensure that communications are as effective as possible.

1.27   These should include, where reasonably practicable:

(a)   Provision of interpretation and translation facilities, for example, in the communication of grievance and other procedures, and of terms of employment.
(b)   Training in English language and in communication skills.[1]
(c)   Training for managers and supervisors in the background and culture of racial minority groups.
(d)   The use of alternative or additional methods of communication, where employees find it difficult to understand health and safety requirements, for example.

- Safety signs; translations of safety notices.
- Instructions through interpreters.
- Instruction combined with industrial language training.

Instructions and pressure to discriminate

1.28   **It is unlawful** to instruct or put pressure on others to discriminate on racial grounds.

(a)   An example of an unlawful instruction is:

- An instruction from a personnel or line manager to junior staff to restrict the numbers of employees from a particular racial group in any particular work.

(b)   An example of pressure to discriminate is:

- An attempt by a shop steward or group of workers to induce an employer not to recruit members of particular racial groups, for example by threatening industrial action.

1.29   **It is also unlawful** to discriminate in response to such instructions or pressure.

1.30   The following recommendations are made to avoid unlawful instructions and pressure to discriminate:

(a)   Guidance should be given to all employees, and particularly those in positions of authority or influence, on the relevant provisions of the law.
(b)   Decision-makers should be instructed not to give way to pressure to discriminate.
(c)   Giving instructions or bringing pressure to discriminate should be treated as a disciplinary offence.

Victimisation

1.31   **It is unlawful** to victimise individuals who have made allegations or complaints of racial discrimination or provided information about such discrimination, for example, by disciplining them or dismissing them. (See also page [250].)

---

1   Industrial language training is provided by a network of local education authority units throughout the country. Full details of the courses and the comprehensive services offered by these units are available from the National Centre for Industrial Language Training, The Havelock Centre, Havelock Road, Southall, Middx.

1.32 It is recommended that guidance on this aspect of the law should be given to all employees and particularly to those in positions of influence or authority.

Monitoring equal opportunity[1]

1.33 It is recommended that employers should regularly monitor the effects of selection decisions and personnel practices and procedures in order to assess whether equal opportunity is being achieved.

1.34 The information needed for effective monitoring may be obtained in a number of ways. It will best be provided by records showing the ethnic origins of existing employees and job applicants. It is recognised that the need for detailed information and the methods of collecting it will vary according to the circumstances of individual establishments. For example, in small firms or in firms in areas with little or no racial minority settlement it will often be adequate to assess the distribution of employees from personal knowledge and visual identification.

1.35 It is open to employers to adopt the method of monitoring which is best suited to their needs and circumstances, but whichever method is adopted, they should be able to show that it is effective. In order to achieve the full commitment of all concerned the chosen method should be discussed and agreed, where appropriate, with trade union or employee representatives.

1.36 Employers should ensure that information on individuals' ethnic origins is collected for the purpose of monitoring equal opportunity alone and is protected from misuse.

1.37 The following is the comprehensive method recommended by the CRE.[2]

Analyses should be carried out of:

(a) The ethnic composition of the workforce of each plant, department, section, shift and job category, and changes in distribution over periods of time.
(b) Selection decisions for recruitment, promotion, transfer and training, according to the racial group of candidates, and reasons for these decisions.

1.38 Except in cases where there are large numbers of applicants and the burden on resources would be excessive, reasons for selection and rejection should be recorded at each stage of the selection process, e.g. initial shortlisting and final decisions. Simple categories of reasons for rejection should be adequate for the early sifting stages.

1.39 Selection criteria and personnel procedures should be reviewed to ensure that they do not include requirements or conditions which constitute or may lead to unlawful indirect discrimination.

1.40 This information should be carefully and regularly analysed and, in order to identify areas which may need particular attention, a number of key questions should be asked.

1.41 Is there evidence that individuals from any particular racial group:

(a) Do not apply for employment or promotion, or that fewer apply than might be expected?
(b) Are not recruited or promoted at all, or are appointed in a significantly lower proportion than their rate of application?
(c) Are underrepresented in training or in jobs carrying higher pay, status or authority?
(d) Are concentrated in certain shifts, sections or departments?

---

1   See the CRE's guide on *Monitoring an Equal Opportunity Policy*.
2   This is outlined in detail in *Monitoring an Equal Opportunity Policy*.

1.42 If the answer to any of these questions is yes, the reasons for this should be investigated. If direct or indirect discrimination is found action must be taken to end it immediately.

1.43 It is recommended that deliberate acts of unlawful discrimination by employees are treated as disciplinary offences.

Positive action[1]

1.44 Although they are not legally required, positive measures are allowed by the law to encourage employees and potential employees and provide training for employees who are members of particular racial groups which have been underrepresented[2] in particular work. (See also page [251].) Discrimination at the point of selection for work, however, is not permissible in these circumstances.

1.45 Such measures are important for the development of equal opportunity. It is therefore recommended that, where there is underrepresentation of particular racial groups in particular work, the following measures should be taken wherever appropriate and reasonably practicable:

(a) Job advertisements designed to reach members of these groups and to encourage their applications: for example, through the use of the ethnic minority press, as well as other newspapers.
(b) Use of the employment agencies and careers offices in areas where these groups are concentrated.
(c) Recruitment and training schemes for school leavers designed to reach members of these groups.
(d) Encouragement to employees from these groups to apply for promotion or transfer opportunities.
(e) Training for promotion or skill training for employees of these groups who lack particular expertise but show potential: supervisory training may include language training.

PART 2
THE RESPONSIBILITIES OF INDIVIDUAL EMPLOYEES

2.1 While the primary responsibility for providing equal opportunity rests with the employer, individual employees at all levels and of all racial groups have responsibilities too. Good race relations depend on them as much as on management, and so their attitudes and activities are very important.

2.2 The following actions by individual employees would be **unlawful**:

(a) Discrimination in the course of their employment against fellow employees or job applicants on racial grounds, for example, in selection decisions for recruitment, promotion, transfer and training.
(b) Inducing, or attempting to induce other employees, unions or management to practise unlawful discrimination. For example, they should not refuse to accept other employees from particular racial groups or refuse to work with a supervisor of a particular racial group.

---

1 The CRE has issued a guide on positive action, entitled, *Equal Opportunity in Employment: Why positive action?*
2 A racial group is underrepresented if, at any time during the previous twelve months, either there was no one of that group doing the work in question, or there were disproportionately few in comparison with the group's proportion in the workforce at that establishment, or in the population from which the employer normally recruits for work at that establishment.

(c) Victimising individuals who have made allegations or complaints of racial discrimination or provided information about such discrimination. (See also page [250].)

2.3 To assist in preventing racial discrimination and promoting equal opportunity it is recommended that individual employees should:

(a) Cooperate in measures introduced by management designed to ensure equal opportunity and non-discrimination.
(b) Where such measures have not been introduced, press for their introduction (through their trade union where appropriate).
(c) Draw the attention of management and, where appropriate, their trade unions to suspected discriminatory acts or practices.
(d) Refrain from harassment or intimidation of other employees on racial grounds, for example, by attempting to discourage them from continuing employment. Such action may be unlawful if it is taken by employees against those subject to their authority.

2.4 In addition to the responsibilities set out above individual employees from the racial minorities should recognise that in many occupations advancement is dependent on an appropriate standard of English. Similarly an understanding of the industrial relations procedures which apply is often essential for good working relationships.

2.5 They should therefore:

(a) Where appropriate, seek means to improve their standards of English.
(b) Cooperate in industrial language training schemes introduced by employers and/or unions.
(c) Cooperate in training or other schemes designed to inform them of industrial relations procedures, company agreements, work rules, etc.
(d) Where appropriate, participate in discussions with employers and unions, to find solutions to conflicts between cultural or religious needs and production needs.

PART 3
THE RESPONSIBILITIES OF TRADE UNIONS

3.1 Trade unions, in common with a number of other organisations, have a dual role as employers and providers of services specifically covered by the Race Relations Act.

3.2 In their role as employer, unions have the responsibilities set out in Part 1 of the Code. They also have a responsibility to ensure that their representatives and members do not discriminate against any particular racial group in the admission or treatment of members, or as colleagues, supervisors, or subordinates.

3.3 In addition, trade union officials at national and local level and shopfloor representatives at plant level have an important part to play on behalf of their members in preventing unlawful discrimination and in promoting equal opportunity and good race relations. Trade unions should encourage and press for equal opportunity policies so that measures to prevent discrimination at the workplace can be introduced with the clear commitment of both management and unions.

Admission of members

3.4 It is unlawful for trade unions to discriminate on racial grounds:

(a) By refusing membership.
(b) By offering less favourable terms of membership.

Treatment of members

3.5 It is unlawful for trade unions to discriminate on racial grounds against existing members:

(a) By varying their terms of membership, depriving them of membership or subjecting them to any other detriment.
(b) By treating them less favourably in the benefits, facilities or services provided. These may include:

- Training facilities.
- Welfare and insurance schemes.
- Entertainment and social events.
- Processing of grievances.
- Negotiations.
- Assistance in disciplinary or dismissal procedures.

3.6 In addition, it is recommended that unions ensure that in cases where members of particular racial groups believe that they are suffering racial discrimination, whether by the employer or the union itself, serious attention is paid to the reasons for this belief and that any discrimination which may be occurring is stopped.

Disciplining members who discriminate

3.7 It is recommended that deliberate acts of unlawful discrimination by union members are treated as disciplinary offences.

3.8 Although they are not legally required, positive measures are allowed by the law to encourage and provide training for members of particular racial groups which have been underrepresented[1] in trade union membership or in trade union posts. (Discrimination at the point of selection, however, is not permissible in these circumstances.)

3.9 It is recommended that, wherever appropriate and reasonably practicable, trade unions should:

(a) Encourage individuals from these groups to join the union. Where appropriate, recruitment material should be translated into other languages.
(b) Encourage individuals from these groups to apply for union posts and provide training to help fit them for such posts.

Training and information

3.10 Training and information play a major part in the avoidance of discrimination and the promotion of equal opportunity. It is recommended that trade unions should:

(a) Provide training and information for officers, shop stewards and representatives on their responsibilities for equal opportunity. This training and information should cover:

- The Race Relations Act and the nature and causes of discrimination.

---

1   A racial group is underrepresented in trade union membership, if at any time during the previous twelve months no persons of that group were in membership, or disproportionately few in comparison with the proportion of persons of that group among those eligible for membership [S.38(5)]. Underrepresentation in trade union posts applies under the same twelve month criteria, where there were no persons of a particular racial group in those posts or disproportionately few in comparison with the proportion of that group in the organisation [S.38(4)].

- The backgrounds of racial minority groups and communication needs.
- The effects of prejudice.
- Equal opportunity policies.
- Avoiding discrimination when representing members.

(b) Ensure that members and representatives, whatever their racial group, are informed of their role in the union, and of industrial relations and union procedures and structures. This may be done, for example:

- Through translation of material.
- Through encouragement to participate in industrial relations courses and industrial language training.

Pressure to discriminate

3.11 **It is unlawful** for trade union members or representatives to induce or to attempt to induce those responsible for employment decisions to discriminate:

(a) In the recruitment, promotion, transfer, training or dismissal of employees.
(b) In terms of employment, benefits, facilities or services.

3.12 For example, they should not:

(a) Restrict the numbers of a particular racial group in a section, grade or department.
(b) Resist changes designed to remove indirect discrimination, such as those in craft apprentice schemes, or in agreements concerning seniority rights or mobility between departments.

Victimisation

3.13 **It is unlawful** to victimise individuals who have made allegations or complaints of racial discrimination or provided information about such discrimination. (See also page [250].)

Avoidance of discrimination

3.14 Where unions are involved in selection decisions for recruitment, promotion, training or transfer, for example through recommendation or veto, **it is unlawful** for them to discriminate on racial grounds.

3.15 It is recommended that they should instruct their members accordingly and examine their procedures and joint agreements to ensure that they do not contain indirectly discriminatory requirements or conditions, such as:

- Unjustifiable restrictions on transfers between departments.
- Irrelevant and unjustifiable selection criteria which have a disproportionately adverse effect on particular racial groups.

Union involvement in equal opportunity policies

3.16 It is recommended that:

(a) Unions should cooperate in the introduction and implementation of full equal opportunity policies, as defined in paragraphs 1.3 & 1.4.
(b) Unions should negotiate the adoption of such policies where they have not been introduced or the extension of existing policies where these are too narrow.
(c) Unions should cooperate with measures to monitor the progress of equal opportunity policies, or encourage management to introduce them where they do not already exist Where appropriate (see paragraphs 1.33–1.35) this may be done

through analysis of the distribution of employees and job applicants according to ethnic origin.

(d) Where monitoring shows that discrimination has occurred or is occurring, unions should cooperate in measures to eliminate it.

(d) Although positive action[1] is not legally required, unions should encourage management to take such action where there is underrepresentation of particular racial groups in particular jobs, and where management itself introduces positive action, representatives should support it.

(f) Similarly, where there are communication difficulties, management should be asked to take whatever action is appropriate to overcome them.

PART 4
THE RESPONSIBILITIES OF EMPLOYMENT AGENCIES

4.1 Employment agencies, in their role as employers, have the responsibilities outlined in Part 1 of the Code. In addition, they have responsibilities as suppliers of job applicants to other employers.

4.2 **It is unlawful** for employment agencies (for exceptions see Race Relations Act):

(a) To discriminate on racial grounds in providing services to clients.

(b) To publish job advertisements indicating, or which might be understood to indicate, that applications from any particular group will not be considered or will be treated more favourably or less favourably than others.

(c) To act on directly discriminatory instructions from employers to the effect that applicants from a particular racial group will be rejected or preferred or that their numbers should be restricted.

(d) To act on indirectly discriminatory instructions from employers i.e. that requirements or conditions should be applied that would have a disproportionately adverse effect on applicants of a particular racial group and which cannot be shown to be justifiable.

4.3 It is recommended that agencies should also avoid indicating such conditions or requirements in job advertisements unless they can be shown to be justifiable. Examples in each case may be those relating to educational qualifications or residence.

4.4 It is recommended that staff should be given guidance on their duty not to discriminate and on the effect which generalised assumptions and prejudices can have on their treatment of members of particular racial groups.

4.5 In particular staff should be instructed:

(a) Not to ask employers for racial preferences.

(b) Not to draw attention to racial origin when recommending applicants unless the employer is trying to attract applicants of a particular racial group under the exceptions in the Race Relations Act.

(c) To report a client's refusal to interview an applicant for reasons that are directly or indirectly discriminatory to a supervisor, who should inform the client that discrimination is unlawful. If the client maintains this refusal the agency should inform the applicant of his or her right to complain to an industrial tribunal and to apply to the CRE for assistance. An internal procedure for recording such cases should be operated.

(d) To inform their supervisor if they believe that an applicant, though interviewed, has been rejected on racial grounds. If the supervisor is satisfied that there are grounds for this belief, he or she should arrange for the applicant to be informed of the right to

---

1   See paragraph 1.44 on positive action.

complain to an industrial tribunal and to apply to the CRE for assistance. An internal procedure for recording such cases should be operated.

(e) To treat job applicants without discrimination. For example, they should not send applicants from particular racial groups to only those employers who are believed to be willing to accept them, or restrict the range of job opportunities for such applicants because of assumptions about their abilities based on race or colour.

4.6 It is recommended that employment agencies should discontinue their services to employers who give unlawful discriminatory instructions and who refuse to withdraw them.

4.7 It is recommended that employment agencies should monitor the effectiveness of the measures they take for ensuring that no unlawful discrimination occurs. For example, where reasonably practicable they should make periodic checks to ensure that applicants from particular racial groups are being referred for suitable jobs for which they are qualified at a similar rate to that for other comparable applicants.

Note
Information on the promotion of equality of opportunity in employment is available from the CRE's Employment Division and from the Department of Employment's Race Relations Advisory Service

COMMISSION FOR RACIAL EQUALITY

The Commission for Racial Equality was set up by the Race Relations Act 1976 with the duties of:

- Working towards the elimination of discrimination.
- Promoting equality of opportunity and good relations between persons of different racial groups.
- Keeping under review the working of the Act, and, when required by the Secretary of State or when it otherwise thinks it is necessary, drawing up and submitting to the Secretary of State proposals for amending it.

Head Office
Elliot House
10/12 Allington Street
London SW1E 5EH
Tel: 0171 828 7022

Birmingham
Alpha Tower (11th Floor)
Suffolk Street Queensway
Birmingham B1 1TT
Tel: 0121 632 4544

Leeds
Yorkshire Bank Chambers
(1st Floor)
Infirmary Street
Leeds LS1 2JP
Tel: 0113 243 4413

Manchester
Maybrook House (5th floor)
40 Blackfriars Street
Manchester M3 2EG
Tel: 0161 831 7782

Leicester
Haymarket House (4th Floor)
Haymarket Shopping Centre
Leicester LE1 3YG
Tel: 0116 251 7852

Scotland
45 Hanover Street
Edinburgh EH2 2PJ
Tel: 0131 226 5186

Wales
Pearl Assurance House
(14th floor)
Greyfriars Street
Cardiff CF1 3AG
Tel: 01222 388977

INDEX

References are to paragraph numbers except entries in *italics* which are to page numbers